# Get a FREE eBook

To register this book, scan the code or go to
**www.manning.com/freebook/sazanavets3**

## By registering you get

- **FREE eBook copy**
  download in PDF and ePub
- **FREE online access**
  to Manning's liveBook platform
- **FREE audio**
  read and listen online in liveBook
- **FREE AI Assistant**
  it knows the book and what you are reading when it answers
- **FREE in-book testing**
  fun tests to lock in your knowledge

In Manning's liveBook platform you can share discussions and comments with other readers, add your own bookmarks and highlights, insert personal notes anywhere on the page, see color versions of all the book's graphics, download source code and other resources, and more!
To register, scan the code or go to www.manning.com/freebook/sazanavets3

MANNING

# *Building Distributed Applications that Work*

## DESIGN, DEBUG, TEST, OBSERVE, SECURE, AND DEPLOY

FIODAR SAZANAVETS

MANNING
SHELTER ISLAND

For online information and ordering of this and other Manning books, please visit www.manning.com. The publisher offers discounts on this book when ordered in quantity. For more information, please contact

Special Sales Department
Manning Publications Co.
20 Baldwin Road
PO Box 761
Shelter Island, NY 11964
Email: orders@manning.com



Manning Publications Co.
20 Baldwin Road
PO Box 761
Shelter Island, NY 11964

Development editor: Ian Hough
Technical editor: Jort Rodenburg
Review editor: Dunja Nikitović
Production editor: Kathy Rossland
Copy editor: Keir Simpson
Proofreader: Jason Everett
Technical proofreader: Srihari Sridharan
Typesetter: Dennis Dalinnik
Cover designer: Marija Tudor

ISBN: 9781633435124

# contents

# preface

I've spent much of my software engineering career building distributed applications hosted in the cloud. These applications are powerful, flexible, and scalable but also traditionally notoriously difficult to build.

Unlike a single monolithic application, a distributed system consists of multiple services, infrastructure dependencies, background processes, databases, message brokers, caches, gateways, and other moving parts. Running the whole thing on a development machine was rarely straightforward. You often had to launch services one by one, emulate the missing pieces, and hope that your local setup was close enough to the real production environment.

Most of the time, it wasn't. As a result, local development often became a loose approximation of the final system. You could test individual components, but you couldn't always test how everything behaved together. Integration and configuration problems, networking mistakes, and dependency mismatches could remain invisible until much later, sometimes revealing themselves after the system had already been deployed.

This situation is one of the central challenges of cloud-native development. The architecture may be distributed, but the developer still needs a reliable way to understand, run, debug, and evolve the system as a whole.

Aspire helps solve this problem. When Aspire was first released, it came as a surprise to much of the .NET community, but its impact on cloud-first systems was immediate. Suddenly, developers had a practical way to describe a distributed application, wire its components together, and launch the whole system locally with far less friction than before.

With Aspire, you can run multiple services, containers, databases, and infrastructure dependencies from a single application model. You can observe how they interact. You can debug them together. You can make your local development environment resemble the real system much more closely than was previously practical.

After all, cloud-native applications aren't just collections of isolated services; they're systems. Their value comes from the way the parts communicate, coordinate, fail, recover, scale, and evolve together. To build them well, you have to understand both the architectural patterns behind them and the tools that help you apply those patterns effectively.

I saw this firsthand while working at Microsoft shortly after Aspire was released. I was part of a large project involving a team of more than 90 people. We were building a distributed system capable of processing large volumes of scientific data. The project started before Aspire existed, so initially, it wasn't built around Aspire. We faced many of the usual problems: difficulty running the full system locally, reliance on emulation, complicated onboarding, and integration issues that were hard to catch early.

Because Aspire was available by that time, the team decided to run a timeboxed proof of concept to see whether the system could be migrated to it. To our pleasant surprise, the migration wasn't as difficult as expected, even for a system as large and complex as the one we were building. When the system was hosted through Aspire, many problems were easier to manage. Developers could launch and test the system locally with far greater confidence. New joiners had fewer setup steps to follow. Integration problems became easier to detect earlier. The system became easier to understand, debug, and evolve.

That experience shaped the way I think about cloud-native development. Since then, I've become an independent consultant, regularly helping teams design and build distributed cloud applications. I often recommend Aspire, not just because it's a useful framework but also because it gives teams a practical way to work with the kinds of architectural patterns that modern cloud systems require.

This book was inspired by that experience. But the book isn't just about Aspire as a product; it's also about building cloud-native distributed applications, using Aspire as the practical tool that allows us to explore the subject properly. Throughout the book, I cover the patterns, decisions, and tradeoffs involved in designing systems made of multiple services and infrastructure components. I also cover local orchestration, service discovery, containers, databases, messaging, caching, observability, deployment, security, and real-world architectural design.

Aspire helps developers make these ideas concrete. It allows us to move from theory to practice quickly. But the goal is broader than learning a single technology. By the end of the book, you should have a stronger understanding of how distributed cloud applications are structured, how their components work together, and how to evolve them from simple beginnings to production-ready systems.

If you haven't worked with Aspire before, I think you'll be amazed by how much friction it removes. More important, I hope that this book helps you become more confident in building cloud-native systems.

# *acknowledgments*

Writing a book is a team sport disguised as a solo activity. I'm grateful to everyone who helped make this one possible.

First, I'm thankful to Manning Publications for agreeing to publish this book and to Andy Waldron, the senior acquisitions editor who commissioned the project. Without you, this book wouldn't have happened.

Thank you to the Aspire team and the wider .NET community for building an ecosystem that's both ambitious and pragmatic and for sharing knowledge so generously. I'm especially thankful to Glenn Condron and Maddy Montaquila from the Aspire development team at Microsoft, who agreed to speak with me and shared the biggest pain points experienced by teams adopting Aspire.

I'm also thankful to the reviewers and early readers who challenged unclear explanations, caught mistakes, and pushed the examples toward real-world usefulness: Alisson Sol, Andy Robinson, Bela Istók, Cameron Presley, David Sellen, Dennis Liabenow, Dmitrii Bychenko, Gajendra Babu Thokala, Georg Piwonka, Giorgio Vilardo, Jayakumar Jayaprakasan, Kenneth Muse, Kyle Laverty, Lars Pesch, Owain Williams, Pravin Pandey, Rajeev Reddy Vishaka, Ricardo Bánffy, Rick Beerendonk, Rob Ruetsch, Roman Fedytskyi, Ronald Goodwin, Sanjay Belaturu Krishnegowda, Soumya Pani, Steve Goodman, Sumit Bhatnagar, Varun Kumar Chowdary Gorantla, Vatroslav Stambuk, Viswanatha Swamy P K, Wayne Mather, and Werner Nindl.

Special thanks to Srihari Sridharan and Jort Rodenburg for their detailed technical reviews. I learned a lot from you! Jort is a principal engineer at QuickMD and the author of *Code Like a Pro in C#* (Manning, 2021). He has extensive experience developing scalable software and leading teams across health care, cybersecurity, and fintech.

To my development editor, Ian Hough, and the production team: thank you for the steady guidance, thoughtful feedback, and patience with the inevitable last-minute changes. This book is better because of you.

Finally, to my family and friends: thank you for giving me support and encouragement and for making space for the long evening and weekend sessions. I couldn't have done this without you.

# about this book

In this book, you'll learn how a modern application evolves from a simple set of services into a production-ready distributed system. Using Aspire as the hands-on foundation, you'll explore the practical patterns behind cloud-native development, including service composition, local orchestration, service discovery, infrastructure integration, observability, deployment, and security.

Through the step-by-step construction of a realistic e-commerce application, you'll gain practical experience with how distributed systems are organized; how their components communicate; and how services connect to databases, caches, message brokers, containers, and other infrastructure dependencies. You'll also work through the kinds of edge cases that make or break real systems, including service discovery with SignalR clients and deployment to cloud environments such as Azure Container Apps and Kubernetes.

## Who should read this book

This book is aimed at .NET developers who want to learn how to use Aspire. Although you don't necessarily need any experience with distributed applications and orchestration, you still need some experience with .NET, C#, and web application development. In particular, you should understand the following:

- Basic C# syntax
- Fundamentals of object-oriented programming
- .NET application startup

- ASP.NET Core application structure
- The use of NuGet packages
- The use of dependency injection in .NET
- Basic understanding of HTTP
- The difference between frontend and backend development

In short, although this book is suitable for junior developers, it isn't suitable as the first book for someone who hasn't learned the basics of using .NET for programming.

## How this book is organized: A road map

This book has four parts that include 10 chapters. Part 1 covers the fundamentals of cloud systems and Aspire:

- Chapter 1—Getting started with distributed systems and Aspire
- Chapter 2—Managing infrastructure components with containers and integrations
- Chapter 3—Using database and storage components

Part 2 is dedicated to hands-on implementation of interactivity and AI integration:

- Chapter 4—Adding order-tracking functionality with SignalR
- Chapter 5—Building a ChatGPT clone with Aspire, Ollama, and Semantic Kernel

Part 3 shows you how to build professional-grade applications:

- Chapter 6—Integration testing and monitoring
- Chapter 7—Components for messaging and caching
- Chapter 8—Application security in Aspire

Part 4 covers production deployment and Aspire system upgrades:

- Chapter 9—Deploying Aspire apps to production
- Chapter 10—Adding legacy apps to Aspire and working with AI agents

## About the code

The book is hands-on, and as such, it relies on a lot of code samples. It follows the "golden thread" pattern, in which each chapter is dedicated to building on top of what was built in the preceding chapter, so we gradually build a system by adding new features and making it more complex.

This book contains many examples of source code, both in numbered listings and inline with normal text. In both cases, source code is formatted in a `fixed-width font like this` to separate it from ordinary text.

In many cases, the original source code has been reformatted; we've added line breaks and reworked indentation to accommodate the available page space in the book. Additionally, comments in the source code have been removed from the listings when the code is described in the text. Code annotations accompany many of the listings, highlighting important concepts.

You can get executable snippets of code from the liveBook (online) version of this book at https://livebook.manning.com/book/building-distributed-applications-that-work. The complete code for the examples in the book is available for download from the Manning website at https://www.manning.com/books/building-distributed-applications-that-work and from GitHub at https://github.com/fiodarsazanavets/aspire-13-examples.

## liveBook discussion forum

Purchase of *Building Distributed Applications that Work* includes free access to liveBook, Manning's online reading platform. Using liveBook's exclusive discussion features, you can attach comments to the book globally or to specific sections or paragraphs. It's a snap to make notes for yourself, ask and answer technical questions, and receive help from the author and other users. To access the forum, go to https://livebook.manning.com/book/building-distributed-applications-that-work/discussion.

Manning's commitment to our readers is to provide a venue where meaningful dialogue between individual readers and between readers and authors can take place. It isn't a commitment to any specific amount of participation on the part of the author, whose contribution to the forum remains voluntary (and unpaid). We suggest that you try asking the author some challenging questions lest their interest stray! The forum and the archives of previous discussions will be accessible from the publisher's website as long as the book is in print.

# *about the author*

**Fiodar Sazanavets** is a senior software engineer, independent consultant, and author specializing in large-scale, data-intensive distributed systems built with .NET and Microsoft Azure. He previously worked at Microsoft and has written several technical books and training courses on .NET, cloud architecture, and software engineering. He is a Microsoft MVP in Developer Technologies.

# *about the cover illustration*

The figure on the cover of *Building Distributed Applications that Work* is "L. Acquaiuolo Ambulante" ("The traveling water seller"), taken from the collection *Customs and Habits of Naples and Its Surroundings, Described and Depicted*, by Francesco de Bourcard, published in 1853. Each illustration is finely drawn and colored by hand.

In those days, it was easy to identify where people lived and what their trade or station in life was by their dress alone. Manning celebrates the inventiveness and initiative of the computer business with book covers based on the rich diversity of regional culture centuries ago, brought back to life by pictures from collections such as this one.

# Part 1

# *From zero to running: Aspire fundamentals*

Aspire is at its best when it shortens the distance between "it builds" and "it runs." In this part, you'll learn the core ideas that make that possible: how Aspire models a distributed application, how it wires projects together, and how it turns dependencies into first-class resources you can run locally with confidence.

We'll start with the simplest possible setup and then add realism: containers, integrations, and the kinds of infrastructure every serious app needs. By the end of part 1, you'll have a working mental model of Aspire's building blocks and enough hands-on familiarity to confidently Aspirify a solution without guessing.

1

# Getting started with distributed systems and Aspire

**This chapter covers**

- Why distributed applications are difficult to run and debug locally
- How Aspire models application services and infrastructure resources
- How AppHost and service defaults configure an Aspire application
- How service discovery connects services without hardcoded addresses

Running one application is easy. Running an application made up of several independently executing parts is rather more difficult.

Consider an online shopping system. Such a system couldn't function if it were just a simple website. It has many moving parts: its storefront needs a catalog API; the catalog API will eventually need a database and a distributed cache; checkout will publish messages to a broker; background services will process orders; and every component will produce logs, traces, and metrics.

In production, these parts work together as one system. A system structured this way is known as a *distributed application*.

On a development machine, though, separate components often have to be started individually. Each resource needs the correct configuration. Services need to know where their dependencies are running. Containers need ports and volumes. One service may start before another is ready. When something fails, its logs may be hidden in one of several terminal windows.

If you're a .NET developer, you can use a tool that solves this major pain point of cloud application development. This tool is Aspire (formerly known as .NET Aspire).

Aspire is designed to make this development experience more manageable. It provides a code-first application model for describing the services and infrastructure resources that form a distributed application. The central project in this model is the *AppHost*. In AppHost code, you declare the resources in the system and describe the relationships between them. Then Aspire can use that model to do the following:

- Start the application's resources together.
- Supply configuration and connection information.
- Coordinate dependencies among resources.
- Enable services to locate one another through service discovery.
- Display resource state and telemetry in a shared dashboard.

The individual services remain independent applications; Aspire doesn't merge them into one executable, and it doesn't replace the production platform on which they'll eventually run. Instead, it gives developers one place to model, run, debug, and observe the complete system.

In this book, you'll use Aspire as the practical foundation for building a realistic cloud-native distributed application. You'll gradually evolve an online shop from a storefront and a small catalog API into a system that uses persistent storage, caching, messaging, background processing, authentication, observability, containers, and deployment configuration.

The goal is to learn more than just Aspire's APIs. As the application evolves, you'll also examine the architectural patterns behind modern distributed systems: how components are composed, how they communicate, how infrastructure is integrated, how failures are diagnosed, and how applications move from local development toward production.

In this chapter, you'll run the first version of the system, inspect its resources in the Aspire dashboard, and connect the storefront to the catalog API without hardcoding the API's network address. These steps establish the application model on which the rest of the book builds.

## 1.1 The online shop as a distributed workflow

The completed online shop will contain several independently running services and infrastructure resources, which together will support the customer journey from browsing products to placing and tracking an order. The application begins with two components:

- *Storefront*—Displays the user interface
- *Catalog API*—Supplies product information to the storefront

When a shopper opens the product catalog, the storefront sends an HTTP request to the catalog API. The API returns the available products, and the storefront presents them to the shopper.

Later chapters expand this basic interaction. The catalog API retrieves information from persistent storage and uses a distributed cache to improve response times. Checkout requests are published through a message broker and processed by a background service. Authentication controls who can place orders, and real-time updates allow customers to follow their deliveries.

The system will also produce logs, metrics, and distributed traces. These signals make it possible to follow a request across multiple components and diagnose failures that would otherwise be difficult to locate.

Figure 1.1 shows the main components of the completed system and the relationships among them. This chapter starts with only the storefront and catalog API. The remaining components will be introduced gradually as the application evolves.

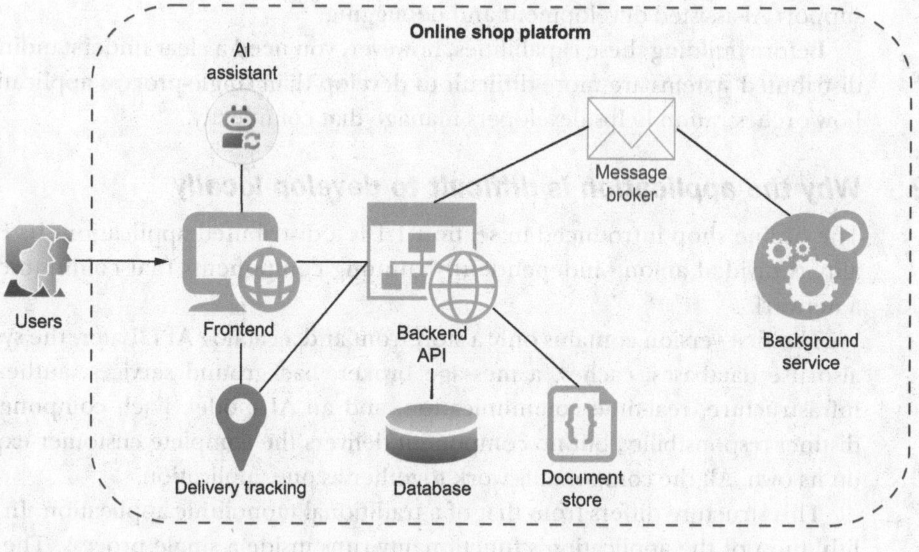


**Figure 1.1 A shopper's request crosses the storefront, API, data stores, and background-processing components. Telemetry makes the complete workflow observable.**

The online shop begins with a simple customer journey. A shopper opens the storefront, browses the product catalog, and views information retrieved from a backend API. In this chapter, you'll use this small starting point to see how Aspire models, runs, and monitors the application's components, and how service discovery allows them to communicate without hardcoded addresses.

As the system evolves, the catalog API will retrieve product information from persistent storage and use caching to improve response times. The application will also store supporting content, such as product reviews and specification files. Authentication and authorization allow anyone to browse the catalog but restrict purchases to registered users.

When a customer places an order, the application hands the longer-running work to a background service through a message broker. This allows the storefront to confirm the order without waiting for every processing step to finish. The system also coordinates access to shared data, prevents conflicting purchases, and provides real-time delivery updates as an order progresses.

Because a request may cross several independently running components, the application needs more than functional code alone. You'll add automated integration tests and observability through logs, metrics, and distributed traces. These capabilities will help you verify the behavior of the complete system and diagnose failures across service boundaries.

Later, the application will gain an AI-powered shopping assistant and be prepared for deployment to cloud and container platforms. You'll learn how to introduce Aspire into existing applications and see how its application model and telemetry can support AI-assisted development and debugging.

Before building these capabilities, however, you need a clear understanding of why distributed systems are more difficult to develop than single-process applications and how orchestration helps developers manage that complexity.

## 1.2 Why the application is difficult to develop locally

The online shop introduced in section 1.1 is a distributed application. Its functionality is divided among independently running components that communicate over a network.

The first version contains only a storefront and a catalog API. Later, the system will also use databases, caches, a message broker, background services, authentication infrastructure, real-time communication, and an AI model. Each component has a distinct responsibility, but no component delivers the complete customer experience on its own. All the components work together as one application.

This structure differs from that of a traditional monolithic application. In a monolith, most of the application's functionality runs inside a single process. The internal modules may still be carefully separated, but they normally communicate through in-process method calls and are started as one executable.

In a distributed application, the boundaries are different. The storefront and catalog API run in separate processes. A database runs as another resource. A message broker or cache may run in a container. Calls that would be simple method invocations inside a monolith become network requests between independently running components. Figure 1.2 illustrates this principle.

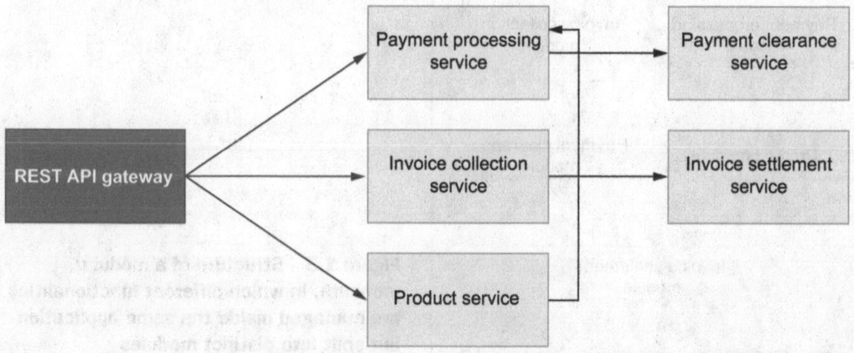


**Figure 1.2 A distributed application consists of several specialist components separated by network connections.**

These boundaries can provide useful architectural flexibility. Individual services can be deployed or scaled separately, for example, and a background service can process work independently of the user-facing application. But those benefits come with additional development complexity.

In this example, the request to the system is initiated through a Representational State Transfer (REST) API, a common architectural style for HTTP communication that allows external clients, such as mobile apps and web pages, to communicate with services hosted on a server. This request triggers a payment process that's handled by separate services, each of which is responsible for an individual action. One service performs invoice collection; another service adjusts the product stock; yet another service clears the payment. Although each service is encapsulated in its own piece of software, all services act together as a whole.

Although each service in a distributed application is technically a separate application, it's meaningless on its own. It serves its purpose only as part of a larger system. In a way, the system is a single application distributed across many components.

This structure is the opposite of the so-called monolithic application, which is a single application that contains all the business logic. Such an application may still consist of many separate modules and libraries, but they would still work together as a single executable. A monolithic application with modularized internal logic is known as a *modular monolith*—a software architecture in which an application is built as a single, unified deployment unit but its internal code is strictly separated into loosely coupled, independent modules. Figure 1.3 shows the structure of a modular monolith.

A monolithic application is easier to build and deploy than a distributed application; after all, it's a single application. You have all its code in one place. You can launch and debug it easily. You can ship and deploy it as a single package. But if you're

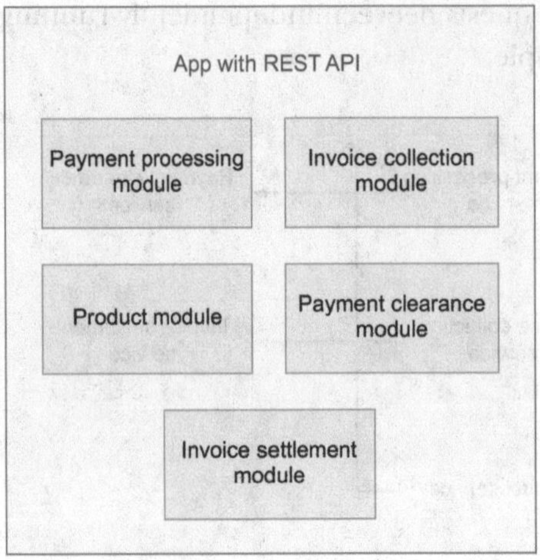


**Figure 1.3 Structure of a modular monolith, in which different functionalities are managed inside the same application but split into distinct modules**

looking to build something scalable that responds quickly, even while it's dealing with large volumes of requests and processing large volumes of data, that application can't stay monolithic forever.

Every major data-intensive application you use, whether it's a social media platform or a popular e-commerce app, is a distributed system. So although distributed systems are more robust than monolithic applications, building them comes with many pain points. Let's discuss the main ones.

### 1.2.1 Starting several resources

A single application normally has one obvious starting point. You run the executable, wait for it to become ready, and begin using it. By contrast, a distributed application may require several resources to start:

- The storefront
- One or more APIs
- Background services
- Databases
- Caches
- Message brokers
- Other supporting infrastructure

Starting these components manually is inconvenient. A developer may have to launch several projects from separate terminal windows, start one or more containers, and confirm that every resource is using the correct configuration.

The order can also matter. The storefront may depend on the catalog API, and the API may depend on a database. A background service may require the message broker to be available before it can begin consuming messages.

Starting a process doesn't necessarily mean that it's ready to accept requests. A database container may be running while it's still initializing. An API process may have started but may not yet be able to connect to its dependencies. Without coordination, the storefront could begin sending requests before the catalog API is ready. The API could start before its database is available. The result may be a temporary failure that disappears when the application is restarted, making the problem difficult to reproduce and diagnose.

### 1.2.2 Managing addresses and configuration

Separately running components must know how to reach one another. Suppose that the storefront sends HTTP requests to the catalog API. To make the call, it needs an address containing a hostname and port, such as `https://localhost:7243`.

That address may be different on another developer's machine. It may also change when a port is already in use. A containerized service may have both an internal container port and a different host port. In a deployed environment, the service may use a Domain Name System (DNS) name rather than a localhost address.

The same problem applies to infrastructure resources. An API may require

- A database connection string
- A cache endpoint
- Message-broker credentials
- An identity-provider address
- Storage configuration

Hardcoding these values makes the application fragile and environment-specific. Maintaining separate configuration files can help, but developers must still make sure that the values match the resources currently running on their machines. The more components the system contains, the more configuration must remain synchronized.

### 1.2.3 Dealing with network boundaries

Inside a single process, one module can usually call another directly. In a distributed application, communication crosses a network boundary.

A network request can fail for reasons that don't exist in a local method call. Following are a few of those reasons:

- The destination service may not be running.
- The service may still be starting.
- The configured address may be incorrect.
- The request may time out.
- The connection may be interrupted.
- The destination may respond slowly or return an error.

Even when every service runs on the same development machine, communication still uses network protocols such as HTTP or WebSocket. Therefore, the application must handle the possibility that a dependency is temporarily unavailable.

This also means that a failure in one component can affect several others. If the catalog API is unavailable, the storefront may start successfully, but the product catalog might not work. If the message broker is unavailable, customers may be able to browse products while order processing fails.

As a result, a distributed application can be partially operational. Understanding which parts are running, which parts are healthy, and which dependencies are failing is an important part of development.

### 1.2.4 Finding failures across multiple components

In a single-process application, most diagnostic information is available in one debugger or one stream of logs. In a distributed application, a single user action may cross several components. Consider a request to display a product:

1. The browser sends a request to the storefront.
2. The storefront calls the catalog API.
3. The catalog API queries a cache.
4. If the product isn't cached, the API queries the database.
5. The result travels back through the API and storefront to the browser.

If the request fails, the visible symptom may appear in the storefront even though the actual cause is in the API, cache, or database or in the configuration between them.

Each component may produce its own logs in a different terminal window. Metrics may be collected separately. A developer may know that the page failed without knowing which network call caused the failure or how long each part of the request took. Distributed tracing helps address this problem by recording how a request travels through the system. Logs, metrics, and traces together provide a more complete picture, but these signals must be collected and presented where developers can use them. Setting up a system to collect distributed tracing in a local development environment isn't easy.

### 1.2.5 Testing the complete workflow

Each service can be tested independently, but isolated tests don't prove that the complete application works. The catalog API may return the correct response when tested on its own. The storefront may render sample product data correctly. But the complete workflow can still fail because

- The storefront uses the wrong service address.
- A required configuration value is missing.
- One service starts before its dependency is ready.
- The API can't connect to its database.
- Serialization formats don't match.
- Authentication or network configuration blocks a request.

As a result, an integration test for a distributed application may have to start several real components, wait for them to become ready, send requests through the application, and inspect the resulting behavior. Coordinating such a test environment manually is difficult. The test setup can become almost as complicated as the application itself.

### 1.2.6 The need for development-time orchestration

These challenges aren't caused by the business logic of the online shop. They arise because the system consists of multiple independently running resources. Developers need a reliable way to do the following:

- Describe which resources belong to the application.
- Start those resources together.
- Express dependencies among the resources.
- Supply addresses and connection information.
- Determine whether each resource is ready and healthy.
- Collect diagnostic information in one place.
- Reproduce the same application topology during integration testing.

Coordinating these activities is a form of orchestration. In this book, the immediate focus is development-time orchestration. The goal is to make the complete distributed application straightforward to run, inspect, debug, and test on a development machine.

Aspire addresses these problems by allowing you to describe the application and its relationships in code. Its AppHost project becomes the central model of the distributed system. Aspire can use that model to start resources, supply configuration, coordinate dependencies, enable service discovery, and present the system through a shared dashboard.

The services still run as independent processes; Aspire doesn't turn the application into a monolith. Instead, it provides a unified development experience for working with all its components. Section 1.3 examines orchestration in detail and shows how Aspire applies it to the online shop.

## 1.3 Overview of orchestration

In distributed applications, *orchestration* refers to the management and coordination of individual services or components within a larger system. When you build a distributed system composed of multiple services, containers, or other components, orchestration is crucial for ensuring that these elements work together seamlessly to achieve the desired outcome. Orchestration involves tasks such as deployment, scaling, health monitoring, and resource allocation across the distributed environment. Figure 1.4 shows how the process of orchestration works.

To understand orchestration, consider what must happen before a shopper can browse the product catalog. The storefront can't retrieve product data unless the catalog API is running. The catalog API may itself depend on a database or cache. Later, order processing will require a message broker and a background service. Each resource must be started with the correct configuration, and dependent services shouldn't begin work until the resources they need are ready.

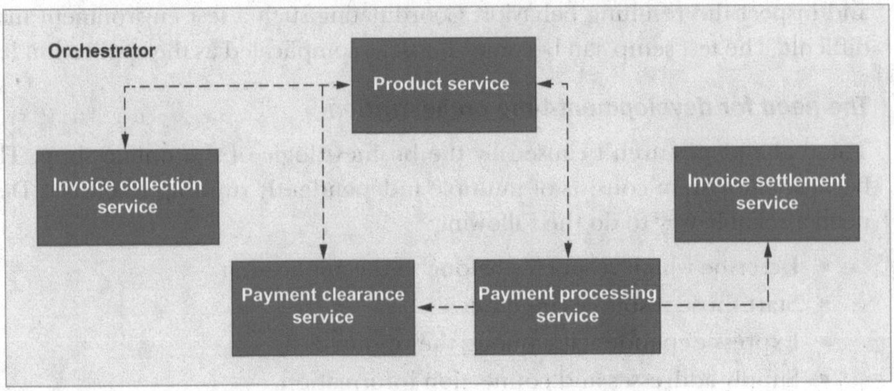


**Figure 1.4 An orchestrator coordinates separate services over the network in a distributed application and ensures that they act as one functioning system.**

An orchestrator coordinates this process. First, it starts the resources that form the application. For the online shop, this may include the storefront, catalog API, database, cache, message broker, and background service. Instead of requiring a developer to launch each component manually, the orchestrator provides a single way to start and manage the complete system.

As the resources start, the orchestrator supplies the configuration they need. The storefront must know how to reach the catalog API, and the API may need connection information for its database and cache. These addresses and connection details can vary among development, testing, and production environments, so they shouldn't be hardcoded into the application.

The orchestrator also tracks dependencies and readiness. A process may be running without being ready to accept requests. A database container, for example, may need time to initialize after it starts. The orchestrator can use health information to determine when a resource is ready and delay dependent services until the resources they require are available.

When the application is running, orchestration provides a view of the system as a whole. If the catalog API becomes unhealthy, developers must see that its failure affects the storefront. In production environments, an orchestration platform may also restart failed instances, route traffic to healthy replicas, or increase the number of running instances when demand grows.

The exact responsibilities depend on the environment. Production orchestration platforms commonly manage deployment, scaling, load balancing, resource allocation, and recovery across servers or clusters. Aspire's immediate role is development-time orchestration. It helps you describe the application's resources and relationships, start them together, supply configuration, assess their health, and inspect them through a shared dashboard.

The services remain independently running components. Orchestration doesn't remove the boundaries between them; it makes those boundaries easier to manage.

## 1.4 How Aspire changes the game

Aspire is a cloud-native application stack designed to simplify the development of modern distributed systems with .NET. Although it's primarily tailored to cloud application development, it can be used to develop any web-hosted application that has at least one external component. Even a simple monolithic application will probably have some sort of database connection and may be connected to a message broker. Aspire makes it easy to integrate these services into a development environment. The principles discussed in this book apply equally to distributed applications hosted in Aspire and to monolithic applications that rely on external components, such as databases and message brokers.

Aspire stands out by providing a streamlined experience for building, running, and monitoring applications that consist of multiple interconnected services. The stack reduces complexity by offering a set of preconfigured components and tools that work together seamlessly, making it easier for developers to manage the entire application life cycle. In addition to making all the services of the distributed application talk to one another in the shared debugger process, Aspire allows those services to integrate easily with necessary infrastructure components, such as databases and message brokers, as shown in figure 1.5.

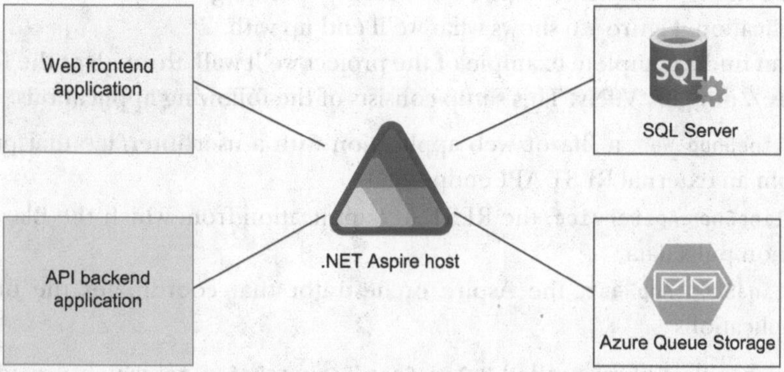


**Figure 1.5 An Aspire host makes separate application services and infrastructure components run as though they're part of a single monolithic application.**

A standout feature of Aspire is its ability to simplify microservice orchestration. Traditionally, running and coordinating multiple services requires a significant amount of boilerplate code and configuration. Aspire addresses this challenge by introducing an intuitive application model that allows developers to define services and their dependencies declaratively. This approach minimizes repetitive code while enhancing the clarity and maintainability of the system's architecture.

Another advantage of Aspire lies in its built-in support for observability. As applications grow in complexity, monitoring their behavior and diagnosing problems become increasingly critical. Aspire integrates with tools such as OpenTelemetry to provide comprehensive tracing, logging, and metrics capabilities out of the box. Developers can track requests as they traverse multiple services, quickly identify performance bottlenecks, and maintain the overall health of their applications without extensive manual instrumentation.

In addition to making orchestration and observability simpler, Aspire is inherently cloud-ready. Applications built with this framework can be effortlessly deployed to cloud platforms such as Microsoft Azure, Amazon Web Services, and any other cloud host. The configuration system is designed to adapt to cloud environments, reducing the friction often associated with moving from local development to production deployment.

Together, these points substantially increase developer productivity and improve the development experience. Aspire helps teams focus on solving business problems rather than wrestle with infrastructure concerns.

## 1.5 Getting started with the Aspire Starter Project

Before you create an Aspire project, you have to set up your development environment. The appendix explains how.

Let's assume that we created a new project based on the Aspire Starter Project template and called the .NET solution `OnlineShop`. We chose this name because throughout this book, we'll showcase Aspire's features by building a fully functioning online shop application. Figure 1.6 shows what we'll end up with.

You can find a complete example of the project we'll walk through at the following link: https://mng.bz/V9Ny. This setup consists of the following applications:

- `OnlineShop.Web`, a Blazor web application with a user interface that pulls data from an external REST API endpoint
- `OnlineShop.ApiService`, the REST API application from which the Blazor application pulls data
- `OnlineShop.AppHost`, the Aspire orchestrator that coordinates the other two applications

There's also a class library called `OnlineShop.ServiceDefaults`, which provides some shared functionality to the applications that Aspire orchestrates.

Next, let's look at how orchestration happens.

## 1.6 Orchestrating with Aspire

To launch the distributed application hosted in Aspire, we have to launch the host application, called `OnlineShop.AppHost` in our example. The host application launches all other applications. If we launch it and wait for all the services to build, we'll see a dashboard that looks like figure 1.7.

If we were to run the host application under an HTTP profile rather than an HTTPS profile, we'd see only one endpoint for each service rather than two. But this scenario applies only to a local development environment.

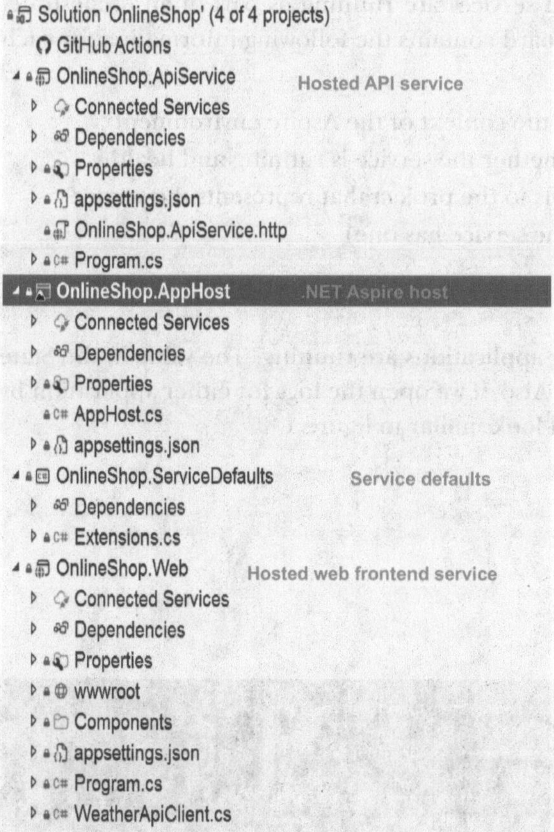


**Figure 1.6 The structure of the Aspire solution**

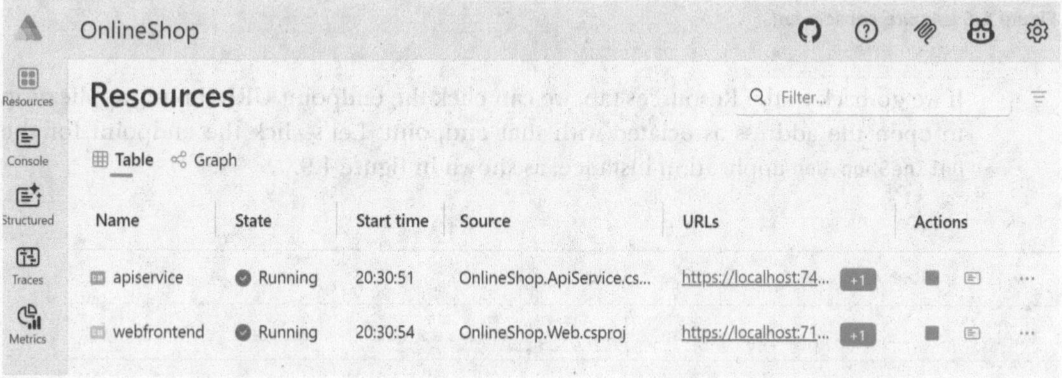


**Figure 1.7 Aspire dashboard**

This dashboard shows which services are running as part of an orchestrated distributed application. The dashboard contains the following information for each service:

- Service type
- Unique name used in the context of the Aspire environment
- State, which tells us whether the service is running and healthy
- Source, which points us to the project that represents the service
- Service endpoint (if the service has one)
- Service logs
- Details of the service

We know that the preceding applications are running. The value in the State column on the dashboard tells us so. Also, if we open the logs for either application by clicking the Console tab, they should look similar to figure 1.8.

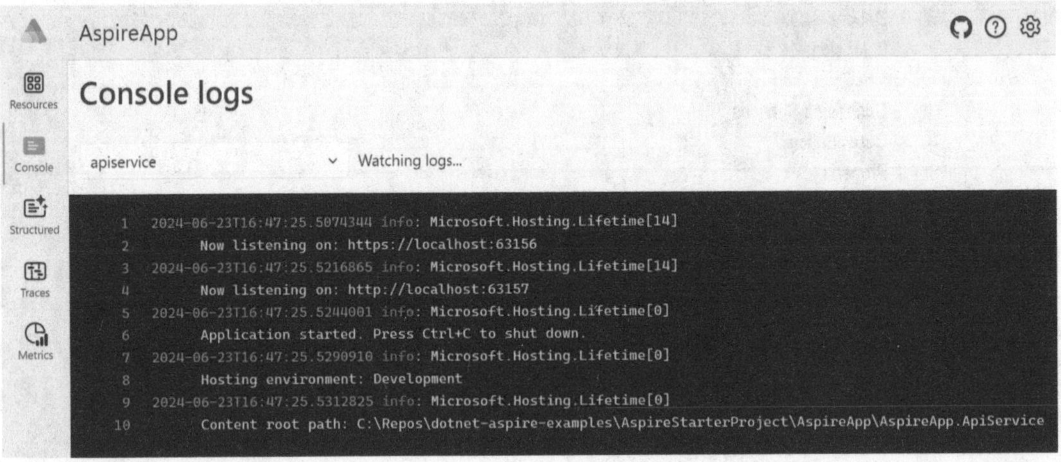


**Figure 1.8 Aspire console log**

If we go back to the Resources tab, we can click the endpoint URL for any application to open the address associated with that endpoint. Let's click the endpoint for the `OnlineShop.Web` application instance, as shown in figure 1.9.

**Figure 1.9 Aspire Resources webfrontend link**

This should open a Blazor UI application, where we can navigate to the Weather tab. This tab contains data that the Blazor application retrieved from the API. It should look similar to figure 1.10, though the exact values may vary.

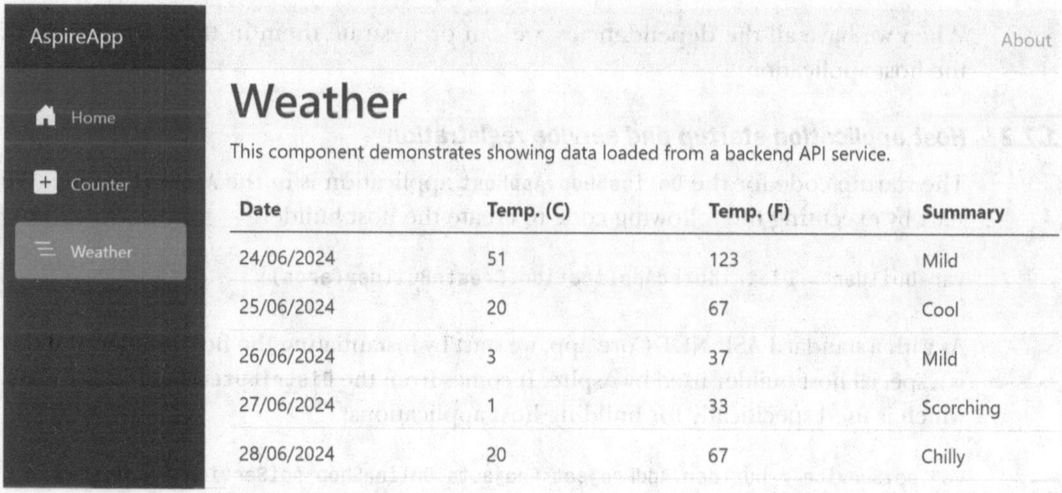


**Figure 1.10 Blazor app hosted in Aspire**

This is how we can get the UI and API to work together. Aspire allows us to see both applications and navigate to their corresponding addresses. But it's more than that.

Next, let's look under the hood of Aspire to see how it handles orchestration.

## 1.7 Setting up Aspire's orchestrator

Aspire is a complex system with a lot to unpack, so we'll start with the basics: the fundamental dependencies that make Aspire work. Then we'll move on to registering applications with the orchestrator.

### 1.7.1 Installing Aspire dependencies

Aspire applications require a specific set of NuGet packages. These packages have already been installed in the default Aspire Starter Project template. Let's go over them to get familiar with what they do.

An Aspire application requires a host application, which acts as the orchestrator. In our playground, the `OnlineShop.AppHost` project plays this role. You can identify the Aspire host project by the following opening tag in its `.csproj` file:

```
<Project Sdk="Aspire.AppHost.Sdk/13.0.1">
```

The host application also has to reference all the applications that it's going to orchestrate. In our case, there are two:

1. `OnlineShop`.Web, a Blazor web application with a user interface that pulls data from an external REST API endpoint
2. `OnlineShop.ApiService`, the REST API application from which the Blazor application pulls data

When we have all the dependencies, we can orchestrate them in the startup code of the host application.

### 1.7.2 Host application startup and service registration

The startup code for the `OnlineShop.AppHost` application is in the `AppHost.cs` file. We start by executing the following code to create the host builder:

```
var builder = DistributedApplication.CreateBuilder(args);
```

As with a standard ASP.NET Core app, we start by instantiating the host builder. But this is a special host builder used by Aspire. It comes from the `DistributedApplication` class, which is used specifically for building host applications:

```
var apiService = builder.AddProject<Projects.OnlineShop_ApiService>("apiservice")
    .WithHttpHealthCheck("/health");
```

This is how we register the API application. The `builder` object has the `AddProject()` method, which includes a generic type specification in angle brackets: `<Projects.OnlineShop_ApiService>`. This type is generated automatically, and its name is constructed as follows:

- The `Projects` part indicates that it's one of the projects from the solution.
- The `OnlineShop_ApiService` part is constructed from the `OnlineShop.ApiService` project name. The dots are replaced with underscores to ensure that it's represented by a single type.

The `WithHttpHealthCheck("/health")` invocation registers the health-check endpoint for the service so that the orchestrator can always tell whether the service is healthy.

This type doesn't exist anywhere in any of our projects; it's autogenerated and constructed from the name of one of our projects. This type has all the code necessary to register that project as an app that the host can orchestrate.

The parameter is the name under which we register the service. In this case, we call it `apiservice`.

### 1.7.3 Registering the UI application

After we register the API, we can register the UI. Here's how it's done in our example project:

```
builder.AddProject<Projects.OnlineShop_Web>("webfrontend")
    .WithExternalHttpEndpoints()
    .WithHttpHealthCheck("/health")
    .WaitFor(apiService)
    .WithReference(apiService);
```

Initially, we do the same thing we did when registering the API service, invoking the `AddProject()` method with a type reference inferred from the `OnlineShop.Web` project. We named this project `webfrontend`.

We're also doing one more thing: invoking the `WithExternalHttpEndpoints()` method to ensure that the web application's endpoints are accessible on an external network, such as the public internet. This is necessary because by default, the services hosted by Aspire are accessible only through Aspire's own internal network.

If you look back at the API service registration, you'll notice that we didn't invoke this method. This means that the API won't be accessible on the public network, making it more secure. The only application that will connect to the API is our `webfrontend` application. And because both the API and `webfrontend` applications are hosted on the same Aspire network, the API service will remain fully accessible to the `webfrontend` app even while it's not accessible to the outside world.

Therefore, we invoke the `WithReference()` method and insert the previously registered API service reference into it so that the Blazor UI application can refer to the API application via service discovery.

We also have the `WaitFor()` method, which ensures that the frontend service starts only after the API service is fully ready. After all, the frontend service pulls data from the API, so some of its functionality won't be available without the API.

If we look at the dashboard again, we see that the services on it have the names `webfrontend` and `apiservice`. These names are arbitrary, but they're the ones we used when registering the services in the startup code of the Aspire orchestrator.

## 1.8 Introducing service defaults

*Service defaults* in Aspire is a collection of extension methods that allow apps to be added to the Aspire orchestrator. These extension methods come as a class library included in the Aspire project template. These extension methods are required for the following tasks:

- Enabling service discovery
- Enabling the orchestrator to assess the health of the applications
- Collecting metrics from the application
- Executing other common functionalities shared by the orchestrated apps

These extension methods come as a class library inside the solution so that they can be modified to fit specific business scenarios. Developers may want to choose a metrics library different from the default one, for example, or they may want to add functionality.

In our setup, the service defaults are represented by the `OnlineShop.ServiceDefaults` project. Because this project is a class library, the purpose of which is to add extension methods for the startup code of ASP.NET Core applications, it has to reference the `Microsoft.AspNetCore.App` framework package. This package gives the library access to types used by ASP.NET Core, such as `IHostApplicationBuilder` and `WebApplication`. We also have to add references to other packages that enable the specific functionality we need, such as service discovery and telemetry.

### 1.8.1 Adding extension methods

The extension methods are in the `Extensions.cs` file in the `OnlineShop.ServiceDefaults` project. The following listing shows that file's contents.

**Listing 1.1 The structure of the `Extensions` class**

```
using Microsoft.AspNetCore.Builder;
using Microsoft.AspNetCore.Diagnostics.HealthChecks;
using Microsoft.Extensions.DependencyInjection;
using Microsoft.Extensions.Diagnostics.HealthChecks;
using Microsoft.Extensions.Logging;
using OpenTelemetry;
using OpenTelemetry.Metrics;
using OpenTelemetry.Trace;

namespace Microsoft.Extensions.Hosting;

public static class Extensions
{
    public static IHostApplicationBuilder
        AddServiceDefaults(
            this IHostApplicationBuilder builder)
    {
        ...
    }

    public static IHostApplicationBuilder
        ConfigureOpenTelemetry(
            this IHostApplicationBuilder builder)
    {
        ...
    }

    private static IHostApplicationBuilder
        AddOpenTelemetryExporters(
            this IHostApplicationBuilder builder)
    {
        ...

    public static IHostApplicationBuilder
        AddDefaultHealthChecks(
            this IHostApplicationBuilder builder)
```

```
    {
        ...
    }

    public static WebApplication
        MapDefaultEndpoints(this WebApplication app)
    {
        ...
    }
}
```

This file contains a combination of extension methods for the IHostApplicationBuilder and WebApplication types, both of which are used in the startup code of ASP.NET Core applications. IHostApplicationBuilder is used to register services that the application can use. The WebApplication type is used to add HTTP endpoints to the application and steps to the request-processing pipeline.

These methods are covered in detail in relevant sections later in this chapter. For now, here's a brief summary of what the methods are used for:

- The ConfigureOpenTelemetry() method registers services that can collect metrics inside the application.
- The AddOpenTelemetryExporters() method configures the functionality that exports metrics from the application so that they can be used to monitor the application.
- The AddServiceDefaults() method invokes these two methods and performs some additional dependency registration, such as adding the services necessary for service discovery.
- The MapDefaultEndpoints() method adds the health-check endpoints to the application.

When we have these methods, we have to invoke them from the startup code of the relevant applications.

### 1.8.2 Using the extension methods

If we open the Program.cs file in the OnlineShop.Web project, we find the following line:

```
builder.AddServiceDefaults();
```

This line invokes the extension method we looked at earlier, registering all dependencies associated with Aspire and allowing the Aspire orchestrator to manage this app. We also have the following invocation farther down the file:

```
app.MapDefaultEndpoints();
```

Again, this line is one of the extension methods we added in the service defaults.

If we open the Program.cs file inside the OnlineShop.ApiService project, we find the same extension methods being invoked.

## 1.9 Service discovery in Aspire

*Service discovery*, a critical aspect of distributed systems and microservices architectures, refers to the process of automatically detecting and registering available services within a network environment. In a microservices architecture, applications are composed of many small independent services that communicate over a network. Service discovery enables these services to locate and communicate with one another dynamically without manual configuration.

Service discovery involves several key components:

- *Service registration*—When a microservice starts, it registers with a service registry or discovery service. This registration typically includes information such as the service's network location (e.g., IP address and port), metadata, and possibly its health status.
- *Service querying*—Other microservices or clients that have to interact with a particular service can query the service registry to discover its location and other relevant details. This querying can be performed dynamically at run time, allowing services to adapt to changes in the network topology or the addition or removal of services. It can also be done statically at compile time through configuration.
- *Dynamic updates*—Service discovery systems support dynamic updates to the registry, allowing services to join or leave the network without disruption. This ensures that the registry always reflects the current state of the system.
- *Load balancing*—Although it's not technically part of service discovery, it's closely related. Service discovery often integrates with load-balancing mechanisms to distribute incoming requests among multiple instances of a service. This integration improves the system's scalability, fault tolerance, and performance by distributing the workload evenly.

The following sections briefly run through the steps required to get discovery up and running.

### 1.9.1 Registering service-discovery components

Before we can enable service discovery with Aspire, we must install the `Microsoft.Extensions.ServiceDiscovery` NuGet package in the applications we want to add to the orchestrator. We'll do this in the `OnlineShop.ServiceDefaults` project.

### 1.9.2 Enabling service discovery

Next, we enable service discovery so the applications can use it. This mechanism enables services hosted in Aspire to communicate by automatically discovering one another's IP addresses. As a developer, all you have to do is label each service with a unique name. The service-discovery infrastructure does the rest.

In our example, the service-discovery components are registered inside the `AddServiceDefaults()` method in the `Extensions.cs` file of the `OnlineShop.ServiceDefaults` class library. Here are the specific calls inside this method that register all the dependencies necessary for service discovery:

- `builder.Services.AddServiceDiscovery()`—Adds core service-discovery components
- `http.AddServiceDiscovery()`—Adds service-discovery components to HTTP clients, enabling them to use labels of other clients as Uniform Resource Identifiers (URIs) instead of the exact IP addresses

### 1.9.3 Using service discovery

When we've registered all the required components, we can start using service discovery. If we open the `Program.cs` file in the `OnlineShop.Web` project folder, we'll find an example of service-discovery use.

First, we must make sure to register all the relevant components, which we do by invoking the `AddServiceDefaults()` extension method. Then, inside a block where we create an HTTP client to connect to the API app, we have the following:

```
client.BaseAddress = new("https+http://apiservice");
```

Normally, we'd use a standard URL as a base address, but not this time. Instead, we're pointing the HTTP client at the name of the service whose address we want to obtain. This name is the one under which we registered the service in the Aspire orchestrator.

In this example, we define the protocol as `https+http`. This means that we try to connect to the service via HTTPS, but if we can't, we use HTTP. Still, HTTPS is preferred.

Then we have a standard colon followed by a double slash, which we use in any URL. Finally, we have the name of the service we want to connect to: `apiservice`.

In this setup, the application registered as `apiservice` can move to a different server. Its address may change. Its port may change. But to our client application, none of this matters because it doesn't know the service's address and doesn't have to. The Aspire host application resolves the correct address for it to connect to.

In this chapter, we studied the structure of the default Aspire Starter Project and got familiar with the fundamental dependencies that make Aspire work. This knowledge will allow us to expand Aspire's capabilities beyond what's offered in the Starter Project, as we'll do in the following chapters. First, however, we'll look more closely at how the built-in monitoring tools are used in Aspire.

## Summary

- Microsoft created Aspire to simplify the process of developing distributed applications.
- Distributed applications are systems that consist of multiple independent services that interact with one another.

- Orchestration is the process of coordinating services inside a distributed system.
- The main benefit of using Aspire is that it lets you run and debug a distributed application from a single place on a development machine, which substantially simplifies development.
- Aspire consists of the Aspire Host project, to which all other projects can connect.
- Different applications hosted by Aspire can pass references to one another when they're registered by the orchestrator.
- The service defaults project is used for shared dependencies that any Aspire-hosted apps can use.
- Service discovery lets you resolve addresses of Aspire-hosted apps by the names under which they were registered in the orchestrator.
- The Aspire orchestrator displays a dashboard that shows the status of all running services.

# Managing infrastructure components with containers and integrations

**This chapter covers**

- Understanding the fundamentals of Docker containers
- Integrating a Keycloak Docker container with Aspire to enable single sign-on (SSO) security
- Understanding Aspire integrations and their benefits over raw Docker containers
- Adding a prebuilt Aspire integration for Redis to an application
- Building a custom Aspire integration library from scratch

In a real-life enterprise-grade application, services need to connect to various infrastructure components, such as databases and message brokers. In this chapter, we discuss two ways infrastructure components can be wired up in an Aspire application:

- By using Docker containers
- Via the Aspire integration libraries

Most enterprise-grade systems require security, and the e-commerce application we're building is no exception. Security is especially important in these kinds of applications. You absolutely don't want anyone to steal your credit card data or make purchases on your behalf! This is why we'll build a system that allows our users to register, log in, and gain the necessary permissions to access the appropriate areas of our app.

This chapter, however, focuses primarily on the infrastructure components. We'll use security-specific infrastructure as an example to learn how infrastructure components in Aspire are set up. Chapter 8 covers the actual security mechanisms and protocols. The goal of this chapter is to practice integrating Aspire with Docker containers and special integration libraries. The fundamental principles covered apply to other types of infrastructure components, not just security-specific ones.

We'll not only add infrastructure components to Aspire but also use Aspire-specific features such as service discovery. This will save us from duplicating the same configuration and references across our system and allow our Aspire-hosted services to connect to one another seamlessly.

To follow this chapter, you have to know what Docker containers are, so that's what we'll look at first.

## 2.1 Docker containers

*Docker* is a technology that allows executable applications to be isolated in so-called containers. This technology is covered in detail in Jeff Nickoloff's excellent book *Docker in Action*, 2nd edition (https://www.manning.com/books/docker-in-action-second-edition). Here, I'll provide an overview.

*Docker containers* are lightweight, portable, isolated environments that allow developers to run applications consistently across different client environments. They encapsulate an application and all its dependencies (such as libraries, binaries, and configuration files) in a single package, as figure 2.1 shows. This ensures that the

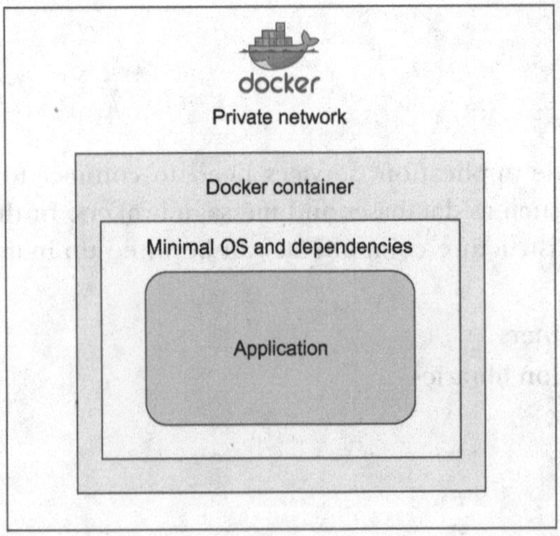


**Figure 2.1 Docker container structure**

application runs the same way regardless of where it's deployed: on a developer's local machine, in a test environment, or in production.

Because containers run in their own isolated environments, they don't interfere with other containers or the host system. This isolation is achieved through Linux kernel-level features such as namespaces and cgroups. Containers can run the Windows operating system (OS), too, but Windows container use cases are relatively rare. Linux remains the most widely used OS inside Docker containers.

Unlike traditional virtual machines, Docker containers share the host system's OS kernel, making them much more lightweight. They don't require a full OS installation for each container, leading to faster startup times, lower resource usage, and easier autoscaling.

Containers can run on any system that has Docker installed, making it easy to move applications between environments (e.g., from development to production) without worrying about compatibility problems. Also, although Docker is a primary containerization technology, it's not the only one available. Docker containers can be hosted by *Podman*, a free, open source, daemonless container engine developed by Red Hat. Docker Engine, by contrast, is commercial software that requires licensing in certain cases.

*Docker images* are the building blocks of Docker containers. They're snapshots or templates that contain everything required to run an application, including the application code, libraries, dependencies, environment variables, and configuration files. When you create a container, you instantiate a Docker image.

The Docker Hub website (https://hub.docker.com/) has a wide collection of Docker images, including popular software packages such as SQL Server, RabbitMQ, the aforementioned Keycloak, and Grafana. You can use all these images directly to launch containers, but you can also use them as base images for other images if you have to add new functionality. Developers can publish public images in Docker Hub that are accessible to everyone or private images that can be accessed only by authorized users.

## 2.2 Keycloak overview

Keycloak is an open source identity and access management solution that provides authentication and authorization services for applications and services. It's designed to make securing applications easy with minimal effort, offering features such as single sign-on (SSO), identity brokering, and user federation. Keycloak acts as an identity provider (IdP), allowing developers to integrate security features into their applications without writing extensive custom code for authentication and authorization.

Although Keycloak is open source software freely available in a Docker container, real commercial enterprises frequently use it for SSO and identity management. They do so because it's relatively simple to set up and includes nearly every feature an IdP solution needs, such as easily customizable login pages that can incorporate any type of company branding.

Keycloak also supports many modern security features such as multifactor authentication. Features that Keycloak doesn't support natively can be enabled through numerous plugins available in its ecosystem. Developers can also write their own custom plugins.

Each Keycloak instance supports multiple domains, known as *realms*. One thing that makes Keycloak easy to set up is that each realm can be easily exported as a JSON file. When we set up a new Keycloak instance, we can import the JSON file to repopulate the instance with OpenID Connect (OIDC) client applications, users, roles, and other settings. Later in this chapter, we'll see an example of importing a Keycloak realm.

## 2.3 Initial setup

Now we're ready to start learning how to host a Keycloak Docker container inside an Aspire app. The sample solution we'll build is available at https://mng.bz/xZ9d.

We'll pick up where we left off in chapter 1. This solution will be our starting point: https://mng.bz/AGvo.

Our initial setup is based on the Aspire Starter Project. This approach makes it easier to see which components have changed compared with the original setup. We're about to apply our first modification to the project and turn it into something that more closely resembles a real enterprise-grade application, with its own dedicated infrastructure components rather than only custom application code.

Besides the Aspire host application, we have the following apps:

- An app named `webfrontend`, which is a frontend Blazor application
- An app named `apiservice`, which is an ASP.NET Core Web API application

Before we launch our Aspire host, we must make sure that the Docker environment is configured on the machine and running. Otherwise, our Keycloak container will fail to start.

## 2.4 Adding a Keycloak container to an Aspire host

Our implementation of the Keycloak integration mechanism is inspired by the GitHub lab created by Damian Edwards, available at https://mng.bz/Z9dR.

We start by putting a `.cs` file with extension methods in the `Extensions` folder of the `OnlineShop.AppHost` project. The file is called `KeycloakHostingExtensions.cs`. It contains the following internal class, which represents an abstraction of a Keycloak container:

```
internal class KeycloakResource(string name) :
    ContainerResource(name),
    IResourceWithServiceDiscovery
{
    public string? ClientSecret { get; set; }
}
```

**NOTE** This class inherits from the `ContainerResource` class, which is used as an abstraction for Docker container resources. It also implements the `IResourceWithServiceDiscovery` interface, which requires it to use common methods used by Aspire-hosted services.

In the same file, we have the static `KeycloakHostingExtensions` class, which contains various extension methods. The following method allows us to pass a service reference and the name of the environment variable that will contain the Keycloak client application secret:

```
public static IResourceBuilder<TResource>
    WithReference<TResource>(
        this IResourceBuilder<TResource> builder,
        IResourceBuilder<KeycloakResource> keycloakBuilder,
        string env)
    where TResource : IResourceWithEnvironment
{
    builder.WithReference(keycloakBuilder);
    builder.WithEnvironment(
        env, keycloakBuilder.Resource.ClientSecret);

    return builder;
}
```

We also have the extension method shown in the following listing, which allows us to launch a Keycloak Docker container inside our app.

**Listing 2.1 Adding a Keycloak container**

```
public static IResourceBuilder<KeycloakResource>
    AddKeycloakContainer(
    this IDistributedApplicationBuilder builder,
    string name,
    int? port = null,
    string? tag = null)
{
    var keycloakContainer = new KeycloakResource(name)     <-- Creating an instance of a Keycloak Docker resource representing a Docker container
    {
        ClientSecret = "some_secret"
    };

    var keycloak = builder
        .AddResource(keycloakContainer)                    <-- Adding a resource to the container builder
        .WithAnnotation(new ContainerImageAnnotation
        {
            Registry = "quay.io",
            Image = "keycloak/keycloak",                   <-- Adding image-specific annotations, such as the image name, registry name, and tags
            Tag = tag ?? "latest"
        })
        .WithHttpEndpoint(port: port,                      <-- Configuring an accessible HTTP port on the container, which is 8080 in Keycloak by default
            targetPort: 8080)
```

```
        .WithEnvironment("KEYCLOAK_ADMIN", "admin")          <-- Adding environment
        .WithEnvironment("KEYCLOAK_ADMIN_PASSWORD",               variables to the
            "admin")                                              container
        .WithEnvironment("WEBAPP_CLIENT_SECRET",
            keycloakContainer.ClientSecret);

    if (builder.ExecutionContext.IsRunMode)         <-- Checking which
    {                                                   parameters to apply to
        keycloak.WithArgs("start-dev");                 the container based on
    }                                                   the run mode
    else
    {
        keycloak.WithArgs("start");
    }

    return keycloak;
}
```

There's quite a lot to take in, so let's go through the code step by step:

1. We're creating a new instance of the `KeycloakResource` class we created earlier. Because this class has a property that stores the client's secret, it allows us to assign any arbitrary value to this property and pass it into both the client and the Keycloak configuration via environment variables.
2. We register this instance in the Aspire orchestrator via the `AddResource()` method. It's similar to the `AddProject()` method we use to register projects as applications hosted by Aspire, but more generic. It allows us to register any type of resource as a hosted service.

   For containers, an alternative registration method is `AddContainer()`. We couldn't use it in our scenario, however, because it gives us less control of the process. The `AddContainer()` method accepts only image name, registry name, and tag as parameters, whereas `AddResource()` allows us to pass any additional parameters that we want. In the preceding example, we were able to pass the client secret via a custom object.
3. We use the next method, `WithAnnotation()`, to specify the details of the Docker image from which we want to build the container. Specifying a tag is optional, but it's good practice to use a specific version in the tag; otherwise, the system will pull the latest version of the image with the `latest` tag. This version may contain breaking changes that will make it incompatible with our application, and the problem may not be easy to debug.
4. We set some environment variable values. In particular, we set the username and password for the admin account and the secret for a specific client app.
5. Finally, we pass some command-line arguments to the container launch command. The next listing shows our final extension method.

**Listing 2.2 Importing the Keycloak realms**

```
public static IResourceBuilder<KeycloakResource>
    ImportRealms(this IResourceBuilder<KeycloakResource>
        builder,
    string source)
{
    builder
        .WithBindMount(source,
            "/opt/keycloak/data/import")
        .WithAnnotation(
            new CommandLineArgsCallbackAnnotation(
                args =>
        {
            args.Clear();
            if (builder.ApplicationBuilder
                .ExecutionContext.IsRunMode)
            {
                args.Add("start-dev");
            }
            else
            {
                args.Add("start");
            }
            args.Add("--import-realm");
        }));

    return builder;
}
```

This method allows us to bind-mount a specific folder in the filesystem that hosts our Aspire application to the `/opt/keycloak/data/` import folder inside the Docker container. Keycloak checks this directory during the initial launch. If the directory contains JSON files with exported realm information, Keycloak imports those files and sets up the realms. We also use this method to demonstrate how bind mounts are set up in Aspire.

A *bind mount* is a Docker feature that allows us to map any arbitrary location in the host machine's filesystem to a specific location in the container's filesystem. Applying it to a folder that contains our realm configuration files makes those files accessible to the software running inside the container.

Because we're mapping the local Keycloak folder to the directory inside the Docker container, we have to create this folder inside our host project directory. We also have to place a JSON file in this folder that will be used for the realm import when the application starts. You can obtain the file at https://mng.bz/RwjZ.

**NOTE** In a real production codebase, the realm import file probably would be placed in a configuration class library or an environment-specific directory rather than in the Aspire host project.

Also, because we need this file to be available with the executable of the host application when it builds, we have to open our `OnlineShop.AppHost.csproj` file and add the following block to it:

```
<ItemGroup>
    <None Update="Keycloak\import.json">
      <CopyToOutputDirectory>PreserveNewest</CopyToOutputDirectory>
    </None>
  </ItemGroup>
```

Now we can see where these extension methods are used by opening the `AppHost.cs` file in the same project. First, we add the appropriate namespace reference at the top of the file:

```
using OnlineShop.AppHost.Extensions;
```

We create our IdP container by placing the following code before any other service definitions:

```
var idp = builder.AddKeycloakContainer(
        "idp", tag: "23.0")
    .ImportRealms("Keycloak")
    .WithExternalHttpEndpoints();
```

Note that we have the `ImportRealms()` method pointing to the Keycloak folder. This folder contains the `import.json` file, which contains all the realm information. We don't need to go into the details of how this file is set up. What's useful to know is that some values are hardcoded, and other values are extracted from environment variables that we saw referenced earlier.

To enable our apps to resolve the address of our Keycloak container, we pass this service reference into the creation script for both the web frontend and API service apps. This is how we pass the container reference to our API app:

```
var apiService = builder
    .AddProject<Projects.OnlineShop_ApiService>("apiservice")
    .WithHttpHealthCheck("/health")
    .WithReference(idp)
    .WaitFor(idp);
```

This is how we pass the container reference into our frontend app:

```
var webFrontend = builder
    .AddProject<Projects.OnlineShop_Web>(
        "webfrontend")
    .WithExternalHttpEndpoints()
    .WithHttpHealthCheck("/health")
    .WithReference(apiService)
    .WithReference(idp,
        env: "Identity__ClientSecret")
    .WaitFor(idp);
```

We're using the version of the `WithReference()` method that uses the client secret because we have to set up this client secret in the UI app for the OIDC flow implementation.

Finally (for a locally hosted development instance only), to fully automate the two-way connection between Keycloak and the applications it secures, we pass the endpoint URLs of the web frontend app into the Keycloak container. The following listing shows what this looks like.

**Listing 2.3 Passing Keycloak references in the Aspire host**

```
if (builder.Environment.IsDevelopment())
{
    var webAppHttp = webFrontend.GetEndpoint("http");
    var webAppHttps = webFrontend.GetEndpoint("https");

    idp.WithEnvironment("WEBAPP_HTTP", () =>
        $"{webAppHttp.Scheme}://{webAppHttp.Host}:{webAppHttp.Port}");

    if (webAppHttps.Exists)
    {
        idp.WithEnvironment("WEBAPP_HTTP_CONTAINERHOST",
            webAppHttps);
        idp.WithEnvironment("WEBAPP_HTTPS", () =>
            $"{webAppHttps.Scheme}://{webAppHttps.Host}:{webAppHttps.Port}");
    }
    else
    {
        idp.WithEnvironment("WEBAPP_HTTP_CONTAINERHOST",
            webAppHttp);
    }
}
```

- Making sure that this logic only executes in the development environment
- Getting the address of the HTTP endpoint of the web frontend application
- Getting the address of the HTTPS endpoint of the web frontend application
- Passing a resource address into an environment variable inside the IdP container
- Checking whether the HTTPS endpoint exists
- Setting other environment variables inside the Keycloak container

You may wonder why we execute this code only in the local development environment, not in production. There's a good reason: calling the `GetEndpoint()` method on a service instance to get its endpoint address always works on a development machine if you run your solution from an IDE. In a deployed application, however, it works only after the host has fully started and the service is already running. This means we would have a circular dependency that's impossible to resolve:

- Keycloak must be launched before its client services; otherwise, those services won't be able to use or connect to the service-discovery feature.
- A Keycloak container has to know the endpoint addresses of its client services; otherwise, the authentication mechanism won't work.

Figure 2.2 illustrates this principle.

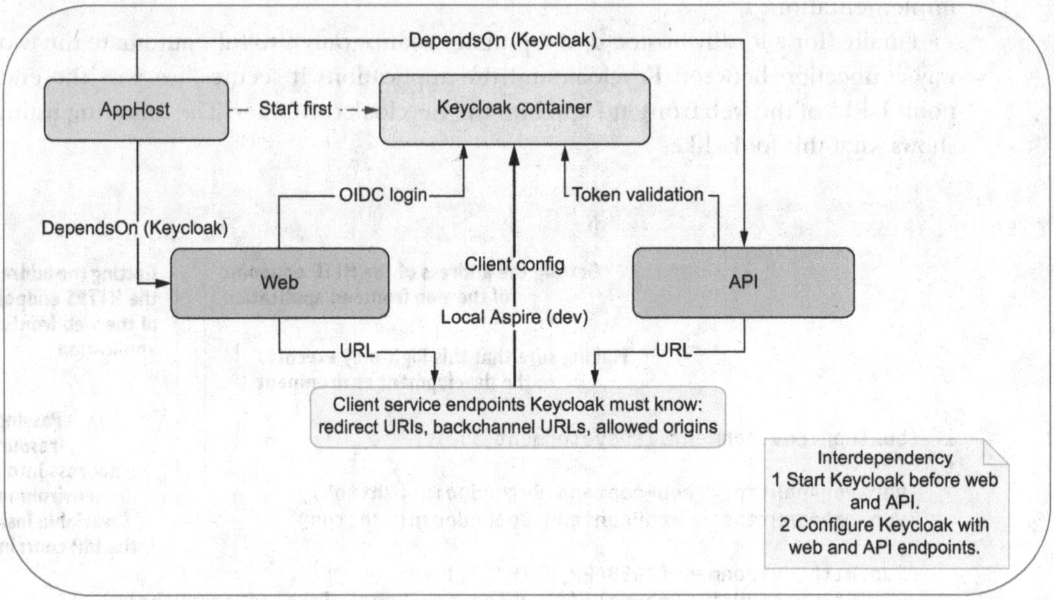


**Figure 2.2 Interdependency between Keycloak container and hosted services**

This problem is easy to solve. Instead of importing the realm when the Keycloak container is created, for example, the realm can be imported after all the client services are up. We can also have separate code paths for a deployed application and a locally hosted instance, as discussed in chapter 9. Nevertheless, passing endpoint references as environment variables when the host launches is still valuable in the development environment because it produces a ready-to-use Keycloak instance that works with other hosted applications right away.

> **NOTE** This situation won't be as much of a problem in a real production environment because a production Keycloak instance won't be transient. Its data and configuration will remain even as new application deployments occur. It will probably run against a persistent database rather than as a separate, fully self-contained container instance. Therefore, it makes perfect sense to configure a production Keycloak realm in a separate step from the application deployment.

Next, we'll see how authentication and authorization are configured in the client app. We'll connect to the IdP endpoint via an `HttpClient` instance that relies on Aspire service discovery.

### 2.4.1 Configuring the web frontend app

A Keycloak realm becomes part of its URL. Therefore, if we want our OIDC-enabled applications to use well-known endpoints, we have to point to an appropriate realm in the address path.

Both the web frontend and API applications have to access this URL, so we must add the following helper method, which is located in the `Extensions.cs` file inside the shared `OnlineShop.ServiceDefaults` project:

```
public static Uri GetIdpAuthorityUri(
    this HttpClient httpClient)
{
    var idpBaseUri = httpClient.BaseAddress
        ?? throw new InvalidOperationException(
            $"HttpClient instance does not have a BaseAddress configured.");
    return new Uri(idpBaseUri, "realms/OnlineShop/");
}
```

Here, we append the `realms/OnlineShop/` path to the base URL that points to the Keycloak IdP. The `realms` part is the standard way to refer to the area that contains different realms. `OnlineShop` is the name of our realm; note that it's case-sensitive.

Next, we register our `HttpClient` instance in the `Program.cs` file of the `OnlineShop.Web` project before the app variable is instantiated:

```
builder.Services.AddHttpClient(
    "OidcBackchannel", o => o.BaseAddress = new("http://idp"));
```

This uses the dependency injection (DI) mechanism to register the client. Then other services within the application can resolve and use this client. Because we passed a reference to a service named `idp` into the web frontend service, the idp path allows us to resolve the endpoint address via the `HttpClient`.

Next, we have to install version 10 or later of the `Microsoft.AspNetCore.Authentication.OpenIdConnect` NuGet package in our web frontend project. This package has all the authentication and authorization middleware we need, so we don't have to reinvent the wheel.

Because we're using a DI-registered `HttpClient` instance, we have to resolve it through an implementation of the `IHttpClientFactory`. One way to do this is to use an extension method for our `AuthenticationBuilder`. We can add this method to the class inside the `AuthExtensions.cs` file, which we can create inside the `OnlineShop.Web` project folder. The following listing shows what it looks like.

**Listing 2.4 Configuring OIDC authentication**

```
using Microsoft.AspNetCore.Authentication;
using Microsoft.AspNetCore.Authentication.OpenIdConnect;
using Microsoft.IdentityModel.Protocols.OpenIdConnect;
```

```
namespace OnlineShop.Web;

public static class AuthExtensions
{
    public static void ConfigureWebAppOpenIdConnect(this
     AuthenticationBuilder authentication)
    {
        // Named options
        authentication.Services
            .AddOptions<OpenIdConnectOptions>(
                OpenIdConnectDefaults.AuthenticationScheme)
            .Configure<
                IConfiguration,
                IHttpClientFactory,
                IHostEnvironment>(Configure);

        // Unnamed options
        authentication.Services.AddOptions<OpenIdConnectOptions>()
            .Configure<
                IConfiguration,
                IHttpClientFactory,
                IHostEnvironment>(Configure);

        static void Configure(
            OpenIdConnectOptions options,
            IConfiguration configuration,
            IHttpClientFactory httpClientFactory,
            IHostEnvironment hostEnvironment)
        {
            var backchannelHttpClient =
                httpClientFactory.CreateClient(
                    "OidcBackchannel");

            options.Backchannel = backchannelHttpClient;
            options.Authority =
                backchannelHttpClient
                    .GetIdpAuthorityUri().ToString();
            options.ClientId = "webapp";
            options.ClientSecret =
                Environment
                    .GetEnvironmentVariable(
                        "Identity__ClientSecret");
            options.ResponseType =
                OpenIdConnectResponseType.Code;
            options.SaveTokens = true;
            options.RequireHttpsMetadata =
                !hostEnvironment.IsDevelopment();
            options.MapInboundClaims = false;
        }
    }
}
```

Let's closely examine what we're doing here. We register the `Configure()` method and map it to the authentication options. Inside this method, we resolve a named `HttpClient` instance that we registered previously by invoking the `CreateClient()` method on the `IHttpClientFactory` instance. Then we pass this client to the `Backchannel` property of the authentication options. We also extract the IdP authority base address from this client and construct the IdP authority URL that we pass to the `Authority` property.

In this example, we use a backchannel to communicate with the Keycloak container. In the context of an HTTP client, a *backchannel* is a communication pathway for secure, direct interactions between a client and a server that aren't exposed outside this communication loop.

Unlike front-channel communication, in which data is sent via the user's browser (e.g., through URL parameters, redirects, or cookies), backchannel communication occurs server-to-server or via a secure HTTP client. This approach is commonly used in authentication, API calls, and data synchronization processes. In this example, backchannel communication also allows us to use the endpoint address resolved from service discovery rather than specify the exact address in the connection settings.

To use the Aspire-specific service discovery feature, we need a backchannel client to connect the application to the IdP instance; otherwise, its address won't be resolved. Service discovery works only in the context of an `HttpClient`.

Because we're using a backchannel, our authority URL doesn't have to be the same as the publicly accessible address of the IdP. It can be the address used inside our internal network. This optimizes network bandwidth use and allows us to restrict public access to particular IdP endpoints.

The remaining options are standard configuration options that work with any type of IdP that relies on the OIDC protocol, not just Keycloak. We take a more detailed look at all these in chapter 8, which is dedicated to the security of both the Aspire orchestrator and the applications hosted on it.

If we go back to the `Program.cs` file, this is how we invoke this extension method, which we can do anywhere before the app variable is instantiated:

```
builder.Services.AddAuthentication(options =>
{
    options.DefaultScheme =
        CookieAuthenticationDefaults.AuthenticationScheme;
    options.DefaultChallengeScheme =
        OpenIdConnectDefaults.AuthenticationScheme;
})
.AddCookie(
    CookieAuthenticationDefaults.AuthenticationScheme)
.AddOpenIdConnect()
.ConfigureWebAppOpenIdConnect();
The following namespace references are required:
using Microsoft.AspNetCore.Authentication.Cookies;
using Microsoft.AspNetCore.Authentication.OpenIdConnect;
using OnlineShop.Web;
```

Our OIDC setup is now complete. But in our system, it's not only the web frontend app that requires authentication; the API endpoint is protected too. In section 2.4.2, we'll ensure that the API app has the right configuration.

### 2.4.2 Configuring API service

To prepare our `OnlineShop.ApiService` project, we install the following NuGet package:

```
Microsoft.AspNetCore.Authentication.JwtBearer
```

Our `OnlineShop.ApiService` project also needs the `AuthExtensions.cs` file with the extension method for authentication configuration. The class inside the file has to be public static. Because we're relying on Bearer token authentication rather than OIDC, our settings are slightly different, but similar principles apply. The next listing shows the main extension method.

**Listing 2.5 Configuring JSON Web Token (JWT) authorization**

```
public static void ConfigureApiJwt(
    this AuthenticationBuilder authentication)
{
    // Named options
    authentication.Services
        .AddOptions<JwtBearerOptions>(
            JwtBearerDefaults.AuthenticationScheme)
        .Configure<
            IConfiguration,
            IHttpClientFactory,
            IHostEnvironment>(Configure);

    // Unnamed options
    authentication.Services.AddOptions<JwtBearerOptions>()
        .Configure<
            IConfiguration,
            IHttpClientFactory,
            IHostEnvironment>(Configure);

    static void Configure(
        JwtBearerOptions options,
        IConfiguration configuration,
        IHttpClientFactory httpClientFactory,
        IHostEnvironment hostEnvironment)
    {
        var backchannelHttpClient =
            httpClientFactory.CreateClient(
                "OidcBackchannel");

        options.Backchannel = backchannelHttpClient;
        options.Authority =
            backchannelHttpClient
                .GetIdpAuthorityUri().ToString();
        options.RequireHttpsMetadata =
            !hostEnvironment.IsDevelopment();
```

```
            options.MapInboundClaims = false;
            options.TokenValidationParameters =
                new TokenValidationParameters
                {
                    ValidateAudience = false
                };
        }
    }
```

We have to reference the following namespaces:

```
using Microsoft.AspNetCore.Authentication;
using Microsoft.AspNetCore.Authentication.JwtBearer;
```

As we can see, we're also using the `HttpClient` for backchannel access to the IdP instance. We still rely on the authority URL that contains the Keycloak realm information in the path.

Now we have to register this client in the project's `Program.cs` file, exactly as we did in the web frontend:

```
builder.Services.AddHttpClient(
    "OidcBackchannel", o => o.BaseAddress = new("http://idp"));
```

This is how we invoke the extension method we previously added in the `Program.cs` file:

```
builder.Services.AddAuthentication(options =>
{
    options.DefaultAuthenticateScheme =
        JwtBearerDefaults.AuthenticationScheme;
    options.DefaultChallengeScheme =
        JwtBearerDefaults.AuthenticationScheme;
})
.AddJwtBearer()
.ConfigureApiJwt();
```

The namespaces we have to reference are

```
using Microsoft.AspNetCore.Authentication.JwtBearer;
using OnlineShop.ApiService;
```

Our Keycloak integration is complete. If we launch our Aspire host, our dashboard will look similar to figure 2.3.

> **TIP** It may take a while for the Keycloak container to be fully ready during the first launch, even after it's shown as green on the dashboard. The reason is that in addition to starting the container, Keycloak has to download some dependencies and configure the environment. If you see an error when navigating to the Keycloak console, that error is likely to autoresolve soon. Wait up to 2 minutes; then refresh the page.

| Name | State | Start time | Source | URLs |
|---|---|---|---|---|
| idp | Running | 20:10:10 | quay.io/keycloak/keycloak:23... | http://localhost:49822 |
| apiservice | Running | 20:10:12 | OnlineShop.ApiService.csproj | https://localhost:7465 +1 |
| webfrontend | Running | 20:10:12 | OnlineShop.Web.csproj | https://localhost:7199 +1 |

**Figure 2.3 Aspire dashboard with a Keycloak container**

We see that the `idp` resource has `Container` as its type and `quay.io/keycloak/keycloak` as its source, which is the fully qualified name of the official Keycloak Docker image. If we click its endpoint URL, we see the page shown in figure 2.4.

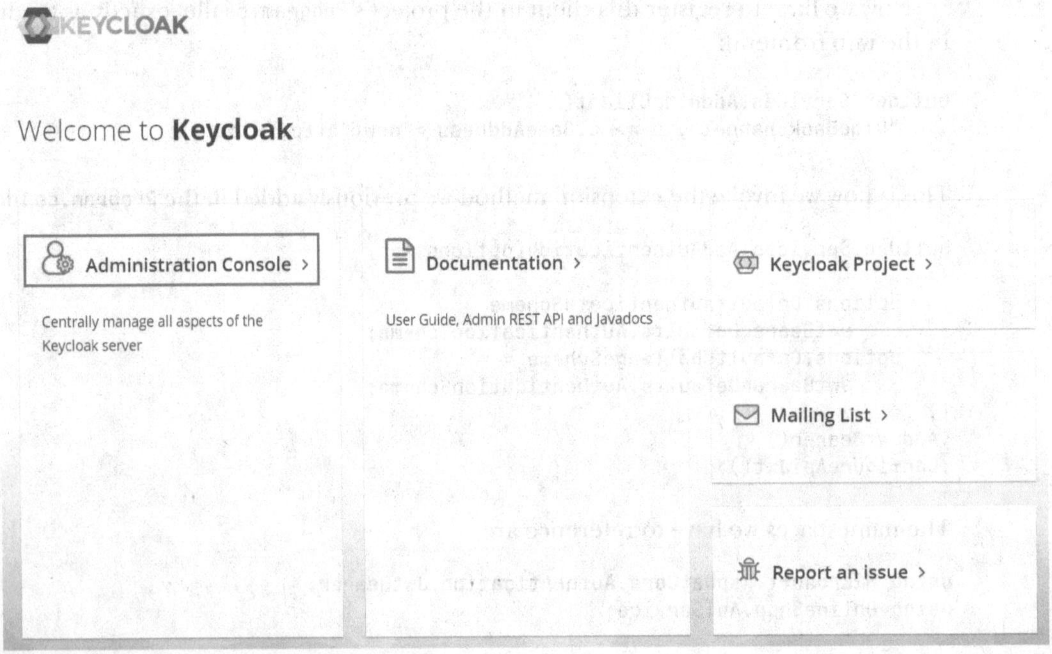


**Figure 2.4 Keycloak admin console**

On this page, clicking the Administration Console option takes us to the login page for our admin account. By default, both the username and password are admin, as shown in figure 2.5.

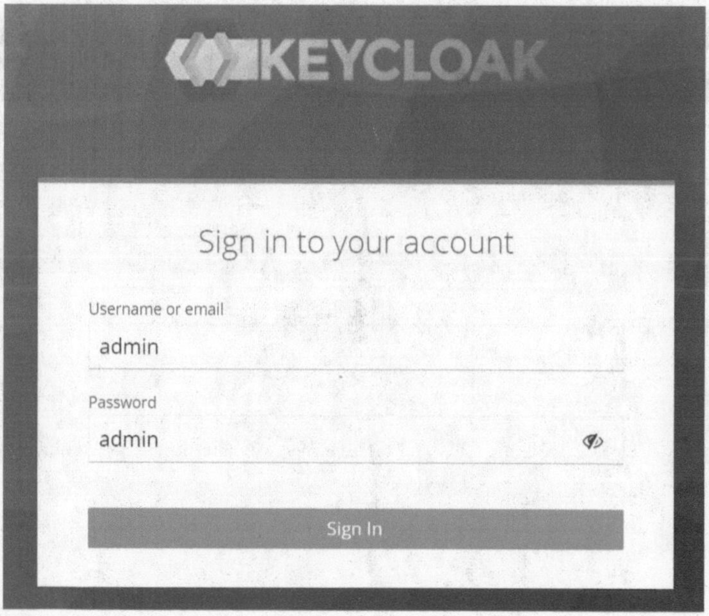


**Figure 2.5 Keycloak admin login page**

After logging in, we can choose the OnlineShop realm from the drop-down list in the top-left corner, as figure 2.6 demonstrates.

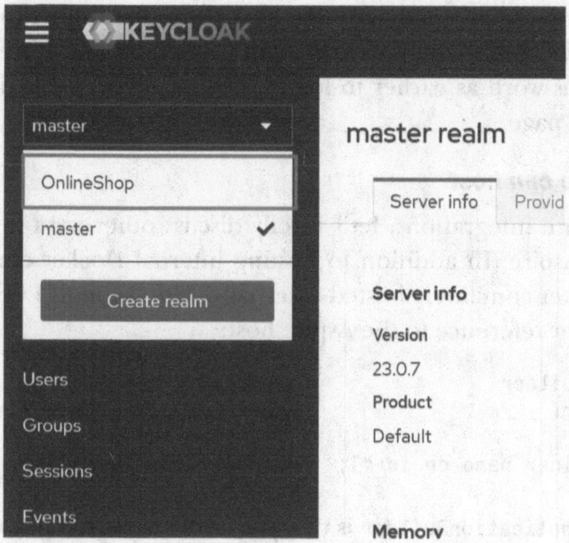


**Figure 2.6 Selecting Keycloak realm**

If we navigate to the Users section, we see a user with the name test@example.com, as shown in figure 2.7.

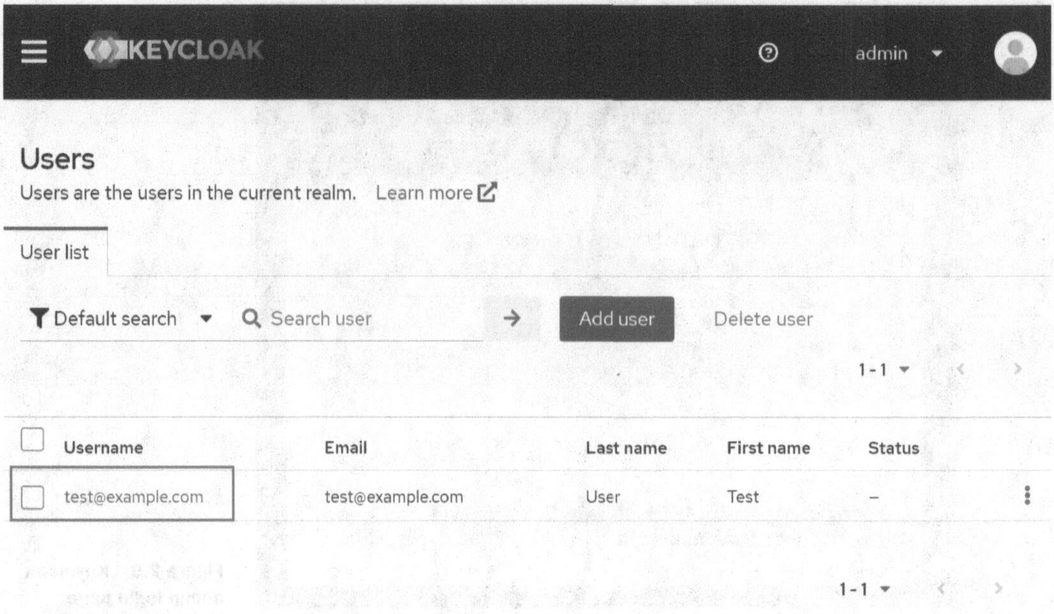


**Figure 2.7 User management panel in Keycloak**

We employ this user to log in to our Blazor frontend app. The user's password is P@$$w0rd1.

If we navigate back to the Aspire dashboard and click the endpoint address of the `webfrontend` app, we're redirected to the Keycloak login page. From there, we can use the same username and password as earlier to log in. After a successful login, we're redirected to the Blazor UI page.

### 2.4.3 Other service types Aspire can host

Before we proceed to Aspire integrations, let's briefly discuss other ways to register containerized services in Aspire. In addition to hosting internal Docker containers, Aspire can connect to Docker containers hosted externally. This is the API we can use to add an external container reference to the Aspire host:

```
IDistributedApplicationBuilder
    .AddExternalContainer(
        "<resource name>",
        "<external container name or id>");
```

In this case, `IDistributedApplicationBuilder` is the type of the `builder` variable in the `AppHost.cs` file of the Aspire host project. For more details, see Anthony Simmon's article at https://mng.bz/26Bg.

Another way to host a service in Aspire is to refer directly to an executable. This is the API for registering executables:

```
IDistributedApplicationBuilder
    .AddExecutable(
        "<resource name>",
        "<command>",
        "<working directory>",
        "<parameters>");
```

Although these concepts are useful to know, use cases for both types of integrations are fairly rare. This is why we won't dedicate much time to them.

By now, you should have a fairly good understanding of how to work with a Keycloak Docker container in Aspire. You should also understand the general principles of how Docker containers are hosted, which you can apply to other containers. Next, we move on to an alternative way of hosting infrastructure components in Aspire.

## 2.5 How Aspire integration libraries differ from containers

In addition to orchestrating projects, executables, and Docker containers, Aspire can orchestrate so-called Aspire integrations (formerly known as Aspire components). These components are special libraries that add popular packages to our distributed application, including the following:

- Databases (e.g., SQL Server, PostgreSQL, and so on)
- Message brokers (e.g., Kafka, Service Bus, and so on)
- Distributed cache (e.g., Redis)

The integrations are based mostly on Docker containers. But the libraries that enable them have a range of extension methods that make it much easier to host these components in Aspire than work with Docker containers directly.

Not all Aspire integrations are based on Docker containers, however. An Aspire integration for a database provider, such as SQL Server, might be configured to connect to a managed SQL Server instance that isn't hosted inside a container. Hosting the SQL Server instance in a container would be a terrible idea unless it's done purely for development or demonstration purposes. Containers are meant to be stateless, which makes them highly unsuitable for storing data. If anything happens to the server that hosts the container, the container will recover, but it will be reset to its original state, so you'll lose all your data.

Different modes of Aspire integrations are covered throughout the book as we build our e-commerce system. In this chapter, we start with the basics. First, we add a basic integration that's optionally available in the starter project template; then we create our own custom integration package so we can get familiar with how Aspire integrations work under the hood.

The easiest way to start learning how Aspire integrations work is to use the Aspire Starter Project with the Redis output caching option.

This project uses Redis for output caching, a performance-optimization technique that stores the dynamically generated output of a web page, or part of a web page, so that it can be served faster on subsequent requests. This reduces the need to reprocess the same data and render the same content repeatedly, improving response time and reducing the load on the server.

By default, output caching is done in the application's memory, which means that if the server restarts or if multiple application instances are running behind a load balancer, output caching no longer works. When the output is cached on Redis, on the other hand, it persists even if the app server restarts and is available to all instances of a distributed application.

For those who are new to Redis, it's an in-memory data structure store commonly used as a database, cache, and message broker. Redis is known for its high performance, flexibility, and rich set of features. Although it stores data in memory, it's hosted separately from the apps that use it and has its own memory. This is why it acts as a distributed cache that many apps can access.

Don't worry—we won't create a new starter project. Instead, we'll add the required components to our own project instance.

## 2.6 Configuring Aspire integrations on the host

A typical Aspire integration consists of two NuGet packages:

- A package that allows you to host an instance of the service on Aspire
- A client package that allows other apps hosted by Aspire to access the service

To install the Redis integration and host a Redis instance on Aspire, we have to reference the `Aspire.Hosting.Redis` package from the host project. In the example repo we referenced earlier, the host project is called `OnlineShop.AppHost`.

After we add the reference to the package, we register it as a service. We'll do this in the `AppHost.cs` file of the `OnlineShop.AppHost` project by executing the following code:

```
var cache = builder.AddRedis("cache");
```

Next, we add a reference to this service to the apps in which we want to use it. In this example, we pass the reference variable to the webfrontend service registration as a parameter of the `WithReference()` method. The full registration of the webfrontend app looks like this:

```
var webFrontend = builder
    .AddProject<Projects.OnlineShop_Web>("webfrontend")
    .WithExternalHttpEndpoints()
    .WithHttpHealthCheck("/health")
    .WithReference(apiService)
    .WithReference(idp, env: "Identity__ClientSecret")
    .WaitFor(idp)
    .WithReference(cache)
    .WaitFor(cache);
```

Because the app registered under the name `webfrontend` is a Blazor web application with an in-browser UI, this is exactly the kind of app in which output caching is important. After we register the integration and pass its reference to a service, we can consume it from that service.

### 2.6.1 Connecting to an integration from a hosted service

Apps inside the host have their own NuGet libraries for connecting to specific components. To enable Redis output caching, we need to reference the `Aspire.StackExchange.Redis.OutputCaching` package in the `OnlineShop.Web.csproj` file. Then we add the following line to the `Program.cs` file:

```
builder.AddRedisOutputCache("cache");
```

> **NOTE** The name we refer to is the name under which we registered the component under in the host app. Service discovery will be used to resolve its address.

With Redis caching enabled, the application caches its output in Redis instead of the local in-memory cache.

### 2.6.2 Viewing integrations in the dashboard

If we launch our playground and wait for the applications to build, we see the `cache` service listed in the dashboard, as shown in figure 2.8.

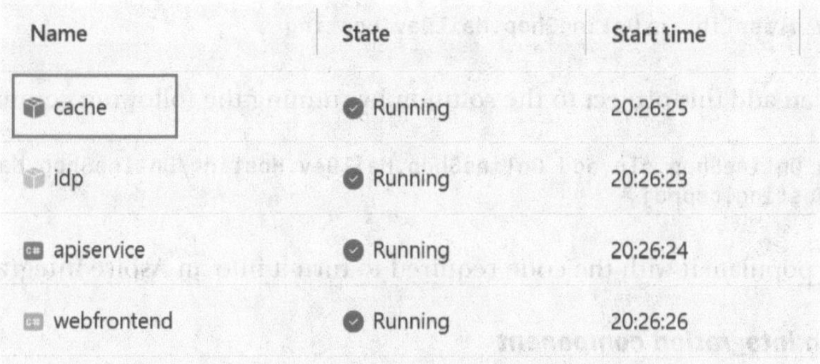


**Figure 2.8 Redis component shown in the Aspire dashboard**

This component is shown as a `Container`, like a Docker container, if it's to be hosted by Aspire because this particular Aspire integration is a Docker container, as most integrations are when run locally. You can also see this on the `Source` tab, where the path starts with `docker.io`.

The setup steps we went through are similar to those for other integration types. But it would be useful for you to know how these integration libraries are structured internally. Let's build our own integration.

## 2.7 Building an Aspire integration library

Earlier in this chapter, we integrated our Aspire setup with a Keycloak container for authentication and authorization. In modern apps that require authentication, users typically receive an email when they register. This email serves two purposes:

- Confirmation that the registration was successful and the system knows about the user
- Verification that the email belongs to the user by getting them to click a confirmation link

Keycloak has this functionality too. Emails require a working Simple Mail Transfer Protocol (SMTP) server. One of the best ways to test this functionality is to emulate an SMTP server in a local environment. That way, the emails can be sent, but nobody receives them accidentally; they'll be visible only on a local development machine.

One of the best tools for this job is the MailDev Docker image, available at https://hub.docker.com/r/maildev/maildev. Let's wrap this image in a custom Aspire component. Our starting point will be the same solution, which we used previously to build the Keycloak Docker container.

First, we add a class library to the `OnlineShop` solution and call it `OnlineShop.MailDev.Hosting`. To do this in any OS in any environment, navigate to the solution folder and execute the following command from your favorite command-line terminal:

```
dotnet new classlib -n OnlineShop.MailDev.Hosting
```

Then you can add this project to the solution by running the following command:

```
dotnet sln OnlineShop.sln add OnlineShop.MailDev.Hosting/OnlineShop.Mail-
    Dev.Hosting.csproj
```

Next, we'll populate it with the code required to turn it into an Aspire integration.

### 2.7.1 Building an integration component

Any Aspire integration package requires the `Aspire.Hosting` NuGet package. To add it to our new project, execute the following command in the command-line interface (CLI):

```
dotnet add OnlineShop.MailDev.Hosting/OnlineShop.MailDev.Hosting.csproj pack-
    age Aspire.Hosting
```

Now we'll populate it with the necessary code. First, we create the `MailDevResource.cs` file and populate it with the following code.

**Listing 2.6 MailDev container component**

```
using Aspire.Hosting.ApplicationModel;

namespace OnlineShop.MailDev.Hosting;

public sealed class MailDevResource(string name) :
    ContainerResource(name), IResourceWithConnectionString
{
    internal const string SmtpEndpointName = "smtp";
    internal const string HttpEndpointName = "http";

    private EndpointReference? _smtpReference;

    public EndpointReference SmtpEndpoint =>
        _smtpReference ??= new(this, SmtpEndpointName);

    public ReferenceExpression ConnectionStringExpression =>
        ReferenceExpression.Create(
            $"smtp://{SmtpEndpoint.Property(EndpointProperty.Host)
                }:{SmtpEndpoint.Property(EndpointProperty.Port)}"
        );
}
```

Extending a base class and implementing an interface; Setting the SMTP endpoint name; Setting the HTTP endpoint name; Setting SMTP endpoint reference; Setting SMTP connection string

Because this class extends `ContainerResource`, it can be used as a base for a Docker container. It also implements `IResourceWithConnectionString`, which allows connections through a connection string. A *connection string* allows client apps to connect to an SMTP server so they can send email through it.

Next, we configure the connection string, the SMTP endpoint, and other items we'll use elsewhere, such as SMTP and HTTP endpoint names. We also add a `MailDevContainerImageTags.cs` file, which we'll populate with the content of the following listing.

**Listing 2.7 Tags for MailDev container**

```
namespace OnlineShop.MailDev.Hosting;

internal static class MailDevContainerImageTags
{
    internal const string Registry = "docker.io";

    internal const string Image = "maildev/maildev";

    internal const string Tag = "2.1.0";
}
```

This class stores constant fields containing the following information:

- The name of the registry from which the image is downloaded
- The name of the Docker image
- The exact version of the image

It's good practice to specify the exact version of the image so that a one-to-one relationship exists between your integration component and the Docker image version on which it relies. This ensures that your integration works consistently and doesn't suddenly start behaving differently, which may happen if you omit the version tag or specify `latest` as the version tag.

Finally, we create a public static `MailDevResourceBuilderExtensions` class. This class contains the extension method that allows this component to be hosted inside Aspire. The next listing shows the method to add.

**Listing 2.8 Method to add a `MailDev` resource**

```
public static IResourceBuilder<MailDevResource> AddMailDev(
    this IDistributedApplicationBuilder builder,
    string name,
    int? httpPort = null,
    int? smtpPort = null)
{
    MailDevResource resource = new(name);      // Create an instance of a MailDev resource.

    return builder.AddResource(resource)
              .WithImage(MailDevContainerImageTags.Image)       // Set the base Docker image for MailDev.
              .WithImageRegistry(MailDevContainerImageTags.Registry)   // Set the Docker registry to pull the image from.
              .WithImageTag(MailDevContainerImageTags.Tag)      // Set the Docker image version tag.
              .WithHttpEndpoint(                                // Configure the HTTP endpoint for the MailDev container.
                  targetPort: 1080,
                  port: httpPort,
                  name: MailDevResource.HttpEndpointName)
              .WithEndpoint(                                    // Configure the SMTP endpoint for the MailDev container.
                  targetPort: 1025,
                  port: smtpPort,
                  name: MailDevResource.SmtpEndpointName);
}
```

We abstracted away the Docker container launch in this extension method. Now we only need to invoke the `AddMailDev()` method from the Aspire host startup.

### 2.7.2 Launching a custom integration from the Aspire host

Before we can launch the MailDev component from the Aspire host, we have to reference the newly created class library from the `OnlineShop.AppHost` project. But the project reference is a special type, so the easiest way to do that is to add it manually. To do so, add this XML element to the `OnlineShop.AppHost.csproj` project file alongside the other project references:

```
<ProjectReference
    Include="..\OnlineShop.MailDev.Hosting\OnlineShop.MailDev.Hosting.csproj"
    IsAspireProjectResource="false" />
```

The important part here is the `IsAspireProjectResource` attribute, which is set to `false`. In the context of Aspire host, any project is automatically treated as an app hosted as an Aspire service, and metadata is generated for it. But that's not what we need; we want to treat it as a standard class library. This attribute allows us to do that.

Next, we open the `AppHost.cs` file inside the `OnlineShop.AppHost` project and add the following `using` statement at the beginning:

```
using OnlineShop.MailDev.Hosting;
```

Finally, after we create the `builder` variable, we add the following line:

```
var maildev = builder.AddMailDev("maildev");
```

Now, if we launch the app, we should see the `MailDev` container running in our dashboard, as figure 2.9 shows.

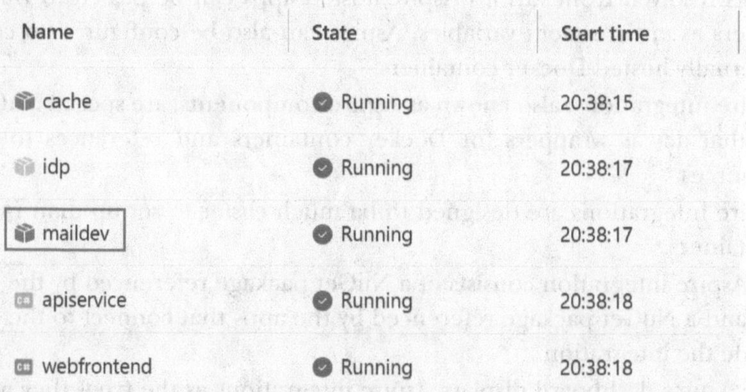


**Figure 2.9 MailDev container running in the Aspire dashboard**

If we click the URL next to it, we see our local email inbox along with links to the additional documentation, as figure 2.10 shows.

**Figure 2.10 MailDev user interface**

In this chapter, we looked at the common principles of hosting Aspire integrations. As an example of an existing integration, we looked at the Redis component used for output caching, which is available in the Aspire Starter Project. But Aspire has many other integration types. The next five chapters (parts 2 and 3) discuss working with other integration types, such as databases and message brokers. We'll start by covering integrations that represent relational SQL databases, which is where we begin adding the functionality that will transform our system into an online shop.

## Summary

- Docker containers provide a consistent hosting environment for apps. They're typically used to host shared infrastructure components, such as IdPs for SSO and databases.
- Docker containers can be added to the Aspire app host by using its native methods. Additional configuration can be implemented via extension methods.
- URLs resolved from various Aspire-hosted apps can be passed to Docker containers as environment variables. Aspire can also be configured to connect to externally hosted Docker containers.
- Aspire integrations, also known as Aspire components, are special NuGet libraries that act as wrappers for Docker containers and references to managed resources.
- Aspire integrations are designed to be much easier to set up than raw Docker containers.
- An Aspire integration consists of a NuGet package referenced by the host project and a NuGet package referenced by the apps that connect to the container inside the integration.
- The Aspire dashboard displays Aspire integrations as the types they wrap, such as Docker containers.
- Although there is an extensive library of existing Aspire integrations, you can create custom ones.

# 3 Using database and storage components

**This chapter covers**

- Connecting Aspire to an existing database instance using connection strings
- Integrating SQL Server and consuming data with both raw SQL and Entity Framework
- Working with other relational databases, including Oracle, PostgreSQL, and MySQL
- Using NoSQL databases such as MongoDB and Azure Cosmos DB
- Connecting to Azure Storage services such as Table Storage and Blob Storage

Aspire can be integrated with many database types, including SQL-based relational database management systems (RDBMSs) and various categories of NoSQL databases, such as document stores and key-value stores. All this can be done via Aspire integration libraries.

This chapter covers both database categories, with examples showing a range of specific data storage technologies in SQL and NoSQL areas. Before we start, however, let's talk about connecting Aspire to an existing database instance. We'll do so by continuing to build our e-commerce app. Our app needs data, such as the products we sell, the orders customers place, and so on. This is what databases are for.

## 3.1 Connecting Aspire to an existing database

Before we look at how to build database resources and let the Aspire host manage them, let's look at how to connect Aspire instances to existing resources. After all, we may already have a fully managed instance of a SQL Server, Oracle, or MongoDB database that we want to connect our system to.

Fortunately, connecting a distributed Aspire application to an existing database works the same way for any database type. Add the following code to the distributed application builder in the `AppHost.cs` file in the Aspire host project:

```
var database = builder.AddConnectionString("database");
```

In this example, `database` is an arbitrary resource name. This value can be anything, but it must point to an entry in the `ConnectionStrings` section of the application settings of the Aspire host application. The value in the settings will be the actual connection string for the database. Here's what such a section would look like in the `appsettings.json` file for the preceding example:

```
"ConnectionStrings": {
    "database": "<a valid SQL database connection string>"
}
```

When the distributed application is registered in the host, the services inside it can resolve the right connection string by specifying the connection name, just as they use any other resource name for service discovery. The Aspire service discovery mechanism takes care of this task, so the services don't need to have the connection string configured in their own settings as long as the variable created from the `AddConnectionString()` method is passed as a reference to all these services.

In section 3.2, we'll see how to use Aspire integrations to host databases internally and fully manage their lifetimes. We'll talk about SQL-based databases first.

## 3.2 SQL database components basics

Here are examples of SQL-based relational database types supported by Aspire:

- SQL Server (including a bespoke Azure version)
- Oracle
- PostgreSQL
- MySQL

Any enterprise-grade application relies on data, so it has data storage technologies integrated with it. SQL-based relational databases are the most popular category of databases used in these applications.

Aspire integrations make it significantly easier to add an RDBMS to your application. You no longer have to manage database connection strings yourself or even configure them in deployment pipelines; the Aspire service discovery mechanism will do the work for you.

Moreover, the integration libraries work both with and without the object-relational mapper, such as Entity Framework (EF). Therefore, you can use the SQL-based databases in the way that you prefer and are accustomed to.

This chapter goes through the main SQL integrations available with Aspire. Before we talk about the individual SQL database types, though, we'll discuss the general principles that all RDBMS integrations follow.

In general, as we saw in chapter 2, each Aspire integration is represented by two types of libraries:

- The host library allows the container with the app to be hosted in a distributed Aspire setup.
- The consumer library allows individual services to interact with the component.

SQL databases are no different; each one has a library that's added to the Aspire host project. The library allows the host to register, configure, and launch the resource with the database management system. This resource is typically a container when you run your system locally. But it can also be configured to deploy a persistent managed database instance when you deploy the system to production, so the data stored in the database doesn't disappear when the container orchestration system moves the containers around.

There are also client libraries for each database type. These libraries allow services to interact with databases by executing queries, inserting data, modifying data, and performing similar operations.

As briefly mentioned earlier, some components have several client libraries to choose among, depending on your preferred approach to working with SQL inside C# code. One client library allows you to use an object-relational mapper, such as Entity Framework, whereas another library works only through a direct interaction via raw SQL.

### 3.2.1 Working with the SQL data model

Regardless of what RDBMS we choose and what library we choose to interact with it, we have to prepare two types of objects:

- Data models representing database entities.
- Data transfer objects transfer this data across application boundaries.

Let's start with the entity model. In C#, this would be a type—usually a class when used in Entity Framework Core (EF Core)—that stores only data and doesn't have any business logic. A single instance of such a class would represent a single record in a database table. Its properties would represent the fields of this record. Each property would have the data type that most closely matches the intended or existing data type of the corresponding field. Such a class would also have properties that map to fields that make sense only in the context of the database, such as the identity field commonly used as the unique identifier that enables relationships through primary and foreign keys.

Because we're building an online store, we need an entity model that represents a product. Therefore, inside the `OnlineShop.ApiService` project, we'll create a folder called `Models`. Inside this folder, we'll create the `Product.cs` file with the following content:

```
using System.ComponentModel.DataAnnotations;

namespace OnlineShop.ApiService.Models;

public class Product
{
    [Key]
    public int Id { get; set; }

    [MaxLength(100)]
    public string Title { get; set; } = string.Empty;

    [MaxLength(2100)]
    public string Summary { get; set; } = string.Empty;

    public decimal Price { get; set; }

    public DateTime DateAdded { get; set; }
}
```

Note that the `Id` property is marked with the `Key` attribute. This property maps to the database-specific identity field that autoincrements when we add new records to the table. Each record has its own unique identity, so it's used as the table index for searching records and as the primary key. Also note that we're using the `MaxLength` attribute on the string properties. This ensures that the corresponding database field is optimized for storing a specific number of characters. Having these limits on the model helps us validate the data before it touches the database.

Next comes the data transfer object (DTO). This data structure transfers data between services or between the client and the server. In our case, DTOs will be returned by the API when the UI service requests product data so that the products can be displayed to the user.

Why can't we use the original data-model entity for this purpose? Well, we can, but this is rarely the most efficient way to go about it for a couple of reasons:

- The database entity may contain some fields that are useless to other services, such as the database-specific identity field. Network bandwidth may be limited, and these fields will use bandwidth for no reason.

- You may have some translation between the original entity and what's displayed to the user. In our context, users care only about the product's name, description, and price; therefore, these fields are the only ones that the DTO will have.

Ideally, when services exchange a DTO, they reference the same contract. Otherwise, if you keep one copy of the DTO definition on the client and another on the server, you run the risk of updating one copy and forgetting to update the other. Therefore, it's a common best practice to keep the same library reference that contains the common DTO definitions for both the client and the server. In our case, we already have the `OnlineShop.ServiceDefaults` project, which is referenced by both the web front-end and the API services. Therefore, we'll create the `Dtos` folder inside this project and place the `ProductDto.cs` file there with the following content:

```
namespace OnlineShop.ServiceDefaults.Dtos;

public record ProductDto(
    string Title,
    string Summary,
    decimal Price
);
```

Before we continue, we have to build one part of our application that will be the same regardless of which RDBMS provider and database mapper we choose: our product UI.

### 3.2.2 Displaying the DTO information in the UI

Our UI is database-agnostic, which is a great example of separation of concerns in a business app. Database changes won't affect the UI, and UI changes won't affect the database. The infrastructure layer is separate from the presentation layer, which is another reason why a separate DTO object exists: it transfers data between the layers so neither layer cares about the implementation details of the other.

Now we'll build a UI layer that adheres to these standards, making some changes to our `OnlineShop.Web` project. First, we'll rename the `WeatherApiClient.cs` file to `ProductsApiClient.cs`. Then we'll apply the changes shown in the following listing so that instead of pulling weather data from the API, it pulls product data.

**Listing 3.1 HTTP client for retrieving product data**

```
using OnlineShop.ServiceDefaults.Dtos;

namespace OnlineShop.Web;

public class ProductsApiClient(HttpClient httpClient)
{
    public async Task<ProductDto[]> GetProductsAsync(int maxItems = 10,
     CancellationToken cancellationToken = default)
    {
        List<ProductDto>? products= null;
```

```
        await foreach (var product in
httpClient.GetFromJsonAsAsyncEnumerable<ProductDto>(
    "/products", cancellationToken))
        {
            if (products?.Count >= maxItems)
            {
                break;
            }
            if (product is not null)
            {
                products ??= [];
                products.Add(product);
            }
        }

        return products?.ToArray() ?? [];
    }
}
```

Sending a HTTP GET request to the /products endpoint of the API

Ensure we only return as many products as we want to display on the page.

Return either the collection of products or an empty array.

**NOTE** After updating this class, we also have to update the dependency injection (DI) registration in the `Program.cs` file to point to the `ProductsApiClient` type inside `builder.Services.AddHttpClient()`.

Now let's get our user interface to use the class. The products will be displayed on the home page of our online shop, so we'll replace the content of the `Home.razor` file (in the `Components` > `Pages` folder) with the content shown in the next listing.

**Listing 3.2 Home page displaying the product data**

```
@page "/"
@using OnlineShop.ServiceDefaults.Dtos
@attribute [StreamRendering(true)]
@attribute [OutputCache(Duration = 5)]

@inject ProductsApiClient ProductsApi

<PageTitle>Products</PageTitle>

<h1>Products</h1>

@if (products == null)
{
    <p><em>Loading...</em></p>
}
else
{
    <table class="table">
        <thead>
            <tr>
                <th>Name</th>
                <th>Price (USD)</th>
                <th>Summary</th>
```

```
                </tr>
            </thead>
            <tbody>
                @foreach (var product in products)
                {
                    <tr>
                        <td>@product.Title</td>
                        <td>@product.Price</td>
                        <td>@product.Summary</td>
                    </tr>
                }
            </tbody>
        </table>
    }

@code {
    private ProductDto[]? products;

    protected override async Task OnInitializedAsync()
    {
        products = await ProductsApi.GetProductsAsync();
    }
}
```

We have to remove the `Counter.razor` and `Weather.razor` files from the Pages folder because we don't need them anymore. Finally, we navigate to the `NavMenu.razor` Razor component (in the `Layout` folder) and remove the NavLink elements pointing to the `/weather` and `/counter` paths. The final content of `NavMenu.razor` should look like the next listing.

**Listing 3.3 Navigation links for the application**

```
<div class="top-row ps-3 navbar navbar-dark">
    <div class="container-fluid">
        <a class="navbar-brand" href="">OnlineShop</a>
    </div>
</div>

<input type="checkbox" title="Navigation menu" class="navbar-toggler" />

<div class="nav-scrollable" onclick="document.querySelector('.navbar-
    toggler').click()">
    <nav class="nav flex-column">
        <div class="nav-item px-3">
            <NavLink class="nav-link" href="" Match="NavLinkMatch.All">
                <span class="bi bi-house-door-fill" aria-hidden="true"></
  span> Home
            </NavLink>
        </div>
    </nav>
</div>
```

Our UI is done. The rest of the chapter is about choices. I'll show you different database implementations, which are mutually exclusive because software teams typically wouldn't use competing database technologies in the same system. Therefore, treat the changes applied in this section as the common starting point for every database type.

## 3.3 Hosting a SQL Server component

First, we'll look at the SQL Server component. To host a SQL Server container with Aspire components, we have to add the NuGet package `Aspire.Hosting.SqlServer` to the Aspire host project. Then we set up this component in the `AppHost.cs` file of the host project:

```
var sql = builder.AddSqlServer("sql").WithLifetime(ContainerLifetime.Persistent);
var sqldb = sql.AddDatabase("sqldb");

var apiService = builder
    .AddProject<Projects.OnlineShop_ApiService>("apiservice")
    .WithHttpHealthCheck("/health")
    .WithReference(idp)
    .WaitFor(idp)
    .WaitFor(sqldb)
    .WithReference(sqldb);
```

Let's examine this code step by step. First, we add a SQL Server component. We assign the name `sql` to the resource but could use any arbitrary name. There are several overloads of the `AddSqlServer()` method. This specific invocation autogenerates the password for the `sa` user, which is used as the default SQL Server admin. The port is assigned automatically too.

Next, we create a database by executing the `AddDatabase()` method with the name of the new database as its parameter. It's important to know that this method's behavior has changed since early versions of Aspire. In version 8, it merely added a reference to a database and a connection string. The actual database had to be created separately. Now it creates the actual database automatically by executing the SQL command appropriate to the database provider. In the SQL Server implementation, this command would be

```
DECLARE @DatabaseName NVARCHAR(128) = N'YourDatabaseName';

IF NOT EXISTS (SELECT 1 FROM sys.databases WHERE name = @DatabaseName)
BEGIN
    DECLARE @SQL NVARCHAR(MAX) = N'CREATE DATABASE ' +
     QUOTENAME(@DatabaseName);
    EXEC(@SQL);
END
```

Because we called our database sqldb earlier, `sqldb` will be used as the value in the square brackets. But the database name can be arbitrary as long as it adheres to the database naming rules.

Remember that the value we pass into the `AddDatabase()` method invocation isn't just the database name but also the name by which the database resource is known for service-discovery purposes. I'll cover this topic later. Please note that we're also invoking the following method while registering the database:

```
WithLifetime(ContainerLifetime.Persistent)
```

Here's why this is important. By default, the SQL Server instance is registered as a Docker container. If we don't make the container lifetime persistent, a new container instance will be launched every time we run the orchestrated application. The old container instance will be destroyed, along with all the data it contains. But with a persistent lifetime, the old container will be reused.

On top of this, other methods allow us to bind-mount the database container to a data volume on a filesystem. As a general rule, though, hosting databases inside Docker in production isn't the best idea. Although Docker provides a convenient way to set up a database quickly in a development environment, it's much better to use a persistent managed database instance in production.

There's also a hybrid approach in which the database server is hosted inside a container in a development environment while the system connects to a managed instance in production. I cover this topic in chapter 9, along with the process of deploying Aspire apps to production.

Let's get back to our code example. We use the `WithReference()` method invocation to insert the database reference into any service that we want to interact with the database. We also use the `WaitFor()` invocation to make sure that the service relying on the database doesn't start until the database is ready.

You can find an example of this setup in the codebase at https://mng.bz/15lX.

If we launch this application, we see both the SQL Server and the database reference in the dashboard (figure 3.1).

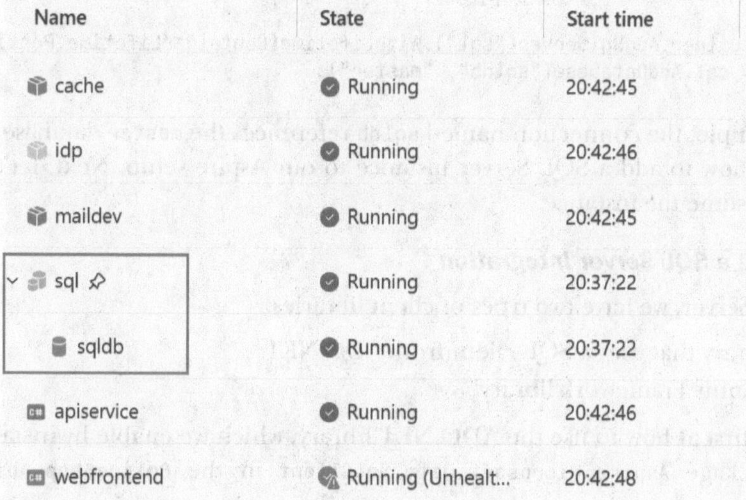


**Figure 3.1 SQL Server component hosted in Aspire**

Let's look at other ways to set up the database. In the following example, we set up our own password for the admin `sa` user in `AppHost.cs` of the Aspire host project:

```
var password = builder.AddParameter("password", secret: true);
var sql = builder.AddSqlServer("sql",
    password).WithLifetime(ContainerLifetime.Persistent);
var sqldb = sql.AddDatabase("sqldb");
```

The password is passed to the `AddSqlServer()` method. The password value is extracted via the `AddParameter()` method, which looks for an entry in the Parameters section of the `appsettings.json` file. It may look like this:

```
{
  "Logging": {
    "LogLevel": {
      "Default": "Information",
      "Microsoft.AspNetCore": "Warning",
      "Aspire.Hosting.Dcp": "Warning"
    }
  },
  "Parameters": {
    "password": "P@$$w0rd"
  }
}
```

We can also pass a specific port number in the `AddSqlServer()` method invocation:

```
var sql = builder.AddSqlServer("sql", port: 3000).WithLifetime(ContainerLife-
    time.Persistent);
var sqldb = sql.AddDatabase("sqldb");
```

This ensures that SQL Server runs on a specific port rather than one assigned automatically by the system. We can also supply the database name to the `AddDatabase()` method:

```
var sql = builder.AddSqlServer("sql").WithLifetime(ContainerLifetime.Persistent);
var sqldb = sql.AddDatabase("sqldb", "master");
```

In this example, the connection named `sqldb` references the `master` database.

This is how to add a SQL Server instance to our Aspire setup. Next, let's look at how to consume the instance.

### 3.3.1 Consuming a SQL Server integration

With SQL Server, we have two types of client libraries:

- A library that uses a SQL client from ADO.NET
- An Entity Framework library

Let's look first at how to use the ADO.NET library, which we enable by installing the NuGet package `Aspire.Microsoft.Data.SqlClient` in the `OnlineShop.ApiService` project.

When we have this NuGet package, we can add the following line to the `Program.cs` file of the consuming project to register the SQL Server client dependencies:

```
builder.AddSqlServerClient("sqldb");
```

This example uses the same name we used when we registered the database resource in the host application. This means that the host will provide the SQL Server connection string. We don't need to construct our own connection string in the client app. But if we ever want to supply our own connection string, we can use different overloads of this method.

This method adds an instance of the `SqlConnection` class to dependency injection (DI) with the appropriate connection string configured. This allows us to execute raw SQL against the SQL Server instance from anywhere in our application code.

Let's see how it's used. As a simple example, we'll use a database to contain the products sold in our online shop. To do so, we add the following block of code to the `Program.cs` file:

```
using (var scope = app.Services.CreateScope())
{
}
```

Inside this block, we resolve the `SqlConnection` instance from the DI container and invoke the `Open()` method to open the connection:

```
var connection = scope.ServiceProvider.GetRequiredService<SqlConnection>();
connection.Open();
```

Although we have both the SQL Server instance and the database configured, we can still use the client to create a new database. This may be useful when each service has its own database (such as in a domain-driven architecture implementation) and the new database hasn't been provisioned by the original Aspire setup. To demonstrate this capability, let's create another database and call it `Shop`. Run the following command:

```
var createDbCommand = new SqlCommand(@"
        IF NOT EXISTS (SELECT *
            FROM sys.databases
            WHERE name = 'Shop')
        BEGIN
              CREATE DATABASE Shop;
        END;", connection);
createDbCommand.ExecuteNonQuery();
```

Next, we create a database table to contain our products:

```
var createTableCommand = new SqlCommand(@"
        USE Shop;
        IF NOT EXISTS (SELECT *
            FROM sysobjects
            WHERE name='Products' and xtype='U')
```

```
        CREATE TABLE Products(
            Id INT PRIMARY KEY IDENTITY,
    Title VARCHAR(100) NOT NULL,

            Summary NVARCHAR(2100) NOT NULL,
            Price DECIMAL(18,2) NOT NULL,
            DateAdded DATE NOT NULL
        )", connection);

createTableCommand.ExecuteNonQuery();
```

`USE Shop` is required to make sure that we're creating a table in the right database. Next, we check whether the database table contains any data:

```
var checkDataCommand =
    new SqlCommand(
        "SELECT COUNT(*) FROM Products",
        connection);
var count = (int)checkDataCommand
    .ExecuteScalar();
```

If the table contains no data, we populate it, as shown in the next listing.

**Listing 3.4 Adding data to a SQL Server database**

```
if (count == 0)
{
    var insertCommand =
        new SqlCommand("""
        INSERT INTO Products (Title, Summary, Price, DateAdded)
        VALUES
        (
            'Wireless Optical Mouse',
            N'Ergonomic wireless optical mouse with adjustable DPI and long
    battery life, suitable for everyday office and home use.',
            24.99,
            '2025-01-05'
        ),
        (
            'Mechanical Gaming Keyboard',
            N'RGB backlit mechanical keyboard with blue switches, anti-
    ghosting keys, and durable aluminum frame.',
            129.99,
            '2025-01-06'
        ),
        (
            '27-inch 4K Monitor',
            N'27-inch UHD 4K monitor with IPS panel, 3840x2160 resolution,
    HDR support, and ultra-thin bezels.',
            399.00,
            '2025-01-07'
        ),
```

```
        (
            'USB-C Docking Station',
            N'Multi-port USB-C docking station with HDMI, DisplayPort,
Ethernet, USB 3.0 ports, and 100W power delivery.',
            179.50,
            '2025-01-08'
        ),
        (
            'External SSD 1TB',
            N'Portable 1TB external SSD with USB 3.2 Gen 2 support,
delivering fast read/write speeds in a compact design.',
            149.99,
            '2025-01-09'
        ),
        (
            'Noise-Cancelling Headphones',
            N'Over-ear wireless headphones with active noise cancellation,
high-fidelity sound, and 30-hour battery life.',
            249.00,
            '2025-01-10'
        ),
        (
            'Webcam Full HD 1080p',
            N'Full HD 1080p webcam with built-in microphone, autofocus, and
low-light correction for video conferencing.',
            69.99,
            '2025-01-11'
        ),
        (
            'Gaming Laptop Backpack',
            N'Water-resistant backpack designed for gaming laptops up to 17
inches, featuring padded compartments and USB charging port.',
            59.95,
            '2025-01-12'
        ),
        (
            'Wi-Fi 6 Router',
            N'Dual-band Wi-Fi 6 router offering high-speed wireless
connectivity, improved range, and support for multiple devices.',
            199.00,
            '2025-01-13'
        ),
        (
            'Portable Laser Printer',
            N'Compact monochrome laser printer suitable for small offices,
offering fast printing speeds and wireless connectivity.',
            289.99,
            '2025-01-14'
        );
        """,
            connection);

        insertCommand.ExecuteNonQuery();
    }
```

Now we can query the database and return its data in our API endpoint, as shown in the next listing.

**NOTE** This example was constructed for demonstration convenience. In a real-life application, database interaction would be abstracted away by the service layer, not done directly in the API endpoint.

**Listing 3.5 Returning data from SQL Server via a `GET` endpoint**

```
app.MapGet("/products",
    ([FromServices] SqlConnection connection) =>
    {
        connection.Open();

        var command = new SqlCommand(@"
            USE Shop;
            SELECT
                Title,
                Summary,
                Price
            FROM Products", connection);
        var products = new List<ProductDto>();

        using (var reader = command.ExecuteReader())
        {
            while (reader.Read())
            {
                products.Add(new ProductDto(
                    Title: reader.GetString(0),
                    Summary: reader.GetString(1),
                    Price: reader.GetDecimal(2)
                ));
            }

            return products.ToArray();
        }
    });
```

Figure 3.2 shows what the home page of our frontend app should look like.

The complete example is available at https://github.com/fiodarsazanavets/aspire-13-examples/tree/main/AppWithSqlServer/OnlineShop.

### 3.3.2 Using Entity Framework

Let's look at how to achieve the same result with Entity Framework. The host remains the same because it still hosts the same SQL Server instance. Only the client changes—that is, how the API service connects to the database. The Entity Framework client library is represented by the NuGet package `Aspire.Microsoft.EntityFrameworkCore.SqlServer`, which we can add to our `OnlineShop.ApiService` project.

## Products

| Name | Price (USD) | Summary |
|---|---|---|
| Wireless Optical Mouse | 24.99 | Ergonomic wireless optical mouse with adjustable DPI and long battery life, suitable for everyday office and home use. |
| Mechanical Gaming Keyboard | 129.99 | RGB backlit mechanical keyboard with blue switches, anti-ghosting keys, and durable aluminum frame. |
| 27-inch 4K Monitor | 399.00 | 27-inch UHD 4K monitor with IPS panel, 3840x2160 resolution, HDR support, and ultra-thin bezels. |
| USB-C Docking Station | 179.50 | Multi-port USB-C docking station with HDMI, DisplayPort, Ethernet, USB 3.0 ports, and 100W power delivery. |
| External SSD 1TB | 149.99 | Portable 1TB external SSD with USB 3.2 Gen 2 support, delivering fast read/write speeds in a compact design. |
| Noise-Cancelling Headphones | 249.00 | Over-ear wireless headphones with active noise cancellation, high-fidelity sound, and 30-hour battery life. |
| Webcam Full HD 1080p | 69.99 | Full HD 1080p webcam with built-in microphone, autofocus, and low-light correction for video conferencing. |
| Gaming Laptop Backpack | 59.95 | Water-resistant backpack designed for gaming laptops up to 17 inches, featuring padded compartments and USB charging port. |
| Wi-Fi 6 Router | 199.00 | Dual-band Wi-Fi 6 router offering high-speed wireless connectivity, improved range, and support for multiple devices. |
| Portable Laser Printer | 289.99 | Compact monochrome laser printer suitable for small offices, offering fast printing speeds and wireless connectivity. |

**Figure 3.2 Products returned from the API endpoint**

Entity Framework represents a database abstraction by using an override of the `DbContext` class. The following code is an example of a `ProductsDbContext` that represents our products database, which we can place in the root of the API project.

**Listing 3.6 `DbContext` implementation for products data**

```
using OnlineShop.ApiService.Models;
using Microsoft.EntityFrameworkCore;

namespace OnlineShop.ApiService;

public class ProductsDbContext : DbContext
{
    public ProductsDbContext(
        DbContextOptions<ProductsDbContext> options) : base(options)
    {
    }

    public DbSet<Product> Products { get; set; }
}
```

When we have the `DbContext`, we can execute the following method inside the `Program.cs` file to register all the database dependencies:

```
builder.AddSqlServerDbContext<ProductsDbContext>("sqldb");
```

This method registers an instance of the `ProductsDbContext` class, which then can be resolved anywhere via DI.

The earlier principles apply. Because we're referencing the `sqldb` connection name, we use the connection string constructed by the Aspire host. But we can customize the connection string via method overrides. The next listing shows the initial database-setup code.

**Listing 3.7 Adding data to the database via a DbContext**

```
using (var scope = app.Services.CreateScope())
{
    var context = scope
        .ServiceProvider
        .GetRequiredService<ProductsDbContext>();

    context.Database.EnsureCreated();

    if (!context.Products.Any())
    {
        var products = new List<Product>
        {
            new Product
            {
                Title = "Wireless Optical Mouse",
                Summary = "Ergonomic wireless optical mouse with adjustable
 DPI and long battery life, suitable for everyday office and home use.",
                Price = 24.99m,
                DateAdded = new DateTime(2025, 1, 5)
            },
            new Product
            {
                Title = "Mechanical Gaming Keyboard",
                Summary = "RGB backlit mechanical keyboard with blue
 switches, anti-ghosting keys, and durable aluminum frame.",
                Price = 129.99m,
                DateAdded = new DateTime(2025, 1, 6)
            },
            new Product
            {
                Title = "27-inch 4K Monitor",
                Summary = "27-inch UHD 4K monitor with IPS panel, 3840x2160
 resolution, HDR support, and ultra-thin bezels.",
                Price = 399.00m,
                DateAdded = new DateTime(2025, 1, 7)
            },
            new Product
            {
                Title = "USB-C Docking Station",
                Summary = "Multi-port USB-C docking station with HDMI,
 DisplayPort, Ethernet, USB 3.0 ports, and 100W power delivery.",
                Price = 179.50m,
                DateAdded = new DateTime(2025, 1, 8)
```

- Resolving DB context from the dependency injection container
- Ensure the database is created if it doesn't already exist.
- Check if any product records already exist.

```
        },
        new Product
        {
            Title = "External SSD 1TB",
            Summary = "Portable 1TB external SSD with USB 3.2 Gen 2
support, delivering fast read/write speeds in a compact design.",
            Price = 149.99m,
            DateAdded = new DateTime(2025, 1, 9)
        },
        new Product
        {
            Title = "Noise-Cancelling Headphones",
            Summary = "Over-ear wireless headphones with active noise
cancellation, high-fidelity sound, and 30-hour battery life.",
            Price = 249.00m,
            DateAdded = new DateTime(2025, 1, 10)
        },
        new Product
        {
            Title = "Webcam Full HD 1080p",
            Summary = "Full HD 1080p webcam with built-in microphone,
autofocus, and low-light correction for video conferencing.",
            Price = 69.99m,
            DateAdded = new DateTime(2025, 1, 11)
        },
        new Product
        {
            Title = "Gaming Laptop Backpack",
            Summary = "Water-resistant backpack designed for gaming
laptops up to 17 inches, featuring padded compartments and USB charging
port.",
            Price = 59.95m,
            DateAdded = new DateTime(2025, 1, 12)
        },
        new Product
        {
            Title = "Wi-Fi 6 Router",
            Summary = "Dual-band Wi-Fi 6 router offering high-speed
wireless connectivity, improved range, and support for multiple
devices.",
            Price = 199.00m,
            DateAdded = new DateTime(2025, 1, 13)
        },
        new Product
        {
            Title = "Portable Laser Printer",
            Summary = "Compact monochrome laser printer suitable for
small offices, offering fast printing speeds and wireless
connectivity.",
            Price = 289.99m,
            DateAdded = new DateTime(2025, 1, 14)
        }
    };
```

```
        context.Products.AddRange(products);      <-- Add products to
        context.SaveChanges();                    <-- the database.
    }
}                                                 Save changes to make sure
                                                  the records are added.
```

Note the `EnsureCreated()` invocation on the `Database` property of the context object. Calling this method creates the database automatically if it doesn't exist.

We don't always want to do this, of course. In many cases, we want to fine-tune the database-creation process, such as by setting a specific collation. But this demonstrates how simple it is to create a database via Entity Framework if we're happy with the default database configuration. Finally, we retrieve the data from the database in the API endpoint:

```
app.MapGet("/products",
    ([FromServices] ProductsDbContext context) => context.Products.ToArray());
```

The `ToArray()` method causes the underlying SQL query to execute, as does its asynchronous version, `ToArrayAsync()`. When the query returns the results, they're converted to an array of `Product` objects. The complete setup of the example is available at https://mng.bz/PwKw.

### 3.3.3 Integrating with Azure SQL Server

Before we explore other SQL database types, let's look briefly at the Microsoft Azure version of SQL Server. Aspire has its own host library for this database and will create and manage an instance of it for you if you deploy your application to Azure. Although we can connect Aspire to an existing Azure SQL Server instance by using the standard SQL Server hosting integration library or the generic `AddConnectionString()` method, it's usually easier to do so via the NuGet package for the Aspire host project, `Aspire.Hosting.Azure.Sql`.

Then we register the SQL Server instance in the startup code of the host application by invoking the `AddAzureSqlServer()` method on the builder:

```
var sql = builder.AddAzureSqlServer("azure-sql");
var sqldb = sql.AddDatabase("sqldb");
```

Although we used a different method to register a SQL Server resource, we used the same `AddDatabase()` method to register the database. This method is universal for adding any type of database when we use the official Aspire integration libraries, whether it's with a SQL-based RDBMS provider or a NoSQL variety.

Interestingly, the `AddAzureSqlServer()` method doesn't add a Docker container if we run it locally. It won't even work locally if we configure it with the default settings. But if we deploy our application to Azure, it automatically creates a managed Azure SQL Server instance in the same resource group as the rest of the application. This makes it the easiest way to integrate Aspire with a SQL Server database if we intend to run it on Azure.

We can still configure our instance so that the local development environment runs the database in a Docker container while Azure uses the managed Azure SQL Server instance. Chapter 9 covers this topic.

By now, you may be asking, "What about the client libraries?" The good news is that both SQL Server client libraries we looked at earlier will work with the Azure SQL Server integration as they do with the standard SQL Server integration. The same libraries also work if our database reference was registered in the host app via the `AddConnectionString()` method. Remember the following caveats:

- The connection string must point to a SQL Server database.
- The name the connection string was registered with must match the name that the client is registered with.
- The connection string resource we registered in the host app must be passed as a reference to the service that has to connect to the database.

This concludes setting up a SQL Server container in Aspire. Next, we'll look at how to do it with other database types. Most of the principles for registering other SQL-based databases are the same as the ones we've already seen, so I'll cover each database provider relatively briefly, focusing on the unique implementation details of each provider.

## 3.4 Hosting an Oracle component

To host an Oracle database in Aspire, install the NuGet package `Aspire.Hosting.Oracle` in the host project. Then create a database server container and the database reference:

```
var oracle = builder.AddOracle("oracle").WithLifetime(ContainerLifetime.Per-
    sistent);
var oracledb = oracle.AddDatabase("oracledb");
```

Once again, both methods have overrides that allow us to customize the database configuration. If we use the default implementation without additional parameters, as shown in the preceding example, it launches an Oracle database inside a Docker container.

Setting the persistent lifetime for our container is even more important for the Oracle database than for any other database type, especially if we want to run and debug our application locally. The Oracle container takes a long time (several minutes) to start. If we don't set the persistent lifetime for the container, we have to endure the slow startup every time we launch our application. Otherwise, we have to suffer only once: the first time we run it.

At this writing, the Oracle component has only an Entity Framework client library. The NuGet package `Aspire.Oracle.EntityFrameworkCore` must be installed in the service that will consume the database, in our case represented by the `OnlineShop.ApiService` project. Then we can execute the following method inside the `Program.cs` file to register the `DbContext` and connect it to the database:

```
builder.AddOracleDatabaseDbContext<ProductsDbContext>("oracledb");
```

Other than this, we use the same Entity Framework and LINQ code that we'd use with other database types. Although different Entity Framework database providers work differently behind the scenes, the top-level abstractions look the same.

**Database connections in Aspire**

Here's a reminder that applies to all other Aspire-specific client libraries for other database providers: each client library works with databases registered via the `AddConnectionString()` method as long as the database that the connection string points to matches the provider type for the client library. Therefore, the preceding registration code still works if we use this method to connect to an existing Oracle database as long as that database is valid. The complete Oracle integration example is at https://mng.bz/Jwpo.

## 3.5 Hosting a PostgreSQL component

PostgreSQL is an extremely popular open source database technology. It's cloud-agnostic, which makes it deployable on any cloud provider, whether it's Azure, Amazon Web Services (AWS), Google Cloud, or even a self-hosted server. The PostgreSQL component is enabled via the NuGet package `Aspire.Hosting.PostgreSQL`. Use the following code to create the database server and the database reference:

```
var postgres = builder.AddPostgres("postgres")
    .WithLifetime(ContainerLifetime.Persistent);
var postgresdb = postgres.AddDatabase("postgresdb");
```

This code uses the same naming pattern as before:

- A provider-specific method to register the database server (in this case, `AddPostgres()`)
- The standard `AddDatabase()` method, which adds the database

Now let's look at suitable clients for connecting our services to this database. As before, these methods can be overridden.

The client services can consume PostgreSQL code through both Entity Framework and raw SQL. To use raw SQL, we can install the NuGet package `Aspire.Npgsql`. Then we can execute the following code inside our `Program.cs` file:

```
builder.AddNpgsqlDataSource("postgresdb");
```

This code registers an instance of the `NpgsqlDataSource` class, which we can insert as a service dependency into the services that need it. If we used the same name in the parameter that we used when we registered the database reference in the host application, the connection string is already configured.

`NpgsqlDataSource` is a standard class for interacting with PostgreSQL databases. This class can create a database connection object, which is used similarly to `SqlConnection`. The next listing shows how to use it to populate the database with data.

**Listing 3.8 Inserting data into a PostgreSQL database**

```
using Npgsql;

using (var scope = app.Services.CreateScope())
{
    var connection = scope.ServiceProvider.GetRequiredService<NpgsqlConnection>();
    await connection.OpenAsync();

    await using (var createTableCmd = new NpgsqlCommand(@"
        CREATE TABLE IF NOT EXISTS products (
            id            INTEGER GENERATED ALWAYS AS IDENTITY PRIMARY KEY,
            title         VARCHAR(100) NOT NULL,
            summary       VARCHAR(2100) NOT NULL,
            price         NUMERIC(18,2) NOT NULL,
            date_added    DATE NOT NULL
        );
    ", connection))
    {
        await createTableCmd.ExecuteNonQueryAsync();
    }

    long count;
    await using (var checkDataCmd = new NpgsqlCommand("SELECT COUNT(*) FROM
     products;", connection))
    {
        count = (long)(await checkDataCmd.ExecuteScalarAsync())!;
    }

    if (count == 0)
    {
        await using var insertCmd = new NpgsqlCommand(@"
            INSERT INTO products (title, summary, price, date_added)
            VALUES
            (
                'Wireless Optical Mouse',
                'Ergonomic wireless optical mouse with adjustable DPI and long
     battery life, suitable for everyday office and home use.',
                24.99,
                DATE '2025-01-05'
            );                                   <- Fewer records have been
                                                    provided for brevity.
        ", connection);

        await insertCmd.ExecuteNonQueryAsync();
    }
}
```

The endpoint to retrieve the products is

```
app.MapGet("/products",
    ([FromServices] NpgsqlConnection connection) =>
    {
        connection.Open();
```

```
        var command = new NpgsqlCommand(@"
            SELECT
                title,
                summary,
                price
            FROM products
            ORDER BY id;", connection);

        var products = new List<ProductDto>();

        using (var reader = command.ExecuteReader())
        {
            while (reader.Read())
            {
                products.Add(new ProductDto(
                    Title: reader.GetString(0),
                    Summary: reader.GetString(1),
                    Price: reader.GetDecimal(2)
                ));
            }
        }

        return products.ToArray();
    });
```

The complete example of this implementation is available at https://mng.bz/wZKO.

An alternative way to interact with a PostgreSQL database is through Entity Framework, which is available through the NuGet package `Aspire.Npgsql.EntityFrameworkCore.PostgreSQL`. Then use the following invocation in the application startup code to register the DB context:

```
builder.AddNpgsqlDbContext<ProductsDbContext>("postgresdb");
```

Then we use the same syntax that we used in the SQL Server and Oracle examples to interact with the database. Entity Framework is designed to abstract away provider-specific database interactions and replace them with standard LINQ syntax. The complete example of this integration is available at https://mng.bz/wZKO.

Aspire supports other RDBMS integrations, such as MySQL, but all of them are based on the fundamental principles I've already covered.

As the examples show, hosting SQL-based relational databases in Aspire is easy. Although we use different libraries for different database types, the principles are largely the same. Following are the important things to remember:

- The `AddDatabase()` method works differently depending on the Aspire version. In the current version of Aspire, it adds the actual database; in version 8, it merely added a connection string, leaving it to the developer to set up the database.
- We can use any library to connect to the database hosted in Aspire, and Aspire-specific NuGet packages allow us to resolve the connection string from the host automatically.

- If we aren't using an Aspire-specific library, the Aspire host still adds the database connection string to the hosted application's settings. We have to pull that string from the entry in the `ConnectionStrings` section of the standard .NET application settings (such as the `appsettings.json` file). The entry has the same name as the database we referenced in the Aspire host (e.g., `sqldb`).

## 3.6 Introduction to NoSQL

*NoSQL* refers to any data storage technology that doesn't adhere to the traditional relational structure. Contrary to the term, some of these database technologies use SQL or at least a language based on SQL. Other than this, they don't consist of standard tables and relationships. There are several types of NoSQL databases, including the following:

- *Document store*—Stores data as documents, often in formats such as JSON and BSON (e.g., MongoDB and Couchbase)
- *Key-value store*—Stores data as key-value pairs, similar to a dictionary (e.g., Redis and DynamoDB)
- *Graph database*—Focuses on relationships between data points, representing data as nodes and edges (e.g., Neo4j and ArangoDB)
- *Column-family store*—Organizes data into columns and rows, but unlike in relational databases, columns can vary between rows (e.g., Cassandra and HBase)

The world of NoSQL has no common database type or standard. The term merely means a data storage technology that doesn't rely primarily on SQL. Even different databases in the same category work differently.

Various NoSQL technologies exist because traditional relational databases aren't always the best solution for certain problems. A key-value store, for example, is the best database choice for a distributed cache because quick data retrieval is the most important feature. Column-family databases are much better suited to data warehousing, which stores large volumes of data. Graph databases are best for building complex connection maps, such as friends-and-connections hierarchies on social media, mind maps, and logistics and supply-chain models. Document stores work well when complex data has to be retrieved frequently and relationships between entities don't matter.

In the next section, we look at hosting various NoSQL and other storage components in Aspire by using its native libraries. The section includes Azure-specific examples, such as Cosmos DB and two types of Azure storage. It also covers MongoDB, which is one of the most popular document storage technologies across technology stacks.

### 3.6.1 Introduction to MongoDB

SQL-based RDBMS databases are great for storing core business data, such as products and orders. But typical e-commerce platforms consist of much more, such as a cart and product reviews. Although this data can also be stored in an RDBMS, other database types may be more suitable. One such type is a document store, which stores related entities in one document. This is how reviews can be associated with a product in the same document, for example.

Next, we'll add product reviews, using one of the most popular document store engines, MongoDB.

If you aren't familiar with MongoDB, it's a NoSQL open source database designed for scalability, flexibility, and ease of development. It stores data in a flexible, JSON-like format called BSON (Binary JSON), which allows more complex data structures than traditional relational databases do.

Unlike SQL databases, MongoDB doesn't rely on tables and rows; instead, it uses collections and documents, making it ideal for handling unstructured or semistructured data. But because it doesn't use tables, MongoDB doesn't have relationships or foreign-key constraints.

The main disadvantage of MongoDB is that it's hard to use when tracking relationships between different entities is important. At the same time, it can perform better than a SQL-based relational database in applications that require fast, iterative development, real-time analytics, or the ability to scale easily. Therefore, it's widely used in e-commerce platforms, social networks, and Internet of Things (IoT) applications.

Also, document databases handle object-relational impedance mismatch better because they store data in a shape that's much closer to the way application code represents it. With SQL-based relational databases, you have to use an object relational mapping (ORM) product such as Entity Framework or verbose translation code to represent table entities as classes in C#. A document store already stores this data similarly to the way objects in the code are structured.

### 3.6.2 Hosting a MongoDB component

To host a MongoDB container in Aspire, we add the NuGet package `Aspire.Hosting.MongoDB` to the Aspire host project. Then, in the startup code of the host application represented by the `AppHost.cs` file, we create a MongoDB server instance and a database reference:

```
var mongo = builder.AddMongoDB("mongo").WithLifetime(ContainerLifetime.Persistent);
var mongodb = mongo.AddDatabase("mongodb");
```

Then we can add the database reference to any service we want to connect to MongoDB by passing the database reference object as a parameter to the `WithReference()` method on that service reference. Here's how to do it:

```
var apiService = builder
    .AddProject<Projects.OnlineShop_ApiService>(
        "apiservice")
    .WithReference(mongodb)
    .WaitFor(mongodb);
```

We can apply some additional configuration to the preceding objects, but these examples are sufficient to launch a MongoDB container inside a distributed Aspire app.

### 3.6.3 Working with a MongoDB client

To interact with data stored in MongoDB from any other service hosted in Aspire, add the NuGet package `Aspire.MongoDB.Driver` reference to that service. Then invoke the following code in the `Program.cs` file to register all relevant MongoDB dependencies:

```
builder.AddMongoDBClient("mongodb");
```

The string value we pass in to the `AddMongoDBClient()` method is the name of the database reference we registered in the host application. Aspire configures the connection string automatically because we're using an Aspire-specific client library. If we want to retrieve the connection string directly, we can find it in the `mongodb` entry of the `ConnectionStrings` section of the application settings. This principle applies to all connection strings passed in to hosted services regardless of the data storage technology.

Next, to represent an individual BSON document stored in a MongoDB database, we need a class with an `Id` or `ObjectId` property as a string. This property stores a unique identifier for each document. The next listing shows what the `ProductReviewsDocument` class and its associated data would look like if it represented a MongoDB document. By convention, this class would be represented by the `ProductReviewsDocument.cs` file, which we'd create inside the project's `Models` folder.

**Listing 3.9 MongoDB-compatible data model**

```
using MongoDB.Bson;
using MongoDB.Bson.Serialization.Attributes;

namespace OnlineShop.ApiService.Models;

public sealed class ProductReviewsDocument
{
    [BsonId]
    [BsonRepresentation(BsonType.ObjectId)]
    public string Id { get; init; } = default!;

    // Matches Product.Id from SQL Server
    public int ProductId { get; init; }

    public double AverageRating { get; set; }

    public int TotalReviews { get; set; }

    public List<ProductReview> Reviews { get; init; } = new();
}

public sealed class ProductReview
{
    public string UserId { get; init; } = default!;

    public int Rating { get; init; }
```

```
    public string Comment { get; init; } = default!;

    public DateTime CreatedAt { get; init; }

    public bool VerifiedPurchase { get; init; }

    public ReviewStatus Status { get; init; } = ReviewStatus.Approved;
}

public enum ReviewStatus
{
    Pending = 0,
    Approved = 1,
    Rejected = 2
}
```

Let's see how to use this class. First, we create the following block inside the `Program.cs` file:

```
using (var scope = app.Services.CreateScope())
{
}
```

Next, we resolve an implementation of the `IMongoClient` interface, which we registered earlier by invoking the `AddMongoDBClient()` method. This object will be used to create a database if it doesn't exist and to create a database collection, which is MongoDB's equivalent of a database table:

```
var mongoClient = scope.ServiceProvider
    .GetRequiredService<IMongoClient>();

var database = mongoClient
    .GetDatabase("ShopDB");

var collection = database
    .GetCollection<ProductReviewsDocument>("ProductReviews");
```

The next step is seeing whether the collection is empty. If so, we populate it with the seed data. To check, we count the documents by executing the following code:

```
var docCount = collection.CountDocuments(FilterDefinition<ProductReviewsDocu-
     ment>.Empty);
```

Next, we populate the collection if the document count is `0`:

```
if (docCount == 0)
{
    var productReviews = new List<ProductReviewsDocument>();

    foreach (var productId in Enumerable.Range(1, 10))
    {
        var reviews = new List<ProductReview>();
```

```
        var numberOfReviews = Random.Shared.Next(1, 5);

        for (var i = 0; i < numberOfReviews; i++)
        {
            reviews.Add(new ProductReview
            {
                UserId = $"user-{Random.Shared.Next(1, 100)}",
                Rating = Random.Shared.Next(3, 6), // 3-5
                Comment = "Great product, works exactly as expected.",
                CreatedAt = DateTime.UtcNow.AddDays(-Random.Shared.Next(1, 30)),
                VerifiedPurchase = Random.Shared.Next(0, 2) == 1,
                Status = ReviewStatus.Approved
            });
        }

        var averageRating = reviews.Average(r => r.Rating);
        productReviews.Add(new ProductReviewsDocument
        {
            ProductId = productId, // matches SQL Products.Id
            AverageRating = Math.Round(averageRating, 2),
            TotalReviews = reviews.Count,
            Reviews = reviews
        });
    }

    collection.InsertMany(productReviews);
}
```

Finally, we add the API endpoint so that it can retrieve the product-review data from the MongoDB database, as shown in the next listing.

**Listing 3.10 `GET` endpoint to return data from MongoDB**

```
app.MapGet("/product-reviews",
    ([FromServices] IMongoClient mongoClient) =>
    {
        var database = mongoClient
            .GetDatabase("ShopDB");

        var collection = database
            .GetCollection<ProductReviewsDocument>(
                "ProductReviews");

        var productReviews = collection
            .Find(FilterDefinition<ProductReviewsDocument>.Empty)
            .ToList();

        return productReviews.ToArray();
    });
```

We're using the standard MongoDB C# Driver, so we can perform any other operations available with this client library. The `Aspire.MongoDB.Driver` package provides only an Aspire-specific wrapper for it.

If we want to, we can build an HTTP client and the UI in the frontend application to display this data the same way we did for the core products list. To see how all the code samples presented in this section integrate into a complete application, go to https://mng.bz/qRpA.

### 3.6.4 Other NoSQL components

Aspire can host NoSQL databases other than MongoDB. One notable database is Azure Cosmos DB. Although it's normally an Azure-specific service, it can be emulated locally via a Docker container. It serves broadly the same business purposes as MongoDB, so I'll cover it only briefly.

Cosmos DB is a globally distributed, multimodel NoSQL database service provided by Microsoft Azure. It's designed to provide high availability, scalability, and low-latency access to data across multiple regions. Cosmos DB is highly versatile, supporting various data models and APIs, making it suitable for a wide range of applications, including real-time analytics, web applications, and IoT systems.

Because Cosmos DB is globally distributed, it allows seamless data replication across multiple Azure regions, ensuring high availability and low-latency data access worldwide. It supports both active-active and active-passive data replication models. Cosmos DB supports multiple data models under a single service, including the following:

- *Document-based data*—For JSON-like documents (e.g., MongoDB API)
- *Key-value stores*—For high-speed access via key-value pairs
- *Column-family data*—Based on wide-column stores (e.g., Cassandra API)
- *Graph data*—For storing and querying graph-based data structures (e.g., Gremlin API)

Cosmos DB is API-agnostic, allowing developers to choose different APIs depending on their use cases. Here are examples of the APIs available:

- *SQL API*—A SQL-like query language for querying JSON documents
- *MongoDB API*—For applications that use MongoDB as a backend
- *Cassandra API*—For applications built on Cassandra
- *Gremlin API*—For graph-based queries
- *Table API*—For key-value data access, similar to Azure Table Storage

Although Cosmos DB requires Azure to be hosted in a production environment, it comes with an emulator, which means we can host an emulated version locally. Aspire has a component that allows us to host an emulated instance of Cosmos DB in a Docker container, as we'll discuss next.

### 3.6.5 Hosting a Cosmos DB component

To enable the Cosmos DB component, add the NuGet package `Aspire.Hosting.Azure.CosmosDB` to the Aspire host application. After we add this package, we can register the Cosmos DB component in our startup code inside the `AppHost.cs` file:

```
var cosmos = builder.AddAzureCosmosDB("cosmos");
```

`AddAzureCosmosDB()` has overloads that allow us to connect to a real Cosmos DB instance hosted in Azure. But we can also execute the following method to make it run in emulated mode, so no connection to Azure is necessary:

```
cosmos.RunAsEmulator();
```

Chapter 9 discusses how code that gets executed for local debugging is separated from production code, so we won't run an emulated Cosmos DB instance in production.

Next, we pass the Cosmos DB component variable in to the `WithReference()` method of the service in which we want to use it:

```
var apiService = builder
    .AddProject<Projects.OnlineShop_ApiService>(
        "apiservice")
    .WithReference(cosmos);
```

### 3.6.6 Connecting to Cosmos DB

In this section, we look at how to interact with the Cosmos DB component from another service hosted by Aspire. The Aspire-specific Cosmos DB client is managed via the NuGet package `Aspire.Microsoft.Azure.Cosmos`.

We can also interact with it through Entity Framework, which is enabled by the NuGet package `Aspire.Microsoft.EntityFrameworkCore.Cosmos`.

To register the Cosmos DB client, add the following code inside the `Program.cs` file:

```
builder.AddAzureCosmosClient("cosmos");
```

The `AddAzureCosmosClient()` invocation registers the Cosmos DB client—that is, the `CosmosClient` object. As before, the name we pass in to this method is the same name we used to register the service in the host app. This allows us to construct the connection string automatically.

Now we're ready to interact with the data stored in Cosmos DB and create suitable data models for it.

## 3.7 Azure Storage integration

With Cosmos DB, we started looking at Azure-specific services that can be emulated locally. Now let's look at other Azure-specific storage services that we can work with in a similar fashion. These services are represented by an Azure Storage account. We'll finish this chapter by integrating our Aspire apps with Azure Storage, starting with Azure Table Storage and then moving to Azure Blob Storage. A sample of a complete Azure Table Storage integration is available at https://mng.bz/7QAm.

If you're new to Azure Storage, here's a brief description. Azure has storage accounts, services dedicated to data storage. Each storage account has several subservices, including the following:

- *Table Storage*—A type of NoSQL database that stores data in separate tables. These tables are flat and aren't related to each other. It's particularly useful for storing reference data. In our example, it would be good for product metadata.
- *Blob Storage*—Equivalent to storing files in the cloud. We can store any kind of file containing any type of data. *BLOB* is an acronym that stands for *binary large object.* Although we can store such data in a SQL database, Blob Storage makes it much easier. In our example, we can use it to store product manuals or spec sheets.
- *Queue Storage*—A service that allows services to exchange messages by using queues. This service acts more like a message broker than a database type; therefore, I cover it later in the book.

### 3.7.1 Hosting Azure Storage components

Now let's see how to integrate Aspire with Table Storage. Because all Azure Storage services are accessible through a storage account, a common Aspire component hosts them all. To enable this component, add the NuGet package `Aspire.Hosting.Azure.Storage` to the Aspire host application project. Then, if we want to host a storage account with Table Storage, we can add the following code to the `AppHost.cs` file:

```
var tables = builder.AddAzureStorage("storage")
    .RunAsEmulator()
    .AddTables("tables");
```

We're invoking the `RunAsEmulator()` method to run the tables in emulated mode. Otherwise, we can use overrides of `AddAzureStorage()` and `AddTables()` to connect the component to real instances of a storage account and Table Storage, respectively.

Next, as always, we pass the Table Storage reference to the service that will use it:

```
var apiService = builder.AddProject<
    Projects.OnlineShop_ApiService>(
        "apiservice")
    .WithReference(tables);
```

### 3.7.2 Interacting with Azure Table Storage

In this section, we interact with Table Storage from another service hosted by Aspire. A project that represents any Aspire-hosted service that has to interact with Table Storage must have the NuGet package `Aspire.Azure.Data.Tables` installed. Then, to register the relevant dependency, we add the following invocation to the `Program.cs` file:

```
builder.AddAzureTableServiceClient("tables");
```

When working with Table Storage, the entity that represents a table entry needs some special columns. Therefore, if we want to work with product metadata entities, we use the class shown in the next listing.

**Listing 3.11 Azure Table Storage model**

```
public sealed class ProductMetadataEntity : ITableEntity
{
    // Required by Table Storage
    public string PartitionKey { get; set; } = default!;
    public string RowKey { get; set; } = default!;

    public DateTimeOffset? Timestamp { get; set; }
    public ETag ETag { get; set; }

    // Business metadata
    public bool ReviewsEnabled { get; set; }
    public bool Featured { get; set; }
    public int MaxReviewsPerUser { get; set; }
}
```

We need two special columns that every table in Table Storage has and that act as unique identifiers for each entity: `PartitionKey` and `RowKey`. The former is necessary so that the data can be partitioned, which is useful when we have a lot of it. The latter represents a unique identifier for each row.

We also need `ETag` and `Timestamp`. The former helps us manage concurrency because several rows can be inserted simultaneously. The latter records the time when the row was inserted or updated.

To seed the Table Storage with data, insert the following block into the `Program.cs` file (or use the existing block where we're already using the service scope):

```
using (var scope = app.Services.CreateScope())
{
}
```

Inside this block, add the following code, which resolves an instance of the previously registered `TableServiceClient` type and uses it to create a table if it doesn't already exist:

```
var tableServiceClient =
    scope.ServiceProvider.GetRequiredService<TableServiceClient>();

var tableClient = tableServiceClient
    .GetTableClient("ProductMetadata");

await tableClient.CreateIfNotExistsAsync();
```

Next, we query the table to see whether it's empty by executing the following code:

```
var existing = tableClient
    .Query<ProductMetadataEntity>(x => x.PartitionKey == "Product")
    .Take(1)
    .Any();
```

Finally, if the table is empty, we execute the following code to populate it with the seed data:

```
if (!existing)
{
    var entities = new List<ProductMetadataEntity>();

    foreach (var productId in Enumerable.Range(1, 10))
    {
        entities.Add(new ProductMetadataEntity
        {
            PartitionKey = "Product",
            RowKey = productId.ToString(),

            ReviewsEnabled = true,
            Featured = productId % 2 == 0,
            MaxReviewsPerUser = 1
        });
    }

    foreach (var entity in entities)
    {
        await tableClient.AddEntityAsync(entity);
    }
}
```

Our table has been populated. All we have to do is set up an API endpoint to retrieve data from it and return it in an HTTP response. The following listing shows how.

**Listing 3.12 Retrieving Azure Table Storage data via a GET request**

```
app.MapGet("/product-metadata",
   async (TableServiceClient tableServiceClient) =>
{
   var tableClient = tableServiceClient
       .GetTableClient("ProductMetadata");

   var metadata = new List<ProductMetadataEntity>();

   var entities = tableClient
       .QueryAsync<ProductMetadataEntity>(
           x => x.PartitionKey == "Product");

   await foreach (var entity in entities)
   {
```

```
        metadata.Add(entity);
    }

    return metadata.ToArray();
});
```

This completes the overview of integrating Aspire with Table Storage. We'll look at Blob Storage next.

### 3.7.3 Integrating with Azure Blob Storage

Blob Storage, also part of an Azure Storage account, is designed for storing files. In this context, we'll use it to store downloadable product specs. A complete application sample that integrates Blob Storage with Aspire is available at https://mng.bz/mZMP.

To host Blob Storage, we use the same NuGet package that we used for Table Storage: `Aspire.Hosting.Azure.Storage`. Then, to host a Blob Storage instance in emulated mode, we use the following code in the `AppHost.cs` file of the host application project:

```
var storage = builder.AddAzureStorage("storage")
    .RunAsEmulator();

var tables = storage
    .AddTables("tables");

var blobs = storage
    .AddBlobs("blobs");


var apiService = builder.AddProject<
    Projects.OnlineShop_ApiService>(
        "apiservice")
    .WithReference(blobs);
```

Let's see how to interact with it. In the service that will interact with the data in Blob Storage, install the NuGet package `Aspire.Azure.Storage.Blobs`.

In our example, we'll store data in a CSV file. To make this format easier to work with, install another NuGet package, `CsvHelper`. After adding both NuGet package references to the project file, insert the following code into the `Program.cs` file:

```
builder.AddAzureBlobServiceClient("blobs");
```

Then, as before, we use the following block to seed the storage with the initial data:

```
using (var scope = app.Services.CreateScope())
{
}
```

Inside this block, we insert the following code:

```
var blobServiceClient =
    scope.ServiceProvider
    .GetRequiredService<BlobServiceClient>();

var containerClient = blobServiceClient
    .GetBlobContainerClient("products");

// Create the container if it doesn't exist
await containerClient.CreateIfNotExistsAsync();

var blobClient = containerClient
    .GetBlobClient("product-specs.csv");

// Check if the blob already exists
if (await blobClient.ExistsAsync())
{
    return;
}
```

This code performs the following tasks:

1. Checks whether a BLOB container called `products` already exists. If not, the container is created.
2. Does the same for a file inside the container called `product-specs.csv`. If a file with this name doesn't exist, it's created.
3. If the file already exists, exits the sequence.

Because we're uploading product specifications as a CSV file, we'll add the following class to our `Model` folder to represent an individual record in that file:

```
namespace OnlineShop.ApiService.Model;

public sealed class ProductSpecCsvRow
{
    public int ProductId { get; set; }
    public string Category { get; set; } = default!;
    public int WarrantyMonths { get; set; }

    public bool ReviewsEnabled { get; set; }
    public bool Featured { get; set; }
    public int MaxReviewsPerUser { get; set; }
}
```

Next, the following code populates a collection with the product specifications:

```
var productSpecs = new List<ProductSpecCsvRow>();

foreach (var productId in Enumerable.Range(1, 10))
{
    productSpecs.Add(new ProductSpecCsvRow
    {
        ProductId = productId,
```

```
            ReviewsEnabled = true,
            Featured = productId % 2 == 0,
            MaxReviewsPerUser = 1,

            Category = productId % 2 == 0 ? "Laptop" : "Peripheral",
            WarrantyMonths = productId % 2 == 0 ? 24 : 12
        });
    }
```

We use the following code to write this data to the CSV file:

```
using (var memoryStream = new MemoryStream())
using (var writer = new StreamWriter(memoryStream, Encoding.UTF8, leaveOpen:
     true))
using (var csv = new CsvWriter(writer, new
      CsvConfiguration(CultureInfo.InvariantCulture)))
{
    csv.WriteRecords(productSpecs);
    writer.Flush();

    memoryStream.Position = 0;
    await blobClient.UploadAsync(memoryStream, overwrite: true);
}
```

We're flushing the writer and setting the memory position back to zero because the BLOB client reads from the memory stream we just wrote the data to.

Finally, we modify the API endpoint to download the file.

**Listing 3.13 Retrieving data from a BLOB container**

```
app.MapGet("/product-specs", async (
   BlobServiceClient blobServiceClient) =>
{
    var containerClient = blobServiceClient
        .GetBlobContainerClient("products");

    var blobClient = containerClient
        .GetBlobClient("product-specs.csv");

    if (!await blobClient.ExistsAsync())
    {
        return Array.Empty<ProductSpecCsvRow>();
    }

    List<ProductSpecCsvRow> productSpecs;

    // Download the CSV from the blob
    var downloadResponse = await blobClient.DownloadAsync();

    using (var stream = downloadResponse.Value.Content)
    using (var reader = new StreamReader(stream))
    using (var csv = new CsvReader(reader, CultureInfo.InvariantCulture))
```

```
    {
        productSpecs = csv
            .GetRecords<ProductSpecCsvRow>()
            .ToList();
    }

    return productSpecs.ToArray();
});
```

This concludes the overview of integrating Azure Blob Storage with Aspire.

## Summary

- The Aspire ecosystem has integrations for four major SQL-based database types: SQL Server, Oracle, PostgreSQL, and MySQL. Although all these integrations rely on different NuGet libraries for hosting inside Aspire, the setup syntax is similar across these libraries.
- When hosting libraries are used with client libraries to register database components, Aspire can generate connection strings automatically.
- All supported database integrations can be managed through Entity Framework, an object-relational mapper that abstracts away SQL interactions in C# code.
- SQL Server, PostgreSQL, and MySQL integrations have client libraries that allow raw SQL database integrations. Oracle integration works only with Entity Framework.
- NoSQL doesn't refer to any specific data storage format. Several database types are classed as NoSQL. Sometimes, NoSQL databases of the same type are set up differently.
- Aspire natively supports integrations with popular NoSQL databases and Azure-native data storage services.
- Various Azure services can use emulators, so we don't have to connect our local development machine to a real Azure instance.

# Part 2

# *Real-time features and AI: Making apps interactive*

Distributed apps aren't just about more services; they're also about better experiences. In this part, you'll use Aspire as the backbone for features that depend on tight feedback loops: real-time updates and AI-powered interactions.

First, you'll add live order tracking with SignalR so users can see state changes as they happen. Then you'll build something more ambitious: a ChatGPT-style app that runs locally with open models using Ollama and integrates intelligence into your application using Semantic Kernel. The goal isn't AI for the sake of AI; it's learning the patterns that make these systems reliable, debuggable, and easy to evolve.

# 4 Adding order-tracking functionality with SignalR

**This chapter covers**

- Using SignalR for real-time two-way communication between client and server
- Using OpenLayers to display interactive maps in the browser
- Building a system capable of handling delivery drivers' location updates in real time

In this chapter, we'll do something interesting with Aspire: build a delivery-tracking app by using SignalR and OpenLayers.

Our app will work similarly to existing popular order-tracking apps, such as Just Eat, Uber Eats, DoorDash, and those used by major e-commerce stores. The user interface will feature a map. The backend of the system will track the delivery driver's coordinates. As soon as the driver moves, the marker on the map will update. We won't have to do anything ourselves, such as refresh the screen. The map will be fully interactive and update automatically, just as it would in a real delivery-tracking app.

To bring this real-time tracking feature to life, we have to solve two main challenges: pushing live data from the server to the browser and rendering that data on an interactive map. We'll use two powerful, specialized libraries for this purpose:

Microsoft's SignalR to manage real-time communication and OpenLayers to display the map.

## 4.1 What is SignalR?

SignalR is a real-time communication library provided by Microsoft as part of ASP.NET Core. It simplifies the process of adding real-time web functionality to applications, enabling server-side code to push content to connected clients in real time. This capability is particularly useful for building features such as live chat, notifications, real-time dashboards, collaborative applications, and gaming.

SignalR enables bidirectional communication between server and client over a single connection. This allows the server to push updates to the client instantly, without the client's having to poll for updates. But in some cases, *long polling*—making constant HTTP requests from the client to check for changes on the server—is a more appropriate approach than server-initiated pushes. In some systems, this mechanism is the only one available because of constraints such as network restrictions. Fortunately, SignalR supports it too.

By default, SignalR works via a protocol known as WebSocket. But if WebSocket connections can't be used for any reason, SignalR can fall back to another transport mechanism, such as server-sent events or the previously mentioned long polling.

Using SignalR is much easier for developers than writing raw WebSockets code or implementing the other supported transport mechanisms manually. SignalR introduces *hubs*, which are high-level APIs for remote procedure calls (RPCs). Hubs allow the server to call methods on the client and vice versa, making client-server interactions easy to manage.

SignalR is highly scalable, making it suitable for large distributed applications, such as those hosted by Aspire. It supports scaling out across multiple servers using backplanes such as Redis, Azure SignalR Service, and SQL Server. This ensures that all clients receive updates, regardless of the server to which they're connected. Following are typical use cases for SignalR:

- Live chat applications, in which SignalR enables real-time messaging between users
- Live notifications because SignalR can push notifications to users instantly, such as stock-price updates or social media alerts
- Live location tracking, of which we'll build an example in this chapter
- Collaborative tools, such as real-time collaboration features in project management apps
- Real-time dashboards because SignalR can update dashboards with live data feeds in applications such as analytics and monitoring systems

**TIP** For more information on SignalR and how it fits into the wider ASP.NET Core ecosystem, see *ASP.NET Core in Action*, 3rd edition, by Andrew Lock (https://mng.bz/5vVz).

## 4.2 Introduction to OpenLayers

The map in our user interface will use OpenLayers, an open source JavaScript library for displaying dynamic, interactive maps on web pages. It allows developers to build robust mapping applications by providing tools for working with geographic data and various map services. OpenLayers is feature-rich and supports multiple mapping formats, making it a versatile choice for web-based geographic information system (GIS) applications.

Like any full-fledged GIS, OpenLayers supports rendering vector and raster layers. Examples of vector data include points, lines, and polygons. Examples of raster data include geographically referenced satellite images of terrain, drawn and digitized maps, and any other pixel-based images that have geographic coordinates. OpenLayers works seamlessly with tiles, vectors, images, and static maps.

Perhaps the biggest advantage of OpenLayers is that it is a freely available JavaScript library. Libraries are also available for other languages, such as TypeScript, Go, Ruby, Java, and Python. The library can be used in any browser, and it has a wide range of functionality that allows developers to manipulate maps, add animations to them, and integrate various types of data with the maps.

Now that we've established the roles of SignalR and OpenLayers, let's put that theory into practice. We'll begin by structuring the Aspire solution and implementing the backend service.

> **TIP** If you want to learn more about OpenLayers or GIS in general, *PostGIS in Action*, 2nd edition, by Regina O. Obe and Leo S. Hsu (https://mng.bz/64xy), will be helpful.

## 4.3 Building a delivery-tracking system

In this section, we'll add the core components of the delivery-tracking system to the e-commerce application we've built so far. We'll focus specifically on the Aspire integration parts of the components rather than the business logic. Therefore, the example we build will work as though an order has already been placed.

We'll implement the full, end-to-end order-processing workflow in chapter 7, integrating our system with message brokers and event-driven functionality. For now, pretend that an order has already been placed when you go through the steps outlined in this chapter, and test your setup afterward. The complete solution is available at https://mng.bz/oZgM.

With the solution structured, we can focus on the core of our application: the `OnlineShop.ApiService` project. This backend service has two primary responsibilities:

- Host a SignalR hub for real-time communication.
- Simulate a stream of location updates.

### 4.3.1 Setting up a SignalR hub

The backend project, `OnlineShop.ApiService`, doesn't need additional NuGet dependencies because SignalR is included in the ASP.NET Core SDK.

Earlier, I mentioned the SignalR hub. The following listing shows an example SignalR hub inside our backend service in the root of the `OnlineShop.ApiService` project.

**Listing 4.1 SignalR hub for order location tracking**

```
using Microsoft.AspNetCore.SignalR;

namespace OnlineShop.ApiService;

public class LocationHub : Hub
{
    public async Task UpdateLocation(
        double latitude,
        double longitude)
    {
        await Clients.All.SendAsync(
            "ReceiveLocationUpdate",
            latitude,
            longitude);
    }
}
```

If you're new to SignalR, here's a breakdownof the code:

- The class `LocationHub` inherits from the `Hub` base class, which comes from the `Microsoft.AspNetCore.SignalR` namespace. We call the class `LocationHub` because its primary purpose is to update the location of the delivery driver. To make it obvious that the class represents a SignalR hub, the name contains the `Hub` suffix.
- Our hub class has a method called `UpdateLocation()`. This method takes two parameters, representing the latitude and longitude, and can be invoked remotely by any connected clients.
- Inside this method, we invoke the `SendAsync()` method on all connected clients. With SignalR, we can send messages to specific clients too. But to keep things simple for demonstration purposes, any connected client will receive the message with our setup.
- Inside this method invocation, the first parameter is a string with the value `ReceiveLocationUpdate`. This is the name of the method delegate on a connected client that acts as an event listener. The event handler with this name will be invoked remotely on the clients when we call the `SendAsync()` method on the server. The remaining parameters of the `SendAsync()` method are passed to the client. We'll see how this works on the client side later in this chapter.

### 4.3.2 Registering a SignalR hub

To make this hub work, we have to register it. If we open the `Program.cs` file of the `OnlineShop.ApiService` project, we find the following line, which registers all the SignalR dependencies:

```
builder.Services.AddSignalR();
```

We also have to associate the hub with an HTTP endpoint by placing the following line just before `app.Run()`:

```
app.MapHub<LocationHub>("/locationHub");
```

In this example, `/locationHub` is an arbitrary URL path relative to the service address. If our service is hosted at `example.com`, the path points to the following address:

```
example.com/locationHub
```

The pathname can be anything, but we gave our path a name that clearly identifies its association with the `LocationHub` class.

Our SignalR hub is fully registered. Next, we'll add logic to the application to simulate periodic changes in location. We'll do so through a background service.

### 4.3.3 Simulating location updates

In our project, let's add a class called `LocationUpdater`. We'll register it as a background service, so the signature of the class will be

```
using Microsoft.AspNetCore.SignalR;

namespace OnlineShop.ApiService;

public class LocationUpdater(
    IHubContext<LocationHub> locationHub) :
    BackgroundService
{
}
```

We're injecting an implementation of a generic `IHubContext` interface that points to the `LocationHub` type. This type allows us to interact with the SignalR clients connected to our hub from outside the hub itself. We don't have to do anything special to register it. The code we reviewed in the `Program.cs` file already registers all the required SignalR dependencies, including the implementation of the `IHubContext` interface. Next, we have this method:

```
private async Task UpdateLocation(
    double latitude,
    double longitude,
    CancellationToken cancellationToken)
```

```
{
    await locationHub.Clients.All.SendAsync(
        "ReceiveLocationUpdate",
        latitude,
        longitude,
        cancellationToken);
}
```

As we can see, the syntax for invoking event handlers on connected clients is pretty much the same as it was inside the `UpdateLocation` method in the `LocationHub` class. We only have to refer to the `Clients` property of the `locationHub` object.

Now let's complete the class by adding the method that will be executed automatically by the runtime in the background:

```
protected override async Task
    ExecuteAsync(
        CancellationToken cancellationToken)
{
    while (!cancellationToken.IsCancellationRequested)
    {
        await Task.Delay(5000, cancellationToken);
        await UpdateLocation(
            51.5074, -0.1276, cancellationToken);

        await Task.Delay(5000, cancellationToken);
        await UpdateLocation(
            51.5074, -0.13, cancellationToken);

        await Task.Delay(5000, cancellationToken);
        await UpdateLocation(
            51.508, -0.14, cancellationToken);
    }
}
```

We send three location updates to the SignalR clients with delays between them in a loop, simulating the movements of a delivery driver. All we have to do now is register this class as a background service. We do so with the following code in the `Program.cs` file:

```
builder.Services.AddSingleton<LocationUpdater>();
builder.Services.AddHostedService(
    sp => sp
        .GetRequiredService<LocationUpdater>());
```

Now that our backend is in place to simulate and transmit location data, our work is half done. Next, we'll build the user-facing portion of the application, the `OnlineShop.Web` project. Its purpose is to connect to the backend service and translate the raw coordinate data into a dynamic marker on an interactive map.

## 4.4 Building the frontend map UI

Let's open the OnlineShop.Web project. The first thing to do is add the SignalR client library. Although server-side SignalR components are included with ASP.NET Core, the client-side components must be explicitly installed. We have to install the NuGet package Microsoft.AspNetCore.SignalR.Client to enable a SignalR client.

Next, we'll add some JavaScript to load the OpenLayers map and handle location updates from the server. We'll create a js folder inside the wwwroot folder and create a file inside it called site.js.

Let's see how this file is populated. First, we declare the following variable. Because this variable is global, we'll have access to the map object from any JavaScript function:

```
var map = null;
```

Next, the following function initializes the map:

```
window.initializeMap = () => {
    map = new ol.Map({
        target: 'map',
        layers: [
            new ol.layer.Tile({
                source: new ol.source.OSM()
            })
        ],
        view: new ol.View({
            center: ol.proj.fromLonLat([-0.1276, 51.5074]),
            zoom: 12
        })
    });
}
```

First, we instantiate the map variable by invoking the Map() method of the ol object. This object comes from the OpenLayers reference library, which we'll add later.

Then we set the map layer, which is required to display the map. In our example, the source is OSM (OpenStreetMap), an open source map of city streets.

Next, we set our view. In our example, we use the latitude and longitude coordinates of London and a 12x zoom. Essentially, when the map loads, we'll see the streets of London close up.

Now we add the following variable to our JavaScript file:

```
window.markerLayer = null;
```

This variable represents the map layer containing the location marker on the map. Every time we receive the delivery driver's new coordinates, the layer is reset, and a new marker is created. This is why we're storing it in a global variable.

Finally, we have this function, which is invoked with parameters representing the latitude and longitude of the new location:

```
window.addMarker = (lat, lon) => {
};
```

Now let's add the logic. First, insert the following code to remove the existing marker from the map:

```
if (window.markerLayer) {
    window.map.removeLayer(window.markerLayer);
}
```

Next, create the new marker based on the provided coordinates:

```
const marker = new ol.Feature({
    geometry: new ol.geom.Point(
        ol.proj.fromLonLat([lon, lat]))
});
```

Make sure that the marker is clearly visible by applying appropriate styling to it:

```
const markerStyle = new ol.style.Style({
    image: new ol.style.Circle({
    radius: 10, // Radius of the circle in pixels
    fill: new ol.style.Fill({
        color: 'rgba(255, 0, 0, 0.8)'
    }), // Fill color (red with 80% opacity)
    stroke: new ol.style.Stroke({
        color: 'black',
        width: 2 }) // Optional stroke (black border)
    })
});
```

Next, apply the style to the marker:

```
marker.setStyle(markerStyle);
```

Create the vector source for the marker, which allows us to display it on the map:

```
const vectorSource = new ol.source.Vector({
    features: [marker]
});
```

Create a vector layer from the vector source:

```
window.markerLayer = new ol.layer.Vector({
    source: vectorSource
});
```

Finally, add the vector layer to the map:

```
window.map.addLayer(window.markerLayer);
```

Our JavaScript for updating the location is complete. Next, we'll register all the appropriate JavaScript and CSS dependencies in the application.

### 4.4.1 Registering frontend dependencies

The `App.razor` file in the `Components` folder is where we register our frontend dependencies.

First, this HTML element in the `head` tag pulls the OpenLayers JavaScript library from a content delivery network (CDN):

```
<script src="https://cdn.jsdelivr.net/npm/ol@v10.3.1/dist/ol.js"></script>
```

We also have the associated stylesheet in the `head` tag:

```
<link rel="stylesheet" href="https://cdn.jsdelivr.net/npm/ol@v10.3.1/ol.css">
```

The reference to the custom JavaScript file goes immediately before the Blazor JavaScript library (`_framework/blazor.web.js`) inside the `body` tag, like so:

```
<script src="js/site.js"></script>
```

We have one more thing to do in the file. By default, the Blazor server app provided in the Aspire template uses a static server rendering mechanism. Although this rendering mode makes the UI load faster, it has some disadvantages. The main disadvantage is that we won't be able to invoke JavaScript code from inside Blazor code.

To fix this problem, we have to make sure that our Blazor components render dynamically. To do so, we add the following attribute to the `HeadOutlet` and `Routes` element references inside the `App.razor` file:

```
@rendermode="InteractiveServer"
```

Now the `HeadOutlet` element should look like this:

```
<HeadOutlet @rendermode="InteractiveServer" />
```

This is what the `Routes` element will look like:

```
<Routes @rendermode="InteractiveServer" />
```

With our frontend dependencies registered and the interactive render mode enabled, we've laid the necessary groundwork. Now we can build the Razor component that will host our map and handle the real-time updates.

### 4.4.2 Building the interactive UI

Before we start building the UI, we need to add the class with an extension method shown in the following listing. To add this class, we create the `Extensions` folder in the `OnlineShop.Web` project and create the `HubConnectionExtensions.cs` file inside it.

**Listing 4.2 Extension class for SignalR service discovery**

```
using Microsoft.AspNetCore.SignalR.Client;

namespace OnlineShop.Web.Extensions;

public static class HubConnectionExtensions
{
    public static IHubConnectionBuilder WithUrl(
        this IHubConnectionBuilder builder,
        string url,
        IHttpMessageHandlerFactory clientFactory)
    {
        return builder.WithUrl(
            url, options =>
        {
            options.HttpMessageHandlerFactory =
                _ => clientFactory.CreateHandler();
        });
    }
}
```

The SignalR connection builder uses this extension method. Remember that we're running an Aspire app and that the backend we want to connect to is located in a separate service. At this writing, service discovery doesn't work automatically with SignalR, so we have to know the IP address of the backend service if we want to connect to the hub.

Still, there's a better way. All we have to do is pass an instance of `IHttpMessageHandlerFactory`. Then associate the `CreateHandler()` method on this instance with the `HttpMessageHandlerFactory` property of the SignalR connection options. Now if the URL that we pass in to the builder refers to one of the named services hosted by Aspire, service discovery will work correctly.

How do we register an instance of the `IHttpMessageHandlerFactory` type? It's simple. All we do is execute the following code inside `Program.cs`:

```
builder.Services.AddHttpClient();
```

Let's create the `OrderTracking.razor` file inside the `Pages` folder of the `Components` folder. Its content starts with the following directives:

```
@page "/tracking"

@using OnlineShop.Web.Extensions
@using Microsoft.AspNetCore.SignalR.Client
```

```
@inject IJSRuntime JSRuntime
@inject IHttpMessageHandlerFactory ClientFactory
```

We inject an instance of the `IJSRuntime` type because it allows us to invoke JavaScript from the C# code. The concrete implementation is mapped automatically by the Blazor setup code. The `ClientFactory` is the `IHttpMessageHandlerFactory` service, which we saw earlier. Then we have this element:

```
<div id="map" style="width: 100%; height: 400px;"></div>
```

Next, we add the following block, which will contain our C# code:

```
@code {
    private HubConnection? hubConnection;

    protected override async Task OnInitializedAsync()
    {
        hubConnection = new HubConnectionBuilder()
            .WithUrl("https://apiservice/locationHub",
                ClientFactory)
            .Build();
    }
}
```

Here, we create an instance of a SignalR connection and configure it to connect to the hub endpoint on the server. Note that we have `apiservice` in the URL because we're executing the `WithUrl()` extension method that we added earlier. This method uses service discovery to resolve the address of the API service.

Next, we add the following life-cycle event-method override:

```
protected override async Task
    OnAfterRenderAsync(bool firstRender)
{
    if (firstRender)
    {
        await JSRuntime
            .InvokeVoidAsync("initializeMap");

        hubConnection?.On<double, double>(
            "ReceiveLocationUpdate",
            async (lat, lon) =>
            {
                await InvokeAsync(async () =>
                {
                    await JSRuntime.InvokeVoidAsync(
                        "addMarker",
                        lat,
                        lon);
                    StateHasChanged();
                });
            });
```

```
        await hubConnection?.StartAsync();
    }
}
```

This life-cycle event method executes automatically when the page finishes rendering. We have to wait for rendering to finish before we try to update the map, so we don't establish the physical SignalR connection until the page is ready.

> **NOTE** This life-cycle event method would never execute if we left the static server-side rendering mode. This is why we made those changes in `App.razor` earlier.

When the page has been rendered, we invoke the `initializeMap` JavaScript function, which initializes the map and displays it on the page. Then we associate some logic with the `ReceiveLocationUpdate` SignalR event handler. When we receive the updated coordinates from the server, we invoke the `addMarker` JavaScript function with these parameters. We're doing this inside the `InvokeAsync()` method to make sure that the logic is associated with the UI thread. We're also invoking `StateHasChanged()` after executing the update to make sure that the UI is partially rerendered.

Finally, we establish the SignalR connection by calling the `StartAsync()` method on the `hubConnection` object.

Before we see how delivery tracking works in our app, we have to add a navigation link to the order-tracking page. To do so, modify the element with the `nav-scrollable` class inside the `NavMenu.razor` file so that it looks like this:

```
<div class="nav-scrollable" onclick="document.querySelector('.navbar-tog-
    gler').click()">
   <nav class="nav flex-column">
       <div class="nav-item px-3">
           <NavLink class="nav-link" href="" Match="NavLinkMatch.All">
               <span class="bi bi-house-door-fill" aria-hidden="true"></span>
    Home
           </NavLink>
       </div>

       <div class="nav-item px-3">
           <NavLink class="nav-link" href="tracking" Match="NavLinkMatch.All">
              <span class="bi bi-list-nested" aria-hidden="true"></span> Track
    Your Order
           </NavLink>
       </div>
   </nav>
</div>
```

If we launch the application, open the frontend app, and navigate to the Track Your Order page, we should see the map, and a marker should appear on it almost immediately, as figure 4.1 shows.

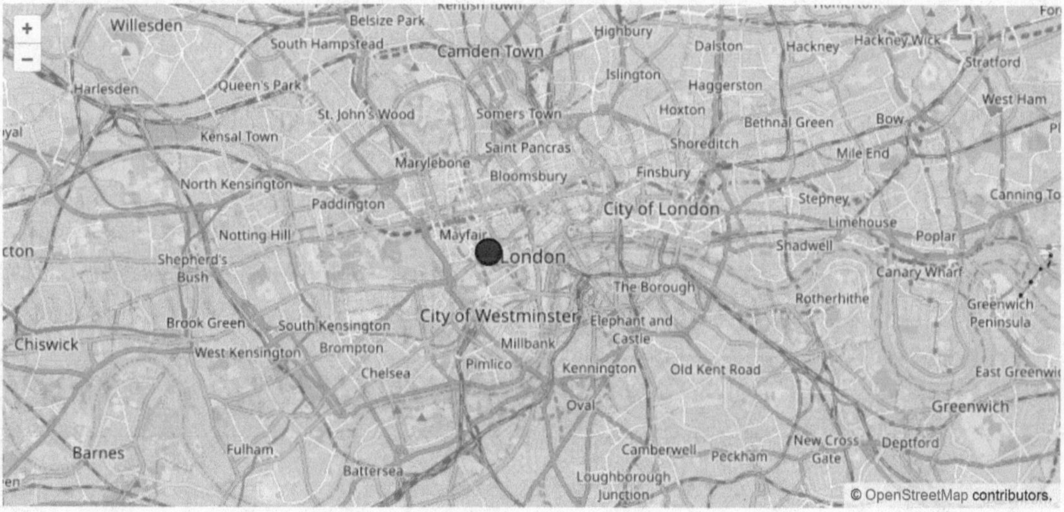


**Figure 4.1 Displaying the marker on the map upon receiving the location update**

With a live marker updating on our map, we have successfully built a complete, real-time distributed application with Aspire. We've seen how to connect a backend data source with a frontend UI using SignalR and how to use Blazor's JavaScript interop to control an interactive map.

## Summary

- In this chapter, we've built a fully interactive map where a user interface persistently connected to the backend server can receive updated locations.
- The persistent connection is managed by SignalR, a library built into ASP.NET Core that facilitates two-way real-time communication between client and server.
- The location is displayed as a marker on an OpenLayers map, which can interact with JavaScript.
- An important point to remember is that for Blazor to manage interactive map updates, it has to render in an interactive mode.
- Interactive updates to an OpenLayers map in Blazor can be managed via Blazor JavaScript interop functionality.
- Any updates to the UI from the Blazor code can be made only after the Razor component has been fully rendered.

# 5 Building a ChatGPT clone with Aspire, Ollama, and Semantic Kernel

**This chapter covers**

- Fundamentals of large language models and how they can be hosted anywhere via Ollama
- Integrating Aspire with Ollama
- Hosting a ChatGPT clone in Aspire
- Building a custom user interface for an intelligent chat app

Large language models (LLMs), such as those used in ChatGPT, Claude, and Copilot, have taken the world by storm. Everyone is talking about them, including technical professionals and nontechnical people, because we can do so many interesting things with them.

Enterprises are increasingly integrating LLMs into their core products. This process is like building your own domain-specific ChatGPT clone that answers questions about your product and acts as a virtual store assistant. The online shop we're building can benefit from AI integration.

Did you know that as a .NET developer, you can integrate any of these models into your application relatively easily regardless of the kind of application you're building and where you intend to run it? You can build any kind of AI functionality into your application as long as LLMs support it. You can use any advanced LLM features, such as retrieval-augmented generation (RAG) and Model Context Protocol (MCP). You can build chatbots, fully autonomous AI agents, you name it.

How do you do it? The answer is Semantic Kernel, a collection of .NET libraries that provide a simple interface for interactions between LLMs and custom code.

It gets even better: not all LLMs charge you extortionate amounts of money to use them. Some are free and open source, with no strings attached; others, such as Meta's Llama, are free with some conditions. You can host these models yourself without relying on someone else's server. The technology that enables this capability is called Ollama. Semantic Kernel supports it, and an existing Aspire integration library is available.

In this chapter, you'll learn to integrate LLM functionality into your distributed Aspire application by building your own locally hosted clone of ChatGPT with a custom-built user interface. And yes, you'll host your own LLM!

## 5.1 Hosting an LLM anywhere with Ollama

To build a ChatGPT-like AI system, we need access to an LLM. We'll host our own LLM inside Aspire. Our first step is enabling the infrastructure component that allows us to do this: an Ollama container.

If you haven't heard of Ollama, it's a lightweight, developer-friendly platform for running LLMs locally or in controlled environments without relying on cloud-hosted AI APIs. It provides a streamlined way to download, manage, and run models such as Llama, DeepSeek, Mistral, and Gemma directly on your machine, with simple commands and minimal setup. The full, rather long list of supported models is available at https://ollama.com/library.

One of Ollama's key benefits is local execution, which gives you full control of your data and model behavior. Because the models run on your own hardware, you avoid sending sensitive information to external servers, which can be critical for privacy, security, and regulatory compliance. Running locally also eliminates recurring API costs and reduces latency because inference happens on your system instead of in network calls to a remote service.

Two other advantages are portability and flexibility. Ollama works on macOS, Linux, and Windows (a native Windows installer is available), and it can run a variety of open source models, letting you choose the best fit for your project rather than be locked into a single vendor's offering. Also, it's hosted inside a Docker container, which makes it deployable anywhere.

The good news is that Aspire can be fully integrated with Ollama. Let's see how. The complete application that we'll build in this chapter is available at https://mng.bz/nZaK.

Typically, Ollama is hosted in a Docker container, which can be launched with a command-line interface (CLI) command similar to the following:

```
docker run -d -p 11434:11434 --name ollama ollama/ollama
```

We can launch it in Aspire as we'd launch any other Docker container. Luckily, we don't have to because Ollama has its own Aspire integration library. Although it's done via a community toolkit rather than an official component made by Microsoft, it still works perfectly.

To start, add a reference to the NuGet package `CommunityToolkit.Aspire.Hosting.Ollama` to your Aspire host project. Next, set up the startup code in the Aspire host. The following listing shows how it's done in the `AppHost.cs` file in the preceding project. We're adding it to the web frontend project rather than the API.

**Listing 5.1 Hosting Ollama in the Aspire host**

```
var builder = DistributedApplication.CreateBuilder(args);

var ollama = builder.AddOllama("ollama")
    .WithLifetime(ContainerLifetime.Persistent)
    .WithDataVolume()
    .WithOpenWebUI();

var phi35 = ollama.AddModel("phi35", "phi3.5");

var webFrontend = builder
    .AddProject<Projects.OnlineShop_Web>("webfrontend")
    .WithExternalHttpEndpoints()
    .WithHttpHealthCheck("/health")
    .WaitFor(phi35)
    .WithReference(phi35)...
```

> **WARNING** Running even a small language model, such as phi3.5, requires a lot of hardware resources. To run the preceding setup, you need a machine with at least 16 GB of RAM. The model itself needs a minimum of 4 GB of free RAM. Therefore, if your machine struggles, you can temporarily disable other resources, such as SQL database and Azure Blob containers, to get the chat functionality to work.

Let's break this code down step by step:

1. Create a standard distributed app builder for Aspire and assign it to the `builder` variable.
2. Create an Ollama container with the following configuration:
   a. Ensure that the container uses a persistent lifetime so we don't have to restart it every time the app restarts and don't have to wait for a large model to download again.
   b. Store the persistent state in local data volumes via the WithDataVolume() invocation.
   c. Add a web-based ChatGPT-like UI for interacting with the Ollama container by invoking the WithOpenWebUI() method.
3. Add a model to Ollama via the `AddModel()` method. We can add any Ollama-supported model. For this example, I chose `phi3.5` because it's one of the

smallest—only 2 GB compared with several hundred GB for Meta's flagship Llama model. The first parameter of the method is the arbitrary name we assigned to the resource (in this case, `phi35`). The second parameter is the actual model name (phi3.5).

4 Pass the model's reference into a web app via the `WithReference()` method.
5 Because the web app depends on the model for its core functionality, pass the model reference into the `WaitFor()` method, ensuring that the web app won't start until the model is fully downloaded and launched.

Now if we launch our application, we should see three items in the dashboard (figure 5.1).

**Figure 5.1 Hosting Ollama in Aspire**

The `phi3.5` model takes a while to download when we launch the app the first time because even though it's relatively small, it's still sizable. To monitor its progress, hover over it. The process may take several minutes, and there may be a delay before the model download starts. Both the custom UI app (`webfrontend`) and Open WebUI (`ollama-openwebui`) will launch after the model has been downloaded and started.

> **NOTE** When you continue building the application beyond this chapter, you may want to remove the Ollama container setup code from `AppHost` because it consumes a lot of hardware resources.

If you navigate to the Open WebUI, you see a user interface very similar to ChatGPT's, as figure 5.2 shows.

In a way, we're already done building a ChatGPT clone. We can already interact with the LLM and receive the answers we ask for. But we came here to learn how to integrate chat-completion functionality with our .NET-based AI agents, not just do what ChatGPT already does. That's what enterprises need; they can't rely only on publicly accessible chatbots. They also have to apply custom UIs, teach the LLMs their enterprise domains, and apply various guardrails so that users don't misuse the chatbot functionality. This is what the new niche of AI engineering is all about, and demand for the skills required to work in this niche is growing rapidly. Therefore, our next step will be to integrate our setup with a tool that allows us to do all these things: Semantic Kernel.

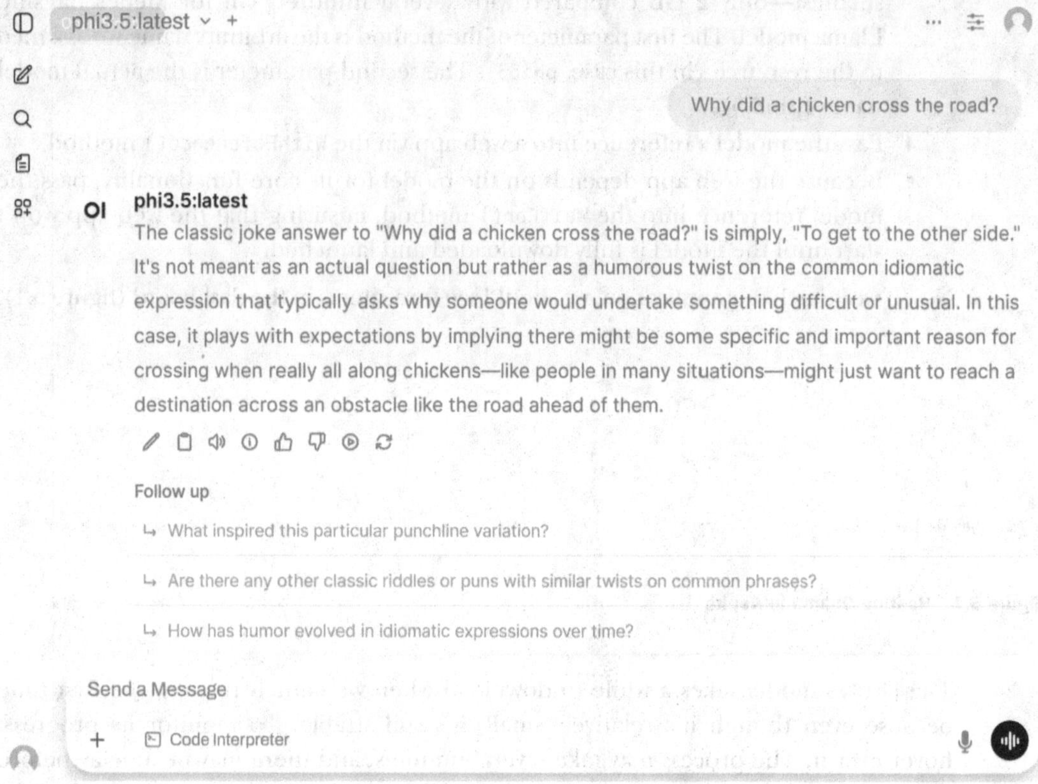


**Figure 5.2 Ollama user interface**

## 5.2 Adding Semantic Kernel

Semantic Kernel has several adapter libraries designed to work with different types of LLM-hosting technologies, such as OpenAI, Microsoft Copilot, and Ollama. It represents the LLM client, so we have to install the relevant packages in the application that will use the chat-completion functionality. In our Aspire example, that application is a hosted web application with the user interface exposed through the web frontend (the `OnlineShop.Web` project).

To enable Semantic Kernel, install the Ollama-specific NuGet package `Microsoft.SemanticKernel.Connectors.Ollama` in this application.

**NOTE** At this writing, this package is in preview. Therefore, to install it, you have to include packages with prerelease versions.

### 5.2.1 Building the chatbot backend

Now, with the package installed, we're ready to build our Semantic Kernel backend. Go to the `Program.cs` file of the project, and add the two following namespace references:

```
using Microsoft.SemanticKernel;
using Microsoft.SemanticKernel.ChatCompletion;
```

Now comes the tricky part. We have to use Aspire's service-discovery mechanism to resolve the address of the Ollama container because Semantic Kernel connects to Ollama via its URI or IP address. How do we do it? With many services, we can pass the container reference into the application and register a `HttpClient` instance with service discovery enabled, like this:

```
builder.Services.AddHttpClient("ollama", c =>
{
    c.BaseAddress = new Uri("http://ollama");
})
.AddServiceDiscovery();
```

In this case, the `http://ollama` URL (which assumes that we named our Ollama container `ollama`) is resolved at runtime to the actual IP address of the Ollama container. But this approach doesn't work with the Ollama community toolkit (at least, not at this writing). This community toolkit wasn't designed to work with Semantic Kernel. Instead, the main client for it was the `OllamaSharp` library, represented by the `CommunityToolkit.Aspire.OllamaSharp` NuGet package in the Aspire ecosystem. Unlike Semantic Kernel, this library connects to an Ollama-hosted model via a connection string rather than an endpoint Uniform Resource Identifier (URI).

The good news is that service discovery works with the connection string. More good news is that you can obtain the actual endpoint address from the connection string. Here's how. First, reference the following namespace:

```
using System.Data.Common;
```

Here's how to extract the connection string, which was passed into the service in the Aspire host project as the reference to the `phi3.5` model:

```
var phiConnectionString = builder.Configuration.GetConnectionString("phi35");
```

`phi35` is the arbitrary name we gave to the resource that represents our model. The connection string is automatically inserted into the `ConnectionStrings` section of the settings under the key that matches that name.

Our next step is extracting the endpoint URI from the connection string:

```
DbConnectionStringBuilder csBuilder = new()
{
```

```
    ConnectionString = phiConnectionString
};

if (!csBuilder.TryGetValue("Endpoint", out var ollamaEndpoint))
{
    throw new InvalidDataException(
        "Ollama connection string is not properly configured.");
}
```

Next, pass the endpoint reference in to the Semantic Kernel registration:

```
builder.Services.AddSingleton(sp =>
{
    IKernelBuilder kb = Kernel.CreateBuilder();
#pragma warning disable SKEXP0070
    kb.AddOllamaChatCompletion(
        modelId: "phi3.5",
        endpoint: new Uri((string)ollamaEndpoint)
    );
#pragma warning restore SKEXP0070

    return kb.Build();
});
```

**NOTE** The Ollama connector API suppressed by the `pragma warning disable` statement is still an experimental feature at this writing.

Then we make sure to register all the other dependencies required to make our Semantic Kernel work:

```
builder.Services.AddSingleton(sp =>
 sp.GetRequiredService<Kernel>()
.GetRequiredService<IChatCompletionService>());
```

The final part is adding the remaining backend functionality for Semantic Kernel.

### 5.2.2 Adding Semantic Kernel backend logic

The functionality we're building into our application is known as *chat completion.* This is what ChatGPT or any other LLM does when you ask it a question. To make chat-completion functionality robust, we must enable *chat history,* which allows the LLM to remember the context of the conversation instead of treating each prompt as an individual, isolated question. To do so, add the interface shown in the next listing.

**Listing 5.2 Interface for the chat-history service**

```
using Microsoft.SemanticKernel.ChatCompletion;

namespace OnlineShop.Web;
```

```
public interface IChatHistoryService
{
    void AddUserMessage(string connectionId, string message);
    ChatHistory GetChatHistory(string connectionId);
    void RemoveHistory(string connectionId);
}
```

Here's what the methods in this interface mean:

- `AddUserMessage()` adds a new chat message to a chat history associated with the same connection ID, which represents a single user session.
- `GetChatHistory()` returns the entire chat history associated with the same session.
- `RemoveHistory()` deletes the chat history when it's no longer needed (that is, when the user disconnects).

The interface uses the `ChatHistory` type; it comes from the `Microsoft.SemanticKernel.ChatCompletion` namespace, which we have to reference. The following listing shows the implementation of this interface.

**Listing 5.3 Chat-history-service implementation**

```
using Microsoft.SemanticKernel.ChatCompletion;

namespace OnlineShop.Web;

public class ChatHistoryService : IChatHistoryService
{
    private readonly Dictionary<string, ChatHistory> _chatHistories = new();

    public void AddUserMessage(string connectionId, string message)
    {
        if (!_chatHistories.TryGetValue(connectionId, out ChatHistory?
     value))
        {                                                    // Check whether a chat history associated with a specific connection ID already exists.
            value = [];
            _chatHistories[connectionId] = value;            // Add a chat history to a dictionary to associate it with a specific connection ID.
        }

        value.AddUserMessage(message);                       // Add a user message to a specific chat history.
    }

    public ChatHistory GetChatHistory(string connectionId)
    {
        return _chatHistories[connectionId];                 // Return a specific chat history based on the connection ID.
    }

    public void RemoveHistory(string connectionId)
    {
        _chatHistories.Remove(connectionId);                 // Remove a chat history from the dictionary.
    }
}
```

As before, we have to reference the `Microsoft.SemanticKernel.ChatCompletion` namespace in the file or globally in the application.

Next, we register this service in the `Program.cs` file. Because the service will be shared across many user sessions and because we have to track all individual user connections, we'll register it as a singleton:

```
builder.Services.AddSingleton<IChatHistoryService, ChatHistoryService>();
```

Next, add a SignalR hub that can accept user prompts from the UI and stream the responses back letter by letter. Streaming the answer instead of returning it all at once makes it look more polished. This is what commercial chatbots typically do. The next listing shows this SignalR hub.

**Listing 5.4 SignalR hub for chat-completion functionality**

```
public class ChatHub : Hub
{
    private readonly Kernel _kernel;
    private readonly IChatCompletionService _chat;
    private readonly IChatHistoryService _chatHistoryService;

    public ChatHub(
        Kernel kernel,
        IChatCompletionService chat,
        IChatHistoryService chatHistoryService)
    {
        _kernel = kernel;
        _chat = chat;
        _chatHistoryService = chatHistoryService;
    }

    public async IAsyncEnumerable<string> StreamAnswer(
        string prompt,
        [EnumeratorCancellation] CancellationToken cancellationToken)
    {
        _chatHistoryService.AddUserMessage(Context.ConnectionId, prompt);

        var settings = new PromptExecutionSettings
        {
        };

        await foreach (var delta in _chat.GetStreamingChatMessageContentsAsync(
            _chatHistoryService.GetChatHistory(
                Context.ConnectionId), settings, _kernel, cancellationToken))
        {
        if (!string.IsNullOrEmpty(delta.Content))
        {
```

- Inject the main Kernel object that performs the core LLM interactions.
- Inject the chat-completion from SemanticKernel.
- Inject the chat-history we created earlier.
- Accept user prompt from the client app, such as UI in the web frontend
- Add a user message to the chat history.
- Configure chat completion settings if required.
- Return the answer to the prompt from the LLM as a streaming context.

```
                yield return delta.Content;     <-- Stream the answer
            }                                       back letter by letter.
        }
    }

    public override async Task OnConnectedAsync()
    {
        Console.WriteLine($"[ChatHub] Connected: {Context.ConnectionId}");
        await base.OnConnectedAsync();
    }

    public override Task OnDisconnectedAsync(Exception? exception)
    {
        Console.WriteLine($"[ChatHub] Disconnected: {Context.ConnectionId}
     {exception?.Message}");
        _chatHistoryService.RemoveHistory(Context.ConnectionId);     <--
        return base.OnDisconnectedAsync(exception);      Remove a chat history
    }                                                     upon a disconnection
}                                                         of a specific client.
```

The `StreamAnswer()` method has its `CancellationToken` parameter annotated with the `EnumeratorCancellation` attribute. This obscure C# language feature is worth explaining. This attribute tells the compiler that a particular `CancellationToken` is supposed to cancel the act of iterating through the stream. In other words, it means "if the caller wants to stop reading items, use this token for that."

This is important because async streams don't produce all their values at the same time; they produce values one by one over time. Cancellation can happen while the caller is still waiting for more items. `EnumeratorCancellation` helps connect the caller's cancellation request to the code inside the async iterator.

This SignalR hub relies on the following namespaces:

```
using Microsoft.AspNetCore.SignalR;
using Microsoft.SemanticKernel;
using Microsoft.SemanticKernel.ChatCompletion;
using System.Runtime.CompilerServices;
```

Each unique client connection has its own connection ID, which allows us to tie its chat history to that user session. The `PromptExecutionSettings` object allows us to configure prompt execution. This is where we can set the so-called *temperature*, which measures how much randomness in the responses we're willing to tolerate.

The final part is registering the SignalR hub. Go back to the application's `Program.cs` file, and add the following expression to the service registrations:

```
builder.Services.AddSignalR();
```

If we want to diagnose problems and see detailed error messages, we can modify it like this:

```
builder.Services.AddSignalR()
    .AddHubOptions<ChatHub>(o => o.EnableDetailedErrors = true);
```

Finally, add the following expression near the bottom of the application middleware in the same file but before either `app.MapRazorComponents<App>()` or `app.MapDefault-Endpoints()`:

```
app.MapHub<ChatHub>("/chat");
```

That's it. Our Semantic Kernel is registered and configured to connect to the Ollama container at runtime. Chat-completion functionality is fully enabled in our distributed app. Now we have to build the UI for it.

## 5.3 Finalizing the user interface

To interact with the SignalR backend, we'll build a JavaScript SignalR client that will display in the browser. This time, we'll use the JavaScript version, so this client will be distinct from the delivery-tracking client that talks to the API backend.

The easiest way to do this is to pull the required library from a publicly available content delivery network (CDN). Open the `App.razor` file in the project to which we added the SignalR hub, and place the following HTML element immediately before the closing head's HTML tag:

```
<script  src="https://cdnjs.cloudflare.com/ajax/libs/microsoft-signalr/9.0.6/
    signalr.min.js" integrity="sha512-kkMt8UThSmWcdXLYFaGZ/U6vyWSNLZMU-
    WQ5SMeF80pGqrEkH5ei9D/3MbVQpB8p7D5C3A4vlX7BpsWTT2BfB6A==" crossori-
    gin="anonymous" referrerpolicy="no-referrer">
</script>
```

### 5.3.1 Adding a SignalR JavaScript client

Now we're ready to build our SignalR client. In the `wwwroot` folder of our project, open the `js` folder, and add a file named `chat.js`. We'll start by populating this file with the following export function:

```
export async function init() {
}
```

This function will be the placeholder for all SignalR-related functionality. All the remaining JavaScript code will be inserted into it. The first thing we'll add is the following guard condition to ensure that the SignalR client has been instantiated. If the client hasn't been instantiated, the condition will output an error to the in-browser console:

```
if (typeof window.signalR === 'undefined') {
    console.error('[chat.js] SignalR client not loaded. Check script tag
     order.');
    return;
}
```

Then create a list of global variables, each representing a specific HTML element on the chat page:

```
const statusEl = document.getElementById('status');
const form = document.getElementById('promptForm');
const promptEl = document.getElementById('prompt');
const sendBtn = document.getElementById('sendBtn');
const stopBtn = document.getElementById('stopBtn');
const clearBtn = document.getElementById('clearBtn');
const copyBtn = document.getElementById('copyBtn');
const outEl = document.getElementById('output');
const countEl = document.getElementById('tokenCount');
```

Next, add the following internal function to set the connection status on the page:

```
function setStatus(text, cls = 'text-bg-secondary') {
    if (!statusEl) return;
    statusEl.className = `badge ${cls}`;
    statusEl.textContent = text;
}
```

Another function ensures that the elements on the page aren't busy while the chat backend is processing the prompt:

```
function setBusy(isBusy) {
    if (sendBtn) sendBtn.disabled = isBusy;
    if (stopBtn) stopBtn.disabled = !isBusy;
    if (promptEl) promptEl.disabled = isBusy;
}
```

Next, add the following function, which updates the number of characters returned by the server so far:

```
function updateCharCount() {
    if (countEl && outEl) countEl.textContent = `${outEl.textContent.length}
     chars`;
}
```

Now we're ready to start configuring the SignalR connection. First, build the URL that will point to the SignalR hub. It will consist of two parts: the base application URL and the `chat` path that points to the SignalR hub:

```
const hubUrl = new URL('chat', document.baseURI).toString();
```

We'll use this URL to build the hub-connection object:

```
let connection = new signalR.HubConnectionBuilder()
    .withUrl(hubUrl, { withCredentials: true })
    .withAutomaticReconnect()
    .configureLogging(signalR.LogLevel.Information)
    .build();
```

Then we'll add event listeners that update UI elements when the client disconnects from the server or reconnects to it or the connection is closed:

```
connection.onreconnecting(() => setStatus('reconnecting…', 'text-bg-warning'));
connection.onreconnected(() => setStatus('connected', 'text-bg-success'));
connection.onclose(() => setStatus('disconnected', 'text-bg-secondary'));
```

With these elements in place, it's time to establish the connection to the hub:

```
try {
    await connection.start();
    setStatus('connected', 'text-bg-success');
    console.log('[chat.js] connection started');
} catch (err) {
    console.error('[chat.js] connection start failed:', err);
    setStatus('disconnected', 'text-bg-danger');
    return;
}
```

Next, add a function that is triggered when a user submits a prompt. The function connects to the SignalR hub and listens for a stream of characters coming back from it:

```
let subscription = null;

async function startStream(prompt) {
    if (!prompt) return;
    outEl.textContent = '';
    updateCharCount();
    setBusy(true);

    const stream = connection.stream('StreamAnswer', prompt);
    subscription = stream.subscribe({
        next: chunk => {
            for (const ch of chunk) outEl.textContent += ch;
            updateCharCount();
            if (outEl.parentElement) {
                outEl.parentElement.scrollTop =
      outEl.parentElement.scrollHeight;
            }
        },
        complete: () => setBusy(false),
        error: err => {
            setBusy(false);
            outEl.textContent += `\n\n[error] ${err?.message ?? err}`;
            updateCharCount();
        }
    });
}
```

Its event listener is attached to the form-submission event:

```
form.addEventListener('submit', async (e) => {
    e.preventDefault();
    await startStream(promptEl.value.trim());
});
```

Next, add event listeners for the Stop, Clear, and Copy buttons:

```
stopBtn.addEventListener('click', () => {
    subscription?.dispose();
    subscription = null;
    setBusy(false);
});

clearBtn.addEventListener('click', () => {
    outEl.textContent = '';
    updateCharCount();
    promptEl.focus();
});

copyBtn.addEventListener('click', async () => {
    try {
        await navigator.clipboard.writeText(outEl.textContent);
        copyBtn.textContent = 'Copied!';
        setTimeout(() => (copyBtn.textContent = 'Copy'), 1000);
    } catch { /* ignore */ }
});
```

Our SignalR client is complete. Let's start building the chat page.

### 5.3.2 Building the chat page

In this section, we'll create a new page for our chat. We'll call the Razor component file `Chat.razor` and place it in the same folder as the `Home.razor` file. Then we'll add the following directives, which set the page path, enable JavaScript interop, and switch on the interactive mode that makes JavaScript work:

```
@page "/chat"
@rendermode InteractiveServer
@inject IJSRuntime JS
```

Next, add the HTML for the chat page, including the input field, the output field, and all the buttons:

```
<div class="container py-4">
    <span id="status" class="badge text-bg-secondary">disconnected</span>

    <form id="promptForm" class="mt-3">
        <textarea id="prompt" class="form-control" rows="4"
     placeholder="Ask…"></textarea>
        <div class="mt-2 d-flex gap-2">
            <button id="sendBtn" type="submit" class="btn btn-primary">Send</
     button>
            <button id="stopBtn" type="button" class="btn btn-outline-
     secondary" disabled>Stop</button>
            <button id="clearBtn" type="button" class="btn btn-outline-danger
     ms-auto">Clear</button>
            <button id="copyBtn" type="button" class="btn btn-outline-
     secondary">Copy</button>
```

```
        </div>
    </form>

    <div class="card mt-4">
        <div class="card-header d-flex justify-content-between align-items-
    center">
            <strong>Response</strong>
            <span id="tokenCount" class="small text-muted">0 chars</span>
        </div>
        <div class="card-body">
            <div id="output" style="white-space:pre-wrap; min-
    height:8rem;"></div>
        </div>
    </div>
</div>
```

Our HTML page is ready, but if we launch our application, it won't do anything because it's not connected to the server. Next, we'll connect the page to the SignalR client.

### 5.3.3 Adding the SignalR client to the page

There are multiple ways to connect the SignalR JavaScript client to the page. The simplest way is to reference the `chat.js` JavaScript file in the HTML. But if we do that in the global HTML envelope in the `App.razor` file, the client will be loaded even for pages on which it can't work. After all, the client relies on specific HTML elements to be present on the page, and we have those elements on our chat page.

Another option is to reference the file in the HTML of the page itself. We could do that, but it isn't good practice. The `script` tags aren't supposed to be referenced inside the HTML body because that would violate the separation of concerns and make the user-facing code and markup less manageable.

Because we're using Blazor, we can load this JavaScript dynamically via JavaScript interop. This is why we enabled this functionality on the page. Add the `code` block to the Razor component as shown in the next listing.

**Listing 5.5 Dynamic loading of the JavaScript file**

```
@code {
    private IJSObjectReference? _module;

    protected override async Task OnAfterRenderAsync(bool firstRender)
    {
        if (firstRender)
        {
            _module =
                await JS.InvokeAsync<IJSObjectReference>("import", "./js/
    chat.js");
            await _module.InvokeVoidAsync("init");
        }
    }
}
```

Ensure we only load the JavaScript file during the first render of the component.

Load the JavaScript file and import the function marked with the export keyword.

Execute the init function that will create the JavaScript client.

Finally, we'll make sure that users can navigate to the chat page. Open the `NavMenu.razor` file, and add the following navigation link to the section with the other links:

```
<div class="nav-item px-3">
    <NavLink class="nav-link" href="chat" Match="NavLinkMatch.All">
        <span class="bi bi-list-nested" aria-hidden="true"></span> Chat
    </NavLink>
</div>
```

Now if we launch our application, navigate to the chat page, and let it load, we should be able to use the chat interface. Figure 5.3 shows what it should look like.

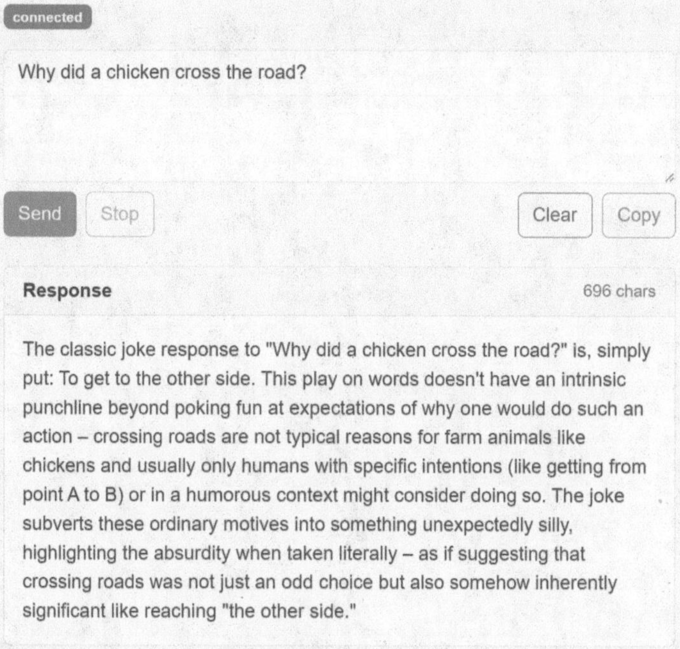


**Figure 5.3 Custom chat interface**

You have successfully built your own Aspire-hosted AI application. You can use this knowledge to build your own AI agents hosted inside distributed systems.

## Summary

- Popular AI applications used for conversations, such as ChatGPT, rely on LLM technology.
- Ollama allows anyone to host LLMs anywhere, free of charge. It can run in Docker containers and can host a wide range of LLMs, including Meta's Llama.

- Aspire has a community toolkit for hosting Ollama. The Ollama community toolkit for Aspire comes with its own frontend, which is similar to ChatGPT and serves the same purpose.
- Semantic Kernel is a Microsoft framework for building AI agents that allows any .NET code to interact with LLMs. It can stream the LLM response letter by letter.
- The official name for the LLM functionality used in chats is chat completion.
- You can use SignalR to build a custom chat interface that supports answer streaming.

# Part 3

# Professional-grade Aspire applications

When the "happy path" works, the real work begins: proving that the system behaves under load, failure, change, and time. This part is about taking what you've built and making it resilient, observable, and safe.

You'll learn how to test distributed systems without turning your test suite into a fragile collection of scripts, how to monitor services so you can see what's happening across boundaries, and how to use messaging and caching in ways that improve performance without sacrificing correctness. Finally, you'll tackle security—not as a checklist but as a set of practical decisions that affect configuration, service-to-service communication, secrets, and deployment.

# 6 Integration testing and monitoring

***This chapter covers***

- Understanding application telemetry and how Aspire processes logs, metrics, and traces
- Seeing how Aspire manages health checks
- Setting up and running integration tests in Aspire
- Using different testing frameworks for integration tests
- Testing the user interfaces of applications hosted by Aspire

In this chapter, we make our application resilient by testing it before deployment to production and monitoring it while it's running in production. We'll start with monitoring because the relevant dependencies are already included in the standard Aspire Starter Project template on which our application is based.

Monitoring applications is crucial for several reasons. It allows us to detect problems such as errors, failures, performance bottlenecks, and security breaches early, and early detection enables proactive responses, minimizing effects on users and the business.

Monitoring also helps ensure that our applications are reliable and available. By tracking uptime, response times, and error rates, we can identify areas for improvement and take steps to improve reliability and availability.

Monitoring can also help us use hardware resources efficiently by providing insights into the performance of our applications and infrastructure. By analyzing metrics such as CPU use, memory use, and response times, we can identify performance bottlenecks, optimize resource allocation, and improve overall system performance.

Another reason we monitor our applications is that doing so helps us understand resource use patterns and trends over time. With this information, we can perform capacity planning and make informed decisions about scaling our infrastructure to meet current and future demands.

There are also direct financial implications. By analyzing metrics related to resource use and performance, we can right-size our infrastructure, eliminate unnecessary expenses, and maximize cost-effectiveness.

Monitoring helps us detect and mitigate security threats and vulnerabilities in our applications and infrastructure. By monitoring access logs, audit trails, and security events, we can identify suspicious activity, enforce security policies, and protect sensitive data from unauthorized access.

Many industries have regulatory requirements and compliance standards that mandate monitoring and reporting of certain metrics and events. Many companies, for example, have service-level agreements (SLAs) that require a certain level of uptime. Monitoring helps ensure compliance with these requirements and facilitates auditing and reporting processes.

Finally, monitoring applications and maintaining high levels of reliability and performance contribute to a positive user experience. By proactively addressing problems and minimizing downtime, we can improve customer satisfaction and loyalty.

Let's look at the different types of monitoring available to us.

## 6.1 Components of monitoring systems

Logging, metrics, and traces are essential components of monitoring systems in distributed environments such as microservices architectures. Each component serves a distinct purpose in providing visibility into the behavior and performance of applications, as shown in figure 6.1. The following sections show how these components are used for monitoring.

### 6.1.1 Logging

*Logging* involves capturing and storing records of events that occur within an application or system. These events can include informational messages, errors, warnings, and debugging information.

Logging tracks the execution flow of applications, record errors and exceptions, and provides diagnostic information for troubleshooting problems. Logs can contain timestamps, severity levels, contextual data, and other relevant details.

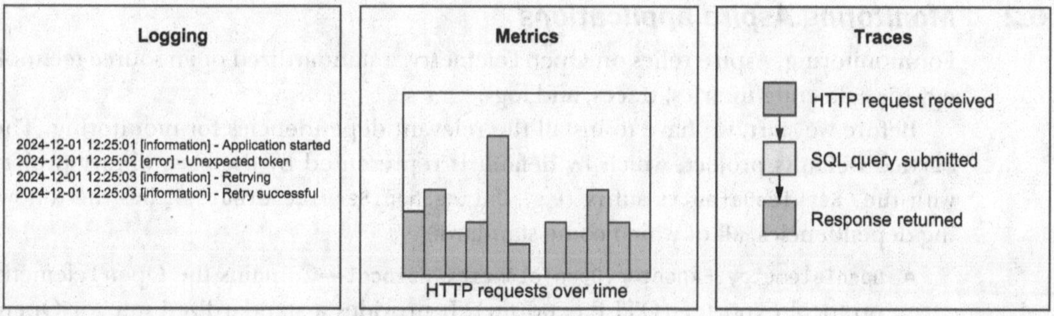


**Figure 6.1 Components of a monitoring system**

Log entries might include HTTP request/response details, database queries, service interactions, and application-specific events. Logs are typically written to files, databases, or centralized logging platforms such as ELK (Elasticsearch, Logstash, Kibana) and Splunk via intermediary systems such as Azure Application Insights.

### 6.1.2 Metrics

*Metrics* are quantitative measurements that provide insight into the performance, resource use, and behavior of applications and systems over time. Metrics are typically numerical values collected at regular intervals.

Metrics monitor the health, performance, and efficiency of applications. They identify trends, anomalies, and performance bottlenecks, and they enable capacity planning and resource optimization.

Common metrics include CPU and memory use, response times, throughput, error rates, and request latency. Metrics are often collected and aggregated using monitoring systems such as Prometheus, Grafana, Graphite, and Datadog.

### 6.1.3 Traces

*Traces* provide end-to-end visibility into the flow of requests as they traverse a distributed system composed of multiple microservices. A trace represents a single request's journey and captures information about each service it interacts with.

Traces diagnose latency problems, identify service dependencies, and understand the overall performance of distributed systems. They enable developers and operators to pinpoint bottlenecks, analyze request flows, and optimize system performance.

Traces consist of *spans*, which represent individual operations within a request. Spans capture timing information, contextual data, and metadata related to each operation. Distributed tracing systems such as Jaeger, Zipkin, and OpenTelemetry collect, visualize, and analyze traces.

Section 6.2 discusses how Aspire uses all these types of monitoring.

## 6.2 Monitoring Aspire applications

For monitoring, Aspire relies on OpenTelemetry, a standardized open source technology for collecting metrics, traces, and logs.

Before we start, we have to install the relevant dependencies for monitoring. The Service Defaults project, which by default is represented by the class library project with the `.ServiceDefaults` suffix (e.g., `OnlineShop.ServiceDefaults`), has the following dependencies, all of which come standard:

- `OpenTelemetry.Exporter.OpenTelemetryProtocol`—Contains the OpenTelemetry protocol exporter (OTLP exporter). It provides a standardized way for OpenTelemetry components (such as SDKs and collectors) to communicate with one another and with backend observability platforms.
- `OpenTelemetry.Extensions.Hosting`—Provides an automated way to start and stop OpenTelemetry's tracing mechanism.
- `OpenTelemetry.Instrumentation.AspNetCore`—Enables the integration of OpenTelemetry components with the ASP.NET Core middleware.
- `OpenTelemetry.Instrumentation.Http`—Allows users to collect telemetry and export it to their backend of choice via HTTP.
- `OpenTelemetry.Instrumentation.Runtime`—Automatically collects metrics associated with the .NET runtime, such as garbage collection, memory use, and thread pools.

The names of all these packages begin with `OpenTelemetry` because they're related to the OpenTelemetry framework. This open source project aims to provide a set of standardized, vendor-agnostic tools and APIs for collecting, processing, and exporting telemetry data (metrics, logs, and traces) from distributed systems and microservices architectures. You can find more information about OpenTelemetry at https://opentelemetry.io/.

Because it's a vendor-agnostic, standardized framework, the Aspire project template uses it as the primary choice for enabling monitoring tools in the application. But we can choose among many alternatives.

## 6.3 Configuring the telemetry

Now that we've added the appropriate packages to enable logging, metrics, and tracing, we can configure them inside the orchestrated applications. If we open the `Extension.cs` file in the `OnlineShop.ServiceDefaults` project, we find the following invocation:

```
builder.ConfigureOpenTelemetry();
```

This invokes the method that registers all dependencies related to telemetry. The method itself also exists in our code. Let's examine it step by step. We begin with the following code:

```
builder.Logging.AddOpenTelemetry(logging =>
{
    logging.IncludeFormattedMessage = true;
```

```
        logging.IncludeScopes = true;
    });
```

This code is how we register OpenTelemetry logging. The setup allows us to collect logs in a format that we can send to a common OpenTelemetry endpoint.

Next is the following block of code, which enables OpenTelemetry metrics to be collected:

```
builder.Services.AddOpenTelemetry()
    .WithMetrics(metrics =>
    {
        metrics.AddAspNetCoreInstrumentation()
            .AddHttpClientInstrumentation()
            .AddRuntimeInstrumentation();
    })
```

Next, we chain-invoke the following methods to allow the traces to be collected:

```
.WithTracing(tracing =>
    {
        tracing.AddAspNetCoreInstrumentation()
            .AddHttpClientInstrumentation();
    });
```

We complete this method by performing the following invocation:

```
builder.AddOpenTelemetryExporters();
```

This method configures the mechanism for sending telemetry to a specific endpoint. If we search our code for the implementation of `AddOpenTelemetryExporters()`, we see that it starts with the following:

```
var useOtlpExporter =
    !string.IsNullOrWhiteSpace(
        builder.Configuration["OTEL_EXPORTER_OTLP_ENDPOINT"]);
```

Essentially, we export the telemetry to the specified OpenTelemetry endpoint only if the endpoint address is set in `OTEL_EXPORTER_OTLP_ENDPOINT`. But even without this setting, this expression still pulls its value, and we have the OpenTelemetry endpoint to send the telemetry to because in the development environment, the value of this setting is `http://localhost:4318` by default. This value won't work in production, but the deployment commands covered in chapter 9 automatically configure telemetry for a deployed production instance.

Finally, we configure the telemetry exporters to export all three types of measurements:

```
if (useOtlpExporter)
{
    builder.Services.AddOpenTelemetry().UseOtlpExporter();
}
```

Now that we know how to configure our application to collect telemetry, let's see how to view that telemetry.

## 6.4 Viewing information in the dashboard

We can see all the measurements in the Aspire dashboard after we launch the app. We can open the Console tab, for example, to view the console logs for any of our services, as figure 6.2 demonstrates.

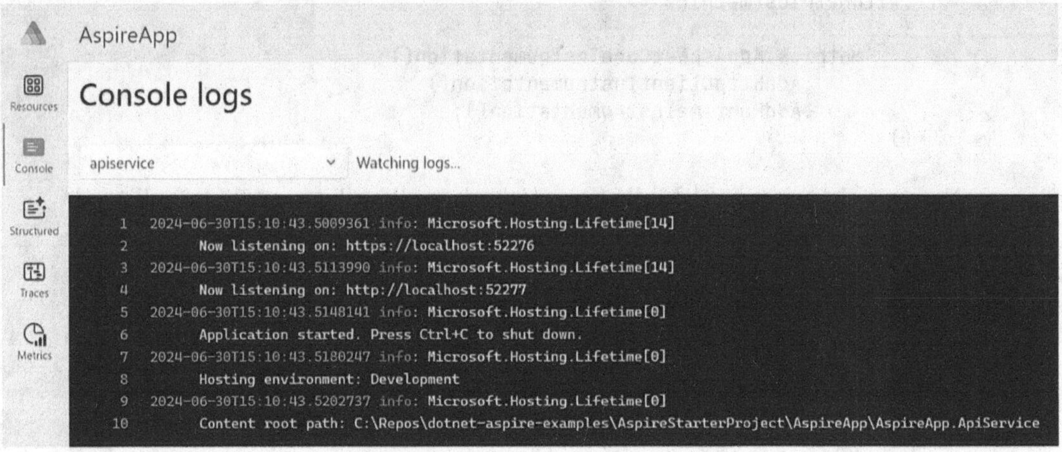


**Figure 6.2 Console logs for an individual service**

We can also open the Structured tab to view the structured logs for all services, as shown in figure 6.3.

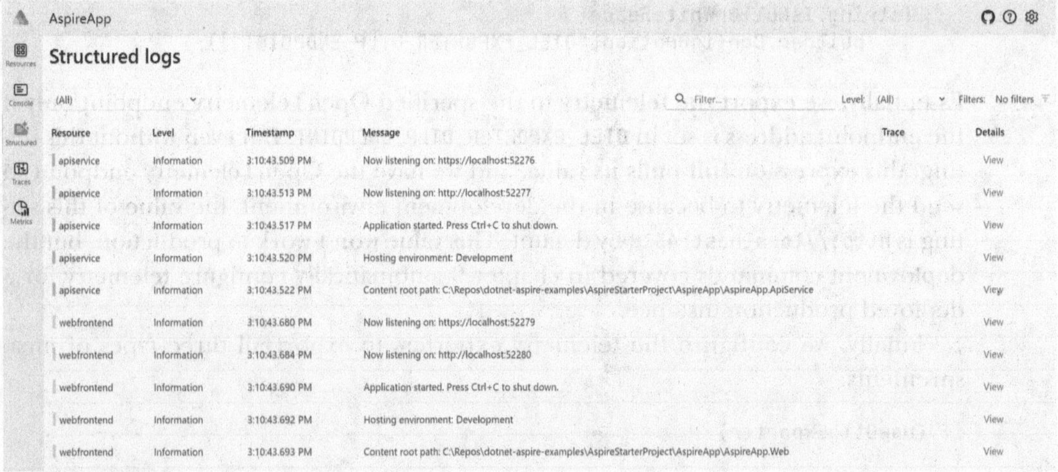


**Figure 6.3 Structured logs in Aspire**

The Traces tab displays information similar to figure 6.4.

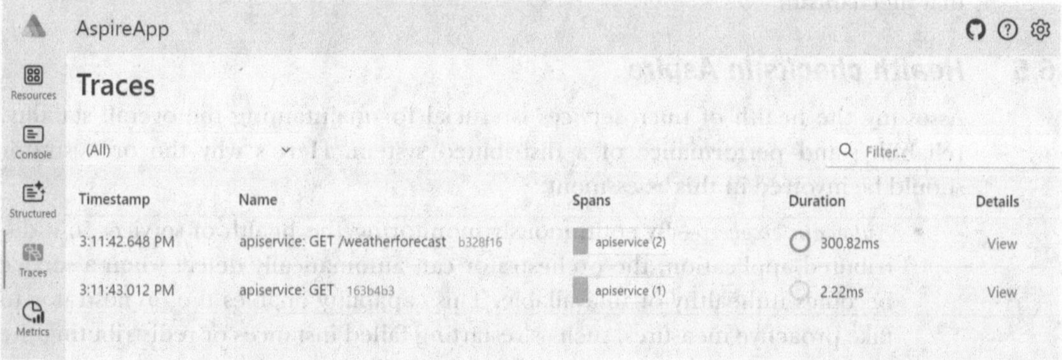


**Figure 6.4 Traces in Aspire setup**

If we open the Metrics tab, we see a wide range of metrics, as shown in figure 6.5.

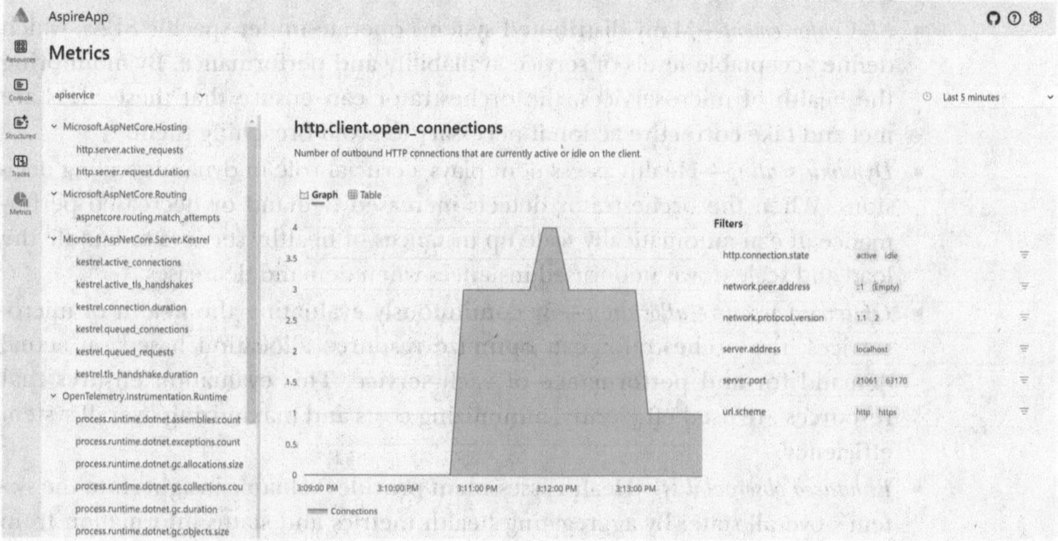


**Figure 6.5 Metrics tab in Aspire**

This is how we can use Aspire to monitor all applications in a single place.

As we've seen in this chapter, Aspire makes it easy to monitor an orchestrated application via its multifunction dashboard. By default, it uses OpenTelemetry, a standardized, platform-agnostic way to collect telemetry. But logging, traces, and metrics aren't the only tools we need to monitor our applications. These tools allow us to see what happened in an application in the past, but we also need a mechanism for determining whether each application is working correctly right now. Section 6.5 covers that mechanism.

## 6.5 Health checks in Aspire

Assessing the health of microservices is crucial for maintaining the overall stability, reliability, and performance of a distributed system. Here's why the orchestrator should be involved in this assessment:

- *Automatic recovery*—By continuously monitoring the health of services in a distributed application, the orchestrator can automatically detect when a service becomes unhealthy or unavailable. This capability enables the orchestrator to take proactive measures, such as restarting failed instances or redistributing the workload to healthy instances without manual intervention.
- *Fault tolerance*—In a distributed architecture, in which services often rely on one another to fulfill requests, the failure of one service can cascade, affecting the entire system. By assessing the health of individual services, the orchestrator can identify and isolate failing services, preventing widespread system failures and maintaining fault tolerance.
- *SLA enforcement*—Many distributed systems operate under specific SLAs, which define acceptable levels of service availability and performance. By monitoring the health of microservices, the orchestrator can ensure that these SLAs are met and take corrective action if necessary to avoid breaching them.
- *Dynamic scaling*—Health assessment plays a crucial role in dynamic-scaling decisions. When the orchestrator detects increased demand or decreased performance, it can automatically scale up instances of healthy services to handle the load and scale down underused instances when demand decreases.
- *Optimized resource allocation*—By continuously evaluating the health of microservices, the orchestrator can optimize resource allocation based on actual demand for and performance of each service. This evaluation ensures that resources are used efficiently, minimizing costs and maximizing overall system efficiency.
- *Enhanced observability*—Health assessment provides valuable insights into the system's overall state. By aggregating health metrics and status information from individual microservices, the orchestrator can provide comprehensive observability and monitoring capabilities, which helps with troubleshooting and performance optimization.

### 6.5.1 Service statuses in Aspire's dashboard

Now let's see how health checks are performed in apps hosted by Aspire. When we look at the Resources tab of the Aspire dashboard, we find the State column in the table displayed there. This column shows the current status of each service managed by Aspire.

Ideally, unless the services were designed for a single run, such as migrations, each service should be shown as Running, with a green check next to it (figure 6.6).

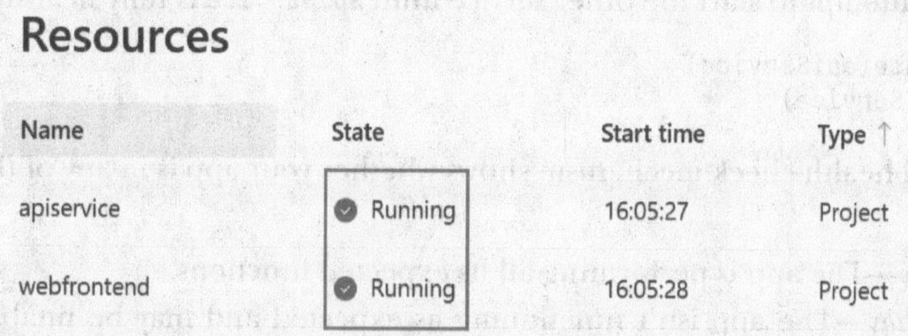


**Figure 6.6 State of services in the Aspire dashboard**

We can check whether this process works correctly by making one of the services throw an exception during startup. We could add the following line to the Program.cs file of the web frontend project before the `app.Run()` method is invoked:

```
throw new InvalidOperationException();
```

If we do this, the dashboard will look like figure 6.7.

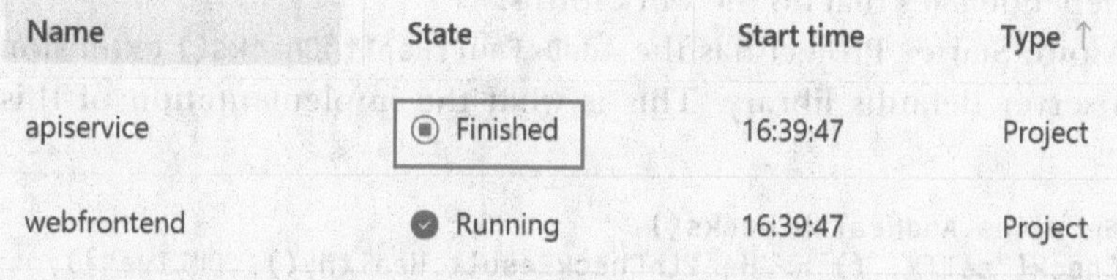


**Figure 6.7 Service startup error shown in the Aspire dashboard**

How does Aspire know whether a particular service is running? That's easy: it uses the health-check endpoint configured on the service. We specify this endpoint when the service is registered by invoking the `WithHttpHealthCheck()` method. When we register our API service, for example, we tell it to expose the health-check endpoint via the `/health` path, like this:

```
var apiService = builder.AddProject<Projects.OnlineShop_ApiService>("apiservice")
    .WithHttpHealthCheck("/health")
```

Then if we pass the API service reference to the other services, this endpoint will be pinged periodically to see whether the service is running and healthy. In the following combination of invocations, the `WithReference()` method enables apiService to be discoverable inside the service into which its reference is passed. The `WaitFor()` method ensures that the orchestrator pings the health-check endpoint of `apiService` regularly and doesn't attempt to start the other service until `apiService` is fully healthy.

```
.WithReference(apiService)
.WaitFor(apiService)
```

The standard health-check mechanism shows whether your app is in any of the following states:

- *Healthy*—The app is performing all its expected functions.
- *Unhealthy*—The app isn't functioning as expected and may be unable to perform its primary functions.
- *Degraded*—The application is operational but performing below optimal levels. There may be problems that don't halt functionality but may impair performance or user experience.

As you've seen, Aspire has a built-in mechanism for performing this type of health check. The next section walks through the process of configuring the health-check endpoint.

### 6.5.2 How health checks are configured inside Aspire apps

To recap, the Aspire orchestrator performs health checks by sending HTTP requests to specific application endpoints. These endpoints generate a specific response to those requests. We don't have to create those endpoints manually; we can register the relevant dependencies that do the work for us.

The Aspire Starter Project has the `AddDefaultHealthChecks()` extension method inside its server defaults library. This is what the implementation of this method looks like:

```
builder.Services.AddHealthChecks()
    .AddCheck("self", () => HealthCheckResult.Healthy(), ["live"]);
```

Here is what's happening:

1. We add the health-check logic by invoking the `AddHealthChecks()` method on the `Services` property of the builder object.
2. We add a specific health check by invoking the `AddCheck()` method.
3. Inside this method, we have a lambda expression that returns a response indicating that our application is healthy.
4. We also add the live tag to the response, which we'll come back to later.

This health-check logic is the simplest we can implement. The health-check endpoint always returns a healthy status while the application is running. If something is wrong with the application, the endpoint becomes inaccessible, and no status is returned.

Now, to make it work, we have to map the appropriate health-check endpoints.

### 6.5.3 Mapping health-check endpoints

To map the health check to the appropriate HTTP endpoints, we have the `MapDefaultEndpoints()` method. This method is invoked in the middleware of all HTTP-enabled applications hosted by Aspire. It adds any default endpoints to the applications, including the health-check endpoints. The health-check endpoints are added by invoking the `MapHealthChecks()` method on the app object. This is how it's invoked:

```
app.MapHealthChecks(HealthEndpointPath);
```

This example is a fairly standard way to register the `/health` path as the basic health-check endpoint. But another health-check endpoint registration allows other applications to get a more detailed look at the application's health state:

```
app.MapHealthChecks(AlivenessEndpointPath, new HealthCheckOptions
    {
        Predicate = r => r.Tags.Contains("live")
    });
```

In these examples, the `HealthEndpointPath` and `AlivenessEndpointPath` variables have the values `"/health"` and `"/alive"`, respectively.

This time, we're registering the `/alive` path, which the orchestrator knows about. This endpoint is more complicated: we're not only checking whether we receive the correct response but also verifying that the response contains the live tag.

When we registered our health-check logic earlier, we accounted for both of these scenarios. While we're returning a valid response, we're also returning the live tag.

### 6.5.4 Monitoring app health in production

If we look closely at the code in the Aspire Starter Project, we see that all health-check endpoints are registered inside the development environment condition, which looks like this:

```
if (app.Environment.IsDevelopment())
```

Does this mean that we do health checks only in the development environment? No. We must do health checks in any environment, especially production. Moreover, we have to use the same endpoints with the same paths.

Still, the production environment has caveats. Because health-check endpoints are accessible like any other public HTTP endpoint, developers must apply appropriate protections to the production versions of them. Such examples aren't included in the standard project template because each scenario has its own implementation based on its specific requirements.

On the other hand, because health-check endpoints typically don't share sensitive information and merely indicate that the application is alive, the developers may choose to enable the same health-check logic in production that they have in the development environment.

Although health checks allow you to assess the real-time state of your services while they're running, it's important to ensure that your application isn't broken before it goes into production. This is what tests are for and what section 6.6 discusses.

## 6.6 Setting up integration tests in Aspire

Before an application can be released to production, it must be thoroughly tested to ensure that it works as expected. It's better to discover and fix bugs before the application is released to users than to release broken software and ruin your reputation in the process.

Aspire includes mechanisms for automating the testing process for the entire distributed system it hosts. Automated test coverage for our software apps is important. Although manual tests sometimes have their place, automated tests allow us to verify our application logic much more efficiently than manual tests can.

Automated tests also allow us to check whether a change in one part of the codebase accidentally broke anything elsewhere, which would be next to impossible to do manually in a complex application. As we add tests for new functionality—or even use the test-driven development (TDD) approach to add the test before we implement the functionality—we retain all the previously added tests for earlier functionality.

Integration tests are a special category of automated tests that allow us to verify that an application or one of its modules works as intended with other components. These tests may use real networks, real HTTP requests, real database connections, and so on.

Traditionally, integration tests were fairly hard to apply to orchestrated distributed applications because such applications have many moving components that must be coordinated. Typically, running all these components is computationally expensive. Therefore, the scope of integration testing in distributed applications is usually limited to interactions among a small number of components.

But Aspire solved this problem quite neatly. Its developers at Microsoft thought ahead to integration tests, so running integration tests against it is almost as easy as running low-level component/unit tests. Moreover, Aspire comes with a template for an integration testing project, so we don't have to search the internet every time we have to add tests to a new distributed application.

### 6.6.1 Adding a test project

The easiest way to set up a test project is to select the Create Test Project option while creating a new Aspire Starter Project application in Visual Studio, as figure 6.8 demonstrates.

If you prefer to use the .NET CLI, you can run the following command to create a new Aspire test project with all the dependencies:

```
dotnet new aspire-xunit
```

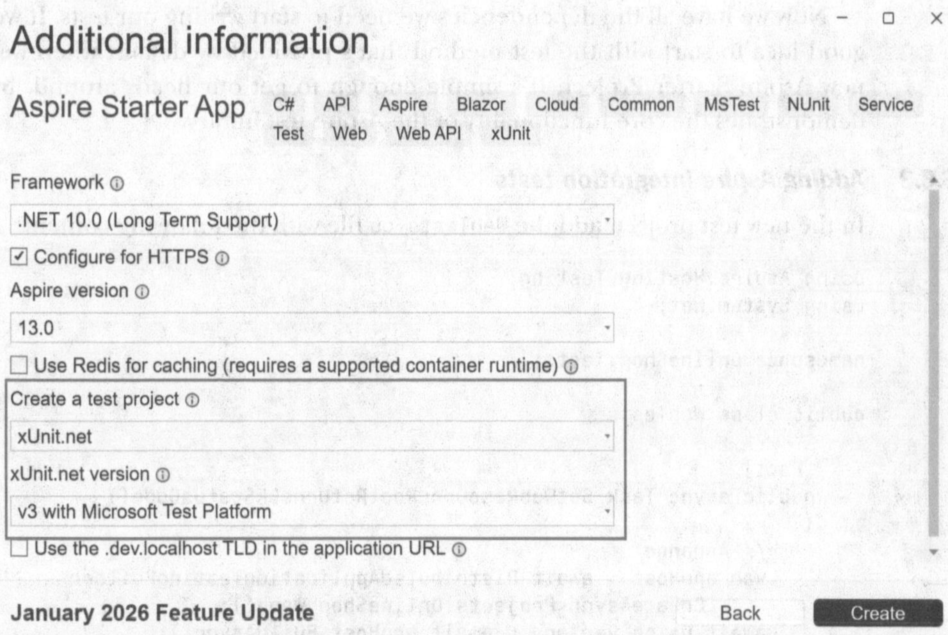


**Figure 6.8 Adding a test project to Aspire app**

By default, the Aspire test project template uses xUnit, but all the concepts we will discuss can also be implemented in NUnit and MSTest. Aspire testing libraries are framework-agnostic and will work with any of these frameworks.

We don't even have to use the default test template. We can create a standard test project in .NET by using any of the testing frameworks and then installing the dependencies specific to Aspire integration testing. Because we already have an application, that's what we'll do next.

### 6.6.2 Installing required dependencies for testing

The GitHub repository at https://mng.bz/MwGn contains an example Aspire project created from the Aspire Starter Project template.

To start, we'll add an xUnit project to our solution and call it `OnlineShop.Tests`. Then, in the new test project, we'll add a reference to the `Aspire.Hosting.Testing` NuGet package, which includes all the components required for Aspire integration testing.

The remaining packages already referenced by the project are related to the testing framework and aren't specific to Aspire. If we used a different testing framework, such as NUnit or MSTest, we'd see different base test packages being referenced.

Because we're testing our entire Aspire application, including its host, we must make sure that our `OnlineShop.Tests` project references the `OnlineShop.AppHost` project.

Now we have all the dependencies we need to start writing our tests. It would be a good idea to start with the test method that's provided by default when we create a new Aspire Starter Project. It's simple enough to get our heads around, but it also demonstrates the core functionality of the Aspire test library.

### 6.6.3 Adding Aspire integration tests

In the new test project, add the `WebTests.cs` file with the following content:

```
using Aspire.Hosting.Testing;
using System.Net;

namespace OnlineShop.Tests;

public class WebTests
{
    [Fact]
    public async Task GetWebResourceRootReturnsOkStatusCode()
    {
        // Arrange
        var appHost = await DistributedApplicationTestingBuilder
            .CreateAsync<Projects.OnlineShop_Web>();
        await using var app = await appHost.BuildAsync();
        await app.StartAsync();

        // Act
        var httpClient = app.CreateHttpClient("webfrontend");
        var response = await httpClient.GetAsync("/");

        // Assert
        Assert.Equal(HttpStatusCode.OK, response.StatusCode);
    }
}
```

This example is a fairly standard example of the arrange-act-assert testing pattern, which states that each test method contains these distinct sections:

- *Arrange*—We set up all the required services to run our test.
- *Act*—We perform the action that we're testing.
- *Assert*—We verify the outcomes of this action.

In this example (and as it's commonly applied in C#), we mark each section with a comment to make the test method as easy to understand as possible. Let's go through this method line by line to understand what it does. The first action we take is the following:

```
var appHost = await DistributedApplicationTestingBuilder
        .CreateAsync<Projects.OnlineShop_Web>();
```

This expression uses the `DistributedApplicationTestingBuilder` type from the `Aspire.Hosting.Testing` library. We invoke the static `CreateAsync<T>()` method to initialize a distributed, orchestrated Aspire application.

The type we specify when we invoke this method is `Projects.OnlineShop_AppHost`, which is the automatically generated representation of our Aspire host project. Essentially, we're creating a test version of our entire Aspire application.

We don't need to delve too deeply into the difference between the test host and a normal host, but it's helpful to know that the test host is much more lightweight. But don't be deceived by the fact that it's lightweight; it still allows us to test all the core functionality of our Aspire app and how its orchestrated services interoperate. The test version of the host still uses real networking and other real dependencies. More information about how this test host works is available at https://mng.bz/4nrV.

In the next two lines, we build the host and start it:

```
await using var app = await appHost.BuildAsync();
await app.StartAsync();
```

We're wrapping the `app` object (which represents the whole Aspire app) in an `await using` scope because it's a disposable object that relies on various unmanaged resources, such as network connections. As soon as the code exits the `using` scope, it cleanly disposes of these resources.

The next expression is

```
var httpClient = app.CreateHttpClient("webfrontend");
```

This expression creates an instance of the `HttpClient` class from the Aspire test host. Because we create it from the Aspire host, we use Aspire service discovery to set its base URL. In this example, we register a Blazor app under the name `webfrontend`. Our HTTP client is configured with the base URL of that app.

Next, we send an HTTP `GET` request to the app's base address, which is denoted by the forward slash:

```
var response = await httpClient.GetAsync("/");
```

Finally, we verify that we received the `OK (200)` response:

```
Assert.Equal(HttpStatusCode.OK, response.StatusCode);
```

Before we move on, here's an important thing to remember: this test launches the entire Aspire host in the background, along with every service it hosts. It honors all interservice dependencies set by `WaitFor()`. Therefore, if we run the test, it takes a long time if we haven't previously created the Ollama container and downloaded the model. To make the tests quicker, we can temporarily remove the following line from the `AppHost.cs` file:

```
.WaitFor(phi35)
```

Next, we'll see how to implement the same method using alternative testing frameworks.

### 6.6.4 Using different testing frameworks

If we want to use NUnit instead of xUnit, we create the test project by executing the following command:

```
dotnet new aspire-nunit
```

In NUnit, our test method would look like this:

```
[Test]
public async Task GetWebResourceRootReturnsOkStatusCode()
{
    // Arrange
    var appHost = await DistributedApplicationTestingBuilder
        .CreateAsync<Projects.OnlineShop_AppHost>();
    await using var app = await appHost.BuildAsync();
    await app.StartAsync();

    // Act
    var httpClient = app.CreateHttpClient("webfrontend");
    var response = await httpClient.GetAsync("/");

    // Assert
    Assert.AreEqual(HttpStatusCode.OK, response.StatusCode);
}
```

The main difference between xUnit and NUnit in this case is the use of `[Test]` instead of `[Fact]` and `Assert.AreEqual()` instead of `Assert.Equal()`. Otherwise, the structure and logic of the test are the same.

If our preferred testing framework is MSTest, we instantiate the test project with the following CLI command:

```
dotnet new aspire-mstest
```

The method looks like this:

```
[TestMethod]
public async Task GetWebResourceRootReturnsOkStatusCode()
{
    // Arrange
    var appHost = await DistributedApplicationTestingBuilder
        .CreateAsync<Projects.OnlineShop_AppHost>();
    await using var app = await appHost.BuildAsync();
    await app.StartAsync();
    // Act
    var httpClient = app.CreateHttpClient("webfrontend");
    var response = await httpClient.GetAsync("/");

    // Assert
    Assert.AreEqual(HttpStatusCode.OK, response.StatusCode);
}
```

In MSTest, the `[TestMethod]` attribute indicates a test method. The assertion uses `Assert.AreEqual()`, similar to NUnit. The rest of the test remains consistent with the structure and logic of the original test.

### 6.6.5 Expanding test functionality

One thing you may have noticed about this test method is that it's simple—so simple that it probably has limited utility. All we're doing is sending a basic HTTP request to the application's home page and verifying that we received a `200` response code.

One way to improve the test is to look at the content returned in the response. This applies to both in-browser applications with a user interface and headless API applications. .NET provides many ways to do this, and each method has pros and cons.

We'll use the `AngleSharp` NuGet package, which allows us to parse HTML on web pages and easily search their content. When we've referenced this NuGet package from our test project, we can create the following helper class with a method that allows us to read the HTTP response object and parse its content.

**Listing 6.1 A helper class for parsing HTML**

```
using AngleSharp;
using AngleSharp.Html.Dom;
using AngleSharp.Io;
using System.Net.Http.Headers;

namespace OnlineShop.Tests.Helpers;

public class HtmlHelpers
{
    public static async Task<IHtmlDocument>
        GetDocumentAsync(HttpResponseMessage response)
    {
        var content = await response
            .Content.ReadAsStringAsync();          // Read the response content into a string.
        var document = await BrowsingContext.New()
            .OpenAsync(
                ResponseFactory, CancellationToken.None);   // Parse the document via ResponseFactory.

        return (IHtmlDocument)document;

        void ResponseFactory(VirtualResponse htmlResponse)
        {
            htmlResponse
                .Address(response.RequestMessage.RequestUri)   // Add address to the parsed response object.
                .Status(response.StatusCode);                  // Add the response status to the parsed object.

            MapHeaders(response.Headers);             // Parse response header.
            MapHeaders(response.Content.Headers);     // Parse the content header from the response.

            htmlResponse.Content(content);            // Parse the content.
```

```
            void MapHeaders(HttpHeaders headers)
            {
                foreach (var header in headers)
                {
                    foreach (var value in header.Value)
                    {
                        htmlResponse.Header(
                            header.Key, value);
                    }
                }
            }
        }
    }
}
```

The method to map headers

Process all the headers.

For each header, process all the values.

Our distributed Aspire app is set up so that a Blazor application fetches data from a separate REST API application to populate its products page, shown in figure 6.9.

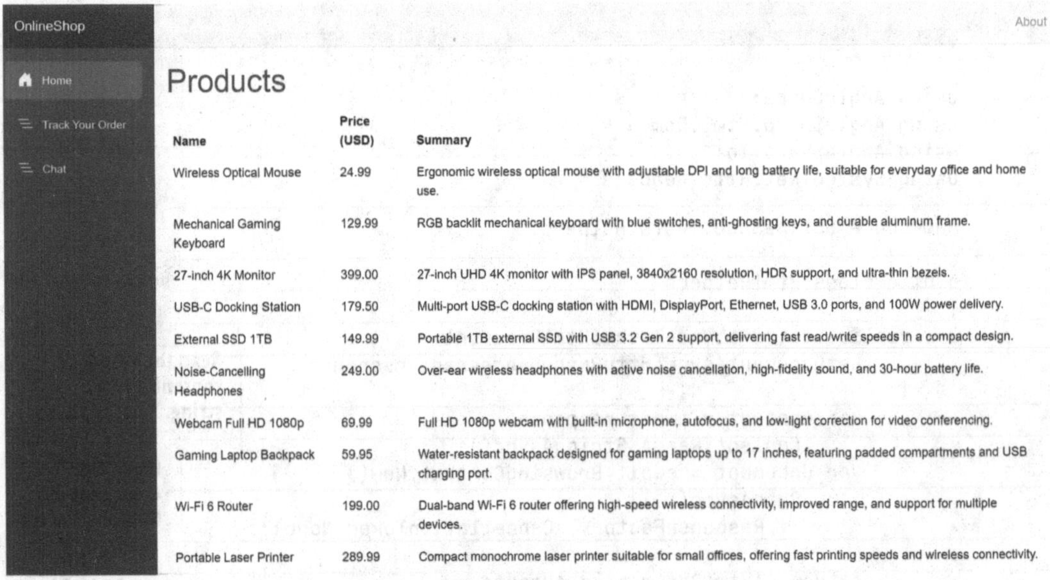


**Figure 6.9 Products page in the Blazor UI app hosted by Aspire**

Let's write a test to see whether the products page has the content we expect to see:

```
[Fact]
public async Task GetProductsReturnsRightContent()
{
    // Arrange
    var appHost = await
        DistributedApplicationTestingBuilder
            .CreateAsync<Projects.OnlineShop_Web>();
```

```
    await using var app = await appHost.BuildAsync();
    await app.StartAsync();

    // Act
    var httpClient = app.CreateHttpClient("webfrontend");

    var response = await httpClient
        .GetAsync("/");
    var responseBody = await HtmlHelpers
        .GetDocumentAsync(response);
    var titleElement = responseBody
        .QuerySelector("h1");

    // Assert
    Assert.Equal(HttpStatusCode.OK, response.StatusCode);
    Assert.NotNull(titleElement);
    Assert.Equal(
        "Products",
    titleElement.InnerHtml);
}
```

In this test method, we aren't simply checking whether the page exists and returns an appropriate response code; we're also reading the page content by passing it to the helper method we created earlier. Then we search for the first `h1` HTML element and check whether its content has the Products title.

Now our test is much more informative. In addition to checking the response status, the test verifies that we get the right output.

### 6.6.6 What about component testing?

Although integration tests are beneficial and often necessary in distributed applications, we can also benefit from testing individual components. These tests are much faster because they don't rely on real networking; they test the code directly.

One of the best ways to write component tests against a Blazor application is to use the `Bunit` NuGet package. Microsoft even endorses this package and mentions it in its documentation, although it's made by the open source community.

We have to install two NuGet packages in our application: `Bunit` and `Bunit.TestDoubles`. The `Bunit` NuGet package uses the previously installed `AngleSharp` as one of its dependencies. To prevent a dependency conflict, it's best to uninstall the existing version of `AngleSharp` before installing `Bunit`.

Let's see how to use this package for testing. Because we don't have any interactive components in the UI yet, we'll use a component from the standard Aspire Starter Project template as an example: the Counter page, shown in figure 6.10.

This page has a button that increments the count onscreen when clicked. We can use `Bunit` to test this functionality. The next listing shows examples of such tests. We can add this file to our test project.

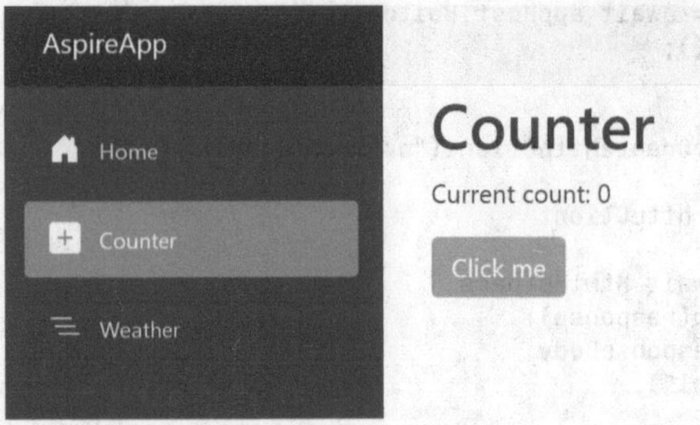


**Figure 6.10 Counter page in Aspire-hosted Blazor application**

**Listing 6.2 bUnit test setup**

```
public class CounterTests : Bunit.TestContext
{
    [Fact]
    public void CounterStartsAtZero()
    {
        // Arrange
        var cut = RenderComponent<Counter>();

        // Assert
        cut.Find("p")
            .MarkupMatches(
                "<p role=\"status\">Current count: 0</p>");
    }

    [Fact]
    public void ClickingButtonIncrementsCounter()
    {
        // Arrange
        var cut = RenderComponent<Counter>();

        // Act
        cut.Find("button").Click();

        // Assert
        cut.Find("p")
            .MarkupMatches(
                "<p role=\"status\">Current count: 1</p>");
    }
}
```

The first test method, `CounterStartsAtZero()`, checks that the initial counter value is `0` by directly rendering the Counter component and checking that the corresponding HTML contains `0` as the count value.

The other test method, `ClickingButtonIncrementsCounter()`, checks that the counter gets incremented when the button is clicked.

This chapter covered monitoring, health checks, and testing. With testing, we focused on setting up and running integration tests in Aspire that can validate entire distributed workflows end to end. We also looked at how to test individual components, which is important for validating detailed behavior inside our applications.

Chapter 8 discusses another important topic, application security, and shows how to protect both the Aspire dashboard and the applications hosted by the Aspire orchestrator.

## Summary

- By default, Aspire uses OpenTelemetry, a standardized and platform-agnostic way of collecting telemetry.
- Logging records relatively detailed information about events happening inside an application.
- Metrics record simple data, such as event counts and event durations.
- Traces link several recorded events so that you can trace the sequence of events.
- Health checks determine whether an app is ready to interact with other systems.
- The Aspire host has its own internal health-checking mechanism, which allows you to see immediately whether any services aren't running as expected.
- The Aspire Starter Project has placeholders for creating health-check endpoints in HTTP-enabled applications hosted by Aspire.
- The exact health-check endpoint implementation is typically environment-specific due to factors such as security.
- Aspire not only allows developers to build distributed, orchestrated applications relatively easily compared with equivalent technologies but also makes it easy to write integration tests against these applications.
- Special libraries let developers add tests to Aspire. The Aspire test libraries are fully compatible with any testing framework available in .NET. Lower-level tests, such as unit tests, can be applied to individual services hosted by Aspire.
- Any library can be used to test individual apps hosted by Aspire, including those that parse HTML and Blazor components.

# 7 Components for messaging and caching

***This chapter covers***

- Understanding the fundamental concepts of message queues and message brokers
- Integrating message brokers with Aspire
- Using distributed caches and distributed locking for thread safety
- Using Redis to implement both distributed locking and caching
- Enabling the Redis management platform in Aspire

It's common for distributed applications to have independent, self-contained services that communicate using message brokers. A *message broker* is a software system that mediates communication among applications, services, or microservices, enabling them to exchange information without being directly connected. It manages the sending, receiving, and routing of messages between systems. This is especially useful in distributed architectures, in which services often have to communicate asynchronously.

Typically, message queues provide this functionality. A service posts a message to a queue without knowing (or even caring) where it will end up. Another service subscribes to the queue, and this receiver service reads the messages from the queue in the order in which they arrive.

When such a service receives a message, it reads the message, extracts any data from it, and performs some actions. After the message is processed, it's removed from the queue or marked as processed, depending on the specific message-broker implementation. Then the next message in the queue is processed, and so on.

Aspire has built-in components that can act as message brokers. In this chapter, we'll look at two of those components: RabbitMQ and Azure Queue Storage. But as we'll see, both rely on the same fundamental principles, which apply equally to other types of message-broker technologies. Figure 7.1 illustrates these principles, showing two typical modes of working with a message broker:

- *Queue-based processing*—Typically, there is only one subscriber to the queue, and after a message has been received and processed by a subscriber, it disappears from the system.
- *Topic-based processing*—There can be many subscribers, each receiving a copy of the next message from the queue.

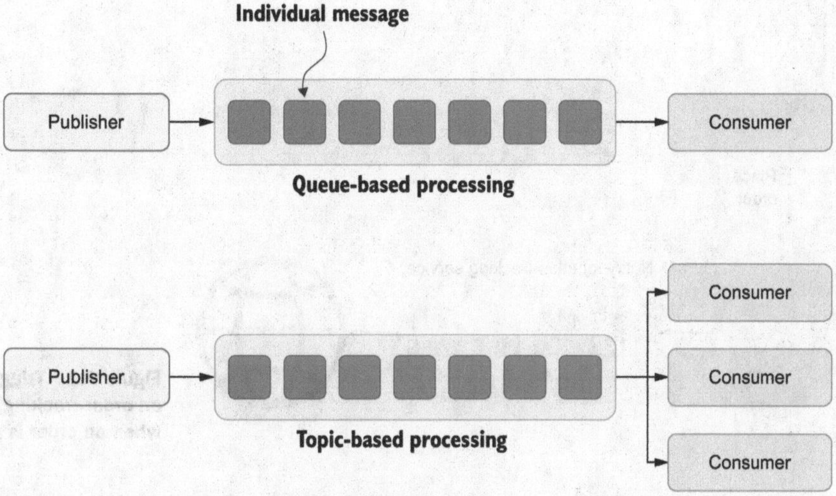


**Figure 7.1 Message-broker workflows**

## 7.1 Working with RabbitMQ

RabbitMQ is a popular open source message broker designed to facilitate communication between distributed systems by managing and routing messages between applications. Built on the Advanced Message Queuing Protocol (AMQP), RabbitMQ enables reliable, asynchronous message delivery across services, making it particularly well suited for microservices and event-driven architectures. Although it can be difficult to set up in production, its relative ease of use, extensive documentation, and flexibility make it a go-to choice for developers building reliable, event-driven systems.

The complete system implementation that relies on RabbitMQ as its message broker is available at https://mng.bz/a92B.

Remember adding order-tracking functionality in chapter 4? At the time, the functionality was fully emulated. We had a page with a map that showed the current location of the delivery driver. But we pretended that the order had been placed.

With a message broker, we can complete this functionality and no longer have to pretend. We'll add the page that allows customers to place orders. When an order is placed, a message is added to the queue in the background to notify the delivery driver.

The user who places the order will see the success message right away because the message broker delegates further work to another service asynchronously. It doesn't matter to the user whether the driver is assigned immediately; what matters is that the order-placing page responds quickly. This is why a background message queue is a suitable solution to this problem. Real e-commerce systems often handle similar workflows this way. Figure 7.2 illustrates our workflow.

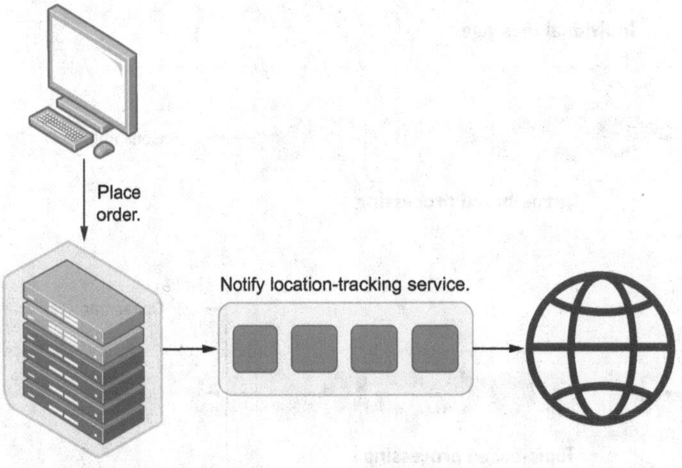


**Figure 7.2 Triggering an order-tracking service when an order is placed**

### 7.1.1 Hosting a RabbitMQ component

To host a RabbitMQ component, we add the NuGet package `Aspire.Hosting.RabbitMQ` to the Aspire host project. Then, to add a RabbitMQ container via the component package, we use the following code in the `AppHost.cs` file:

```
var rabbitmq = builder.AddRabbitMQ("rabbitmq");
var apiService =
    builder.AddProject<Projects.OnlineShop_ApiService>("apiservice")
    .WithHttpHealthCheck("/health")
    .WithReference(rabbitmq)
    .WaitFor(rabbitmq)...
```

We're now ready to set up RabbitMQ dependencies inside our API service hosted by Aspire, which will allow us to send and consume messages across these services. First, however, we have to add the order-processing functionality that will trigger the message broker.

### 7.1.2 Adding order-processing functionality

First, we go into the `OnlineShop.Web` project and open the `ProductsApiClient.cs` file. Then we add the following method, which will allow us to make an order. This method takes a dictionary in which a product ID is mapped to the quantity to be ordered:

```
public async Task<HttpResponseMessage> MakeOrder(Dictionary<int, int> basket)
{
    return await httpClient.PostAsJsonAsync($"/api/orders", basket);
}
```

Because our `ProductDto` object doesn't currently store the product ID, which we'll need to identify a product uniquely for an order, we'll modify it to look like this:

```
public record ProductDto(
    int Id,
    string Title,
    string Summary,
    decimal Price
);
```

Next, we open the `Program.cs` file and locate the original `/products` endpoint. We have to modify the logic inside it to make sure that the `Id` field from the original database entity is mapped to the data transfer object (DTO) that gets returned to the calling client:

```
app.MapGet("/products",
    ([FromServices] SqlConnection connection) =>
    {
        connection.Open();

        var command = new SqlCommand(@"
            USE Shop;
            SELECT
                Id,
                Title,
                Summary,
                Price
            FROM Products", connection);
        var products = new List<ProductDto>();

        using (var reader = command.ExecuteReader())
        {
            while (reader.Read())
            {
                products.Add(new ProductDto(
                    Id: reader.GetInt32(0),
```

```
                Title: reader.GetString(1),
                Summary: reader.GetString(2),
                Price: reader.GetDecimal(3)
            ));
        }

        return products.ToArray();
    }
});
```

Now we have to modify our database-creation script so that it accepts orders. We add classes that represent two things:

- Overall order information
- Order items that are mapped to individual products

The order can be represented by the following class, which we'll place in the `Models` folder of the `OnlineShop.ApiService` project:

```
public class Order
{
    [Key]
    public int Id { get; set; }

    public double TotalAmount { get; set; }
}
```

Each order item can be represented by the following class:

```
public class OrderItem
{
    public int OrderId { get; set; }
    public int ProductId { get; set; }
    public int Quantity { get; set; }
}
```

Next, we go back to the `Program.cs` file and locate the script that creates the original Products table in the database. We have to modify it so that it creates the Orders and OrderItems tables based on the new entities. Here's what such a script might look like if we use a raw SQL Server client:

```
var createTableCommand = new SqlCommand(@"
USE Shop;

-- Products table
IF NOT EXISTS (
    SELECT *
    FROM sysobjects
    WHERE name='Products' AND xtype='U'
)
BEGIN
    CREATE TABLE Products (
```

```
        Id INT PRIMARY KEY IDENTITY,
        Title VARCHAR(100) NOT NULL,
        Summary NVARCHAR(2100) NOT NULL,
        Price DECIMAL(18,2) NOT NULL,
        DateAdded DATE NOT NULL
    );
END

-- Orders table
IF NOT EXISTS (
    SELECT *
    FROM sysobjects
    WHERE name='Orders' AND xtype='U'
)
BEGIN
    CREATE TABLE Orders (
        Id INT IDENTITY PRIMARY KEY,
        TotalAmount DECIMAL(18,2) NOT NULL
    );
END

-- OrderItems table
IF NOT EXISTS (
    SELECT *
    FROM sysobjects
    WHERE name='OrderItems' AND xtype='U'
)
BEGIN
    CREATE TABLE OrderItems (
        OrderId INT NOT NULL,
        ProductId INT NOT NULL,
        Quantity INT NOT NULL,

        CONSTRAINT PK_OrderItems PRIMARY KEY (OrderId, ProductId),

        CONSTRAINT FK_OrderItems_Orders
            FOREIGN KEY (OrderId) REFERENCES Orders(Id),

        CONSTRAINT FK_OrderItems_Products
            FOREIGN KEY (ProductId) REFERENCES Products(Id)
    );
END
", connection);
```

Finally, we'll add the user interface for placing orders. Go back to the `OnlineShop.Web` project, and open the `Home.razor` file, which lists our available products. We'll keep it simple to demonstrate how message-broker integrations work in Aspire. Instead of building an elaborate user interface, we'll add only the minimal functionality required for the user to place an order. This page will serve as both the product list and the basket, showing the total amount and allowing the user to place the order. The following listing shows what this Razor component will look like after the modification.

**Listing 7.1 UI for placing orders**

```
@page "/"
@using OnlineShop.ServiceDefaults.Dtos
@attribute [StreamRendering(true)]
@attribute [OutputCache(Duration = 5)]

@inject ProductsApiClient ProductsApi

<PageTitle>Products</PageTitle>

<h1>Products</h1>

@if (products == null)
{
    <p><em>Loading...</em></p>
}
else
{
    <table class="table">
        <thead>
            <tr>
                <th>Name</th>
                <th>Price (USD)</th>
                <th>Summary</th>
                <th style="width: 280px;">Basket</th>
            </tr>
        </thead>
        <tbody>
            @foreach (var product in products)
            {
                var qty = GetQuantity(product.Id);

                <tr>
                    <td>@product.Title</td>
                    <td>@product.Price</td>
                    <td>@product.Summary</td>
                    <td>
                        <div style="display:flex;
                            gap:8px; align-items:center; flex-wrap:wrap;">
                            <button class="btn btn-sm btn-primary"
                                    @onclick="() => AddToBasket(product.Id)">    ◁ Add to basket button.
                                Add to Basket
                            </button>

                            <button class="btn btn-sm btn-outline-danger"
                                    @onclick="() => RemoveFromBasket(product.Id)"
                                    disabled="@(qty == 0)">    ◁ Remove from basket button.
                                Remove From Basket
                            </button>

                            <span class="btn btn-sm btn-secondary disabled"
                                  aria-disabled="true"
```

```
                                            style="pointer-events:none;">
                                        Quantity ordered: @qty
                                    </span>
                                </div>
                            </td>
                        </tr>
                }
            </tbody>
        </table>

        @if (TotalQuantity > 0)
        {
            <div class="mt-3 p-3 border rounded" style="display:flex; justify-
   content:space-between; align-items:center; gap:12px; flex-wrap:wrap;">
                <div>
                    <strong>Total price:</strong> @TotalPrice.ToString("0.00") USD
                    <span class="text-muted">(@TotalQuantity item@(TotalQuantity == 1
   ? "" : "s"))</span>
                </div>

                <button class="btn btn-success"
                        @onclick="PlaceOrderAsync"
                        disabled="@isPlacingOrder">
                    @(isPlacingOrder ? "Placing..." : "Place order")
                </button>
            </div>

            @if (!string.IsNullOrWhiteSpace(orderStatus))
            {
                <p class="mt-2">@orderStatus</p>
            }
        }
    }

@code {
    private ProductDto[]? products;

    private readonly Dictionary<int, int> basket = new();

    private bool isPlacingOrder;
    private string? orderStatus;

    protected override async Task OnInitializedAsync()
    {
        products = await ProductsApi.GetProductsAsync();
    }

    private int GetQuantity(int productId)
        => basket.TryGetValue(productId, out var qty) ? qty : 0;

    private void AddToBasket(int productId)
    {
        basket.TryGetValue(productId, out var qty);
        basket[productId] = qty + 1;
```

Show product quantity selected for the order.

If any products are selected, display the total price and the button for placing the order.

In-memory basket tracking the selected quantity for each product

Add to basket method.

```
        // ensure UI updates immediately
        orderStatus = null;
        StateHasChanged();
    }

    private void RemoveFromBasket(int productId)      <-- Remove from basket method.
    {
        if (!basket.TryGetValue(productId, out var qty) || qty <= 0)
            return;

        qty--;

        if (qty <= 0)
            basket.Remove(productId);
        else
            basket[productId] = qty;

        orderStatus = null;
        StateHasChanged();
    }

    private int TotalQuantity => basket.Values.Sum();

    private decimal TotalPrice
    {
        get
        {
            if (products == null || basket.Count == 0)
                return 0m;

            decimal total = 0m;

            foreach (var (productId, qty) in basket)
            {
                var product = products.FirstOrDefault(p => p.Id == productId);
                if (product is null) continue;

                total += (decimal)product.Price * qty;
            }

            return total;
        }
    }

    private async Task PlaceOrderAsync()      <-- Place order method
    {
        if (TotalQuantity <= 0)
            return;

        isPlacingOrder = true;
        orderStatus = null;

       try
        {
            var payload = new Dictionary<int, int>(basket);
```

```
                var response = await ProductsApi.MakeOrder(payload);

                if (response.IsSuccessStatusCode)
                {
                    orderStatus = "Order placed successfully.";
                    basket.Clear();                                    <-- Clear the basket
                }                                                          upon successful
                else                                                       order placement.
                {
                    orderStatus = $"Failed to place order. Status:
            {(int)response.StatusCode} {response.ReasonPhrase}";
                }
            }
            catch (Exception ex)
            {
                orderStatus = $"Failed to place order: {ex.Message}";
            }
            finally
            {
                isPlacingOrder = false;
                StateHasChanged();
            }
        }
    }
```

### 7.1.3 Sending messages via RabbitMQ

In this section, we'll add the endpoint for accepting order placement and wire it up to RabbitMQ. In our example setup, different parts of the API service publish messages to a queue in RabbitMQ and consume them from the same queue.

To integrate this service with RabbitMQ, install the NuGet package `Aspire.RabbitMQ.Client` in the `OnlineShop.ApiService` project. Then add the following code to the `Program.cs` file, using the original name we registered the RabbitMQ component under as a parameter:

```
builder.AddRabbitMQClient("rabbitmq");
```

Next, we add the endpoint that both accepts an order and places a message on a queue, telling the background services that an order has been placed. We'll start by adding a placeholder for the `POST` endpoint mapping:

```
app.MapPost("/api/orders", async (
    Dictionary<int, int> basket,
    [FromServices] SqlConnection dbConnection,
    [FromServices] IConnection rabbitConnection) =>
 { });
```

Then we insert the following code into the body of the endpoint mapping, which verifies that the basket isn't empty and that it contains items with a quantity greater than `0`:

```
if (basket is null || basket.Count == 0)
    return Results.BadRequest("Basket is empty.");

var items = basket
    .Where(kvp => kvp.Value > 0)
    .ToDictionary(kvp => kvp.Key, kvp => kvp.Value);

if (items.Count == 0)
    return Results.BadRequest("Basket contains no items with quantity > 0.");
```

Next, we open the database connection, begin a transaction, and place the `try/catch` block so that the transaction is rolled back if any errors occur:

```
if (dbConnection.State != ConnectionState.Open)
    await dbConnection.OpenAsync();

int orderId;
decimal totalAmount;

await using var tx =
    (SqlTransaction)await
     dbConnection.BeginTransactionAsync(IsolationLevel.ReadCommitted);

try
{

}
}
catch (Exception ex)
{
    await tx.RollbackAsync();
    return Results.Problem($"Order creation failed: {ex.Message}");
}
```

Now we populate the `try` body with the database operations. We'll begin by querying the products using the product IDs from the order to calculate the total order amount:

```
var productIds = items.Keys.ToList();
var inParams = string.Join(", ", productIds.Select((_, i) => $"@p{i}"));

var priceLookup = new Dictionary<int, decimal>();

await using (var cmd = new SqlCommand($@"
    SELECT Id, Price
    FROM Products
    WHERE Id IN ({inParams});",
    dbConnection, tx))
{
    for (int i = 0; i < productIds.Count; i++)
        cmd.Parameters.AddWithValue($"@p{i}", productIds[i]);

    await using var reader = await cmd.ExecuteReaderAsync();
    while (await reader.ReadAsync())
```

```
        priceLookup[reader.GetInt32(0)] = reader.GetDecimal(1);
}

totalAmount = items.Sum(i => priceLookup[i.Key] * i.Value);
```

Then we create the order entry in the database:

```
await using (var cmd = new SqlCommand(@"
    INSERT INTO Orders (TotalAmount)
    VALUES (@totalAmount);
    SELECT CAST(SCOPE_IDENTITY() AS INT);",
    dbConnection, tx))
{
    var p = cmd.Parameters.Add("@totalAmount", SqlDbType.Decimal);
    p.Precision = 18;
    p.Scale = 2;
    p.Value = totalAmount;

    orderId = (int)(await cmd.ExecuteScalarAsync() ?? 0);
}

if (orderId <= 0)
    return Results.Problem("Failed to create order.");
```

Finally, we create order items linked to the products in the order and commit the transaction:

```
await using (var cmd = new SqlCommand(@"
    INSERT INTO OrderItems (OrderId, ProductId, Quantity)
    VALUES (@orderId, @productId, @quantity);",
    dbConnection, tx))
{
    cmd.Parameters.Add("@orderId", SqlDbType.Int).Value = orderId;
    var pProductId = cmd.Parameters.Add("@productId", SqlDbType.Int);
    var pQuantity = cmd.Parameters.Add("@quantity", SqlDbType.Int);

    foreach (var (productId, qty) in items)
    {
        pProductId.Value = productId;
        pQuantity.Value = qty;
        await cmd.ExecuteNonQueryAsync();
    }
}

await tx.CommitAsync();
```

After the initial `try/catch` block, we create a queue for the order:

```
await using var channel = await rabbitConnection.CreateChannelAsync();

const string queueName = "orders.created";

await channel.QueueDeclareAsync(
    queue: queueName,
```

```
    durable: true,
    exclusive: false,
    autoDelete: false,
    arguments: null);
```

Here, we create a message queue named `orders.created`. We also configure the following settings for the queue:

- `durable`—Determines whether the queue should survive a RabbitMQ server restart. When the setting is `false`, the queue isn't saved to disk and will be lost if RabbitMQ restarts. When the setting is `true`, the queue persists even after a server restart.
- `exclusive`—Indicates whether the queue is exclusive to this connection. When the setting is `true`, the queue can be used only by the current connection and deleted when the connection is closed. Here, `false` means that the queue can be used by multiple connections and won't be deleted when the connection closes. In our example, either option is fine.
- `autoDelete`—Specifies whether the queue should be deleted automatically when the last consumer unsubscribes. When the setting is `false`, the queue isn't deleted even if no consumers are listening to it.
- `arguments`—Provides optional additional arguments for the queue. Passing `null` means that this queue has no extra configurations. Arguments can be used to set policies such as message lifespan, known as time to live (TTL), maximum message length, and similar parameters.

Next, we publish the message to the queue and return a success response to the calling client:

```
var message = JsonSerializer.Serialize(new { orderId });
var body = Encoding.UTF8.GetBytes(message);

var props = new BasicProperties
{
    Persistent = true
};

await channel.BasicPublishAsync(
    exchange: "",
    routingKey: queueName,
    mandatory: false,
    basicProperties: props,
    body: body);

return Results.Created($"/api/orders/{orderId}", new
{
    OrderId = orderId,
    TotalAmount = totalAmount
});
```

As we can see, each message is JSON containing the order ID. In section 7.1.4, we'll look at the code that consumes those messages.

> **NOTE** The `exchange` parameter is left blank. This probably wouldn't be the case in a real production system, which routes different types of messages to different exchanges. But because we're using a simple end-to-end message flow, using the default exchange is absolutely fine.

### 7.1.4 Consuming RabbitMQ messages

The consumer of our messages will be the `LocationUpdater` background service. We'll modify it to listen to the `orders.created` message queue. When it receives a message, it creates an initial order-tracking location, which we can assume is the default location of our warehouse. The next listing shows the modified class.

**Listing 7.2 Messages consumed**

```
using Microsoft.AspNetCore.SignalR;
using RabbitMQ.Client;
using RabbitMQ.Client.Events;
using System.Text;
using System.Text.Json;

namespace OnlineShop.ApiService;

public sealed class LocationUpdater(
    IHubContext<LocationHub> locationHub,
    IConnection rabbitConnection) : BackgroundService
{
    protected override async Task ExecuteAsync(CancellationToken stoppingToken)
    {
        await using var channel =
            await rabbitConnection.CreateChannelAsync(cancellationToken:
      stoppingToken);

        const string queueName = "orders.created";

        await channel.QueueDeclareAsync(
            queue: queueName,
            durable: true,
            exclusive: false,
            autoDelete: false,
            arguments: null,
            cancellationToken: stoppingToken);

        await channel.BasicQosAsync(
            prefetchSize: 0,
            prefetchCount: 1,
            global: false,
            cancellationToken: stoppingToken);

        var consumer = new AsyncEventingBasicConsumer(channel);
```

Open the RabbitMQ channel.

Declare queue if it doesn't exist.

Set the queue channel configuration.

Create the message consumer.

```
        consumer.ReceivedAsync += async (sender, args) =>
        {
            try
            {
                var json = Encoding.UTF8.GetString(args.Body.ToArray());
                var message =
    JsonSerializer.Deserialize<OrderCreatedMessage>(json);

                if (message is null)
                {
                    await channel.BasicNackAsync(
                        args.DeliveryTag, false, false, stoppingToken);
                    return;
                }

                await SetInitialDeliveryLocation(
                    message.OrderId,
                    stoppingToken);

                await channel.BasicAckAsync(
                    args.DeliveryTag,
                    multiple: false,
                    cancellationToken: stoppingToken);
            }
            catch
            {
                await channel.BasicNackAsync(
                    args.DeliveryTag,
                    false,
                    requeue: true,
                    cancellationToken: stoppingToken);
            }
        };

        await channel.BasicConsumeAsync(
            queue: queueName,
            autoAck: false,
            consumer: consumer,
            cancellationToken: stoppingToken);

        await Task.Delay(Timeout.Infinite, stoppingToken);
    }

    private async Task SetInitialDeliveryLocation(
        int orderId,
        CancellationToken cancellationToken)
    {
        await Task.Delay(3000, cancellationToken);
        await UpdateLocation(orderId, 51.5074, -0.1276, cancellationToken);
    }

    private async Task UpdateLocation(
        int orderId,
```

**Add an event handler to the consumer that gets triggered when a message is received.**

**Deserialize a message received from the queue.**

**Set unsuccessful delivery if the message is null.**

**Set the initial delivery location for tracking.**

**Acknowledge successful message processing.**

**Set the consumer to listen to the messages.**

**Set the background service to run infinitely until the application is terminated.**

```
            double latitude,
            double longitude,
            CancellationToken cancellationToken)
        {
            await locationHub.Clients.All.SendAsync(
                "ReceiveLocationUpdate",
                latitude,
                longitude,
                cancellationToken);
        }

        private sealed record OrderCreatedMessage(int OrderId);
    }
```

When we launch the application, it may initially take some time for the RabbitMQ container to download and start. This delay is expected due to the container's large size. When the application has launched, we should no longer see a location pin on the map on the order-tracking page; it will appear only when we place an order.

If we're setting only the initial location, how can it be updated? We can do that via the `LocationHub`. Another SignalR client, such as the delivery driver's mobile device, can send requests to the `UpdateLocation` endpoint with the new coordinates.

Our location-tracking system isn't complete, and we could make additional improvements. Still, we've achieved our goal of integrating the RabbitMQ publishers and consumers into our Aspire setup.

## 7.2 Working with Azure Queue Storage

In this section, we look at an alternative message broker: Azure Queue Storage. It's not a separate service but (as discussed in chapter 3) part of an Azure Storage account, alongside Azure Table Storage and Azure Blob Storage.

Azure Queue Storage provides a simple, reliable, and scalable way to store large numbers of messages for asynchronous communication between applications or services. Unlike messaging solutions like Azure Service Bus and RabbitMQ, which offer advanced messaging features, Azure Queue Storage is a straightforward, cloud-based queue storage service designed for basic task management and simple communication needs. The complete solution that uses Azure Queue Storage is available at https://mng.bz/X7l6.

We use the same principles we used with RabbitMQ. The order-placement endpoint generates the messages and puts them in a queue. The location-tracking background service consumes the messages and updates the location information. This demonstrates how to use a different message broker for the same purpose.

### 7.2.1 Hosting an emulated Azure Queue Storage component

Azure Queue Storage is part of the standard Azure Storage component, along with Table Storage and Blob Storage. Therefore, we have to reference the same NuGet package, `Aspire.Hosting.Azure.Storage`, in the Aspire host project.

Here's how we create the Queue Storage reference in the `AppHost.cs` file and pass it to both the web frontend and the API services:

```
var storage = builder.AddAzureStorage("storage")
    .RunAsEmulator();


var queues = storage.AddQueues("queues");

builder
    .AddProject<Projects.OnlineShop_ApiService>(
        "apiservice")
    .WaitFor(queues)
    .WithReference(queues)...
```

### 7.2.2 Sending messages via Azure Queue Storage

Now we're ready to start sending and receiving messages. The NuGet package we have to reference from our API project is `Aspire.Azure.Storage.Queues`. This is how we register the Queue Storage client in the `Program.cs` file of both applications:

```
builder.AddAzureQueueServiceClient("queues");
```

**NOTE** The name we pass into the method is the same name we used to register the Queue Storage reference within the Aspire host project.

The service we have to resolve where we intend to use the queue is `QueueServiceClient`. This is what the signature of the order-placement API endpoint will look like:

```
app.MapPost("/api/orders", async (
    Dictionary<int, int> basket,
    [FromServices] SqlConnection dbConnection,
    [FromServices] QueueServiceClient queueServiceClient) =>
```

Where we would put the message in the queue, we create a queue client and the queue, if it doesn't exist:

```
var queueClient = queueServiceClient
    .GetQueueClient("orders-created");
queueClient.CreateIfNotExists();
```

**NOTE** We called our queue `orders-created` rather than `orders.created` because a dot is an invalid character in an Azure Queue Storage name, whereas it's a conventional word separator in a RabbitMQ queue.

Finally, we send the message:

```
var message = JsonSerializer.Serialize(new { orderId });

queueClient.SendMessage(message);
```

That covers the publishing part. As we can see, Azure Queue Storage is simpler to work with than RabbitMQ.

### 7.2.3 Consuming Azure Queue Storage messages

Here's how the messages are consumed. If we open the `LocationUpdater` service, this is what the class signature should look like:

```
public sealed class LocationUpdater(
    IHubContext<LocationHub> locationHub,
    QueueServiceClient queueServiceClient) : BackgroundService
```

We have to reference the following namespaces:

```
using Azure.Storage.Queues;
using Azure.Storage.Queues.Models;
using System.Text.Json;
```

Finally, here's the logic inside the `ExecuteAsync()` method:

```
var queueClient = queueServiceClient
    .GetQueueClient("orders-created");
await queueClient.CreateIfNotExistsAsync();

while (!stoppingToken.IsCancellationRequested)
{

    QueueMessage[] messages = queueClient
    .ReceiveMessages(maxMessages: 10);

    foreach (var message in messages)
    {
        var body =
    JsonSerializer.Deserialize<OrderCreatedMessage>(message.MessageText);

        await SetInitialDeliveryLocation(
                body.OrderId,
                stoppingToken);
    }
}
```

We run an infinite loop, which terminates only when a cancellation is issued. For each iteration, we read a batch of 10 messages and process them all in a for-each block.

This concludes our overview of using Azure Queue Storage inside a distributed Aspire application.

Aspire supports a variety of message brokers. In this chapter, we've looked at two of them, but the underlying principles are the same for other message-broker types.

Message brokers are important in almost any distributed architecture because not all communication between services should happen synchronously. When we use message queues, applications can process messages in the background without affecting user experience.

## 7.3 Overview of distributed cache and lock

*Distributed caching* is a mechanism for storing frequently accessed data in a shared, high-performance data store that spans multiple servers or nodes. This type of caching is typically used to improve application performance and scalability in distributed systems.

When we use a cache, we store data in random-access memory (RAM) rather than on a disk unless the cache is a special-purpose on-disk cache. Reading data from RAM is much faster than interacting with storage disks, so caches can improve application performance significantly, especially when the cache is hit often. This is especially important when we're dealing with large volumes of data.

When we use a tool like Redis, the same cache can be shared among separate applications and even separate physical machines. If one application populates the cache, other applications can access it too. This is why such a cache is called *distributed.* Figure 7.3 shows how distributed caching enables several applications to access the same cache even if they didn't populate it originally.

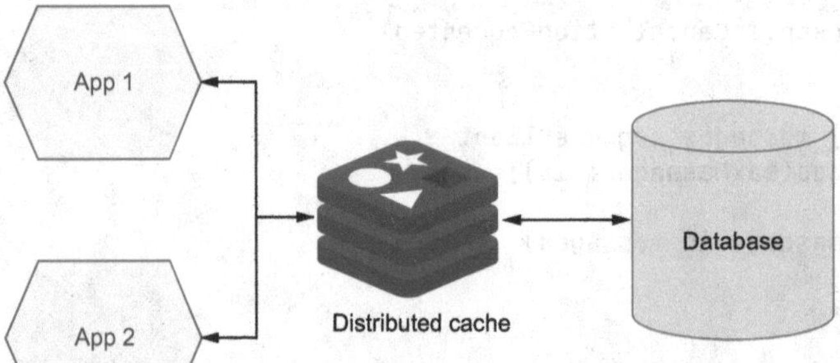


**Figure 7.3 Multiple applications accessing the same distributed cache**

*Distributed locking* is a technique for managing concurrent access to shared resources in a distributed system. It ensures that only one process or thread can access a resource at a time, preventing race conditions and ensuring consistency.

A distributed lock uses a special data structure within a distributed cache that is used for locking. Because it's distributed, it can be used to lock resources not only for separate threads within the same application but also for separate applications. Figure 7.4 demonstrates this principle.

Distributed locking is often implemented with the same tools and mechanisms that enable distributed caching. In a way, a distributed lock is a type of cache with named locks cached in memory, possibly on another machine. Let's see how Redis enables both techniques.

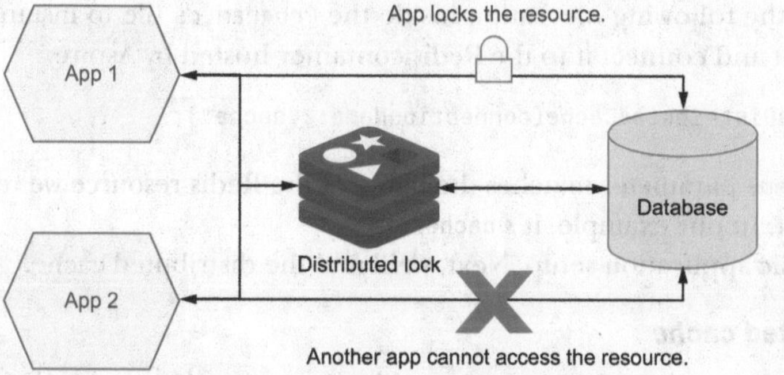


**Figure 7.4 Distributed locking controls which applications can access a database resource.**

## 7.4 Setting up Redis for caching and locking

To see how both mechanisms can be applied in applications hosted by Aspire, we'll use the setup at https://mng.bz/64xo. We'll start by adding the necessary dependencies to the Aspire host to make it host a Redis component.

### 7.4.1 Installing a Redis component

To install the Redis component, add the NuGet package `Aspire.Hosting.Redis` to the Aspire host application.

This package is the one we used in chapter 2 to demonstrate output caching. The component will contain a Redis instance, as it did before, but we'll use it for a different purpose. The code inside our `AppHost.cs` file that registers the Redis component looks like this:

```
var cache = builder.AddRedis("cache")
    .WithRedisCommander();
```

**NOTE** Make sure to pass its reference into the API service because we'll use it for both caching and locking.

We're creating a Redis component instance and passing its reference to the API application. Note the invocation of `WithRedisCommander()`. This call creates another container instance with the service called Redis Commander. We can use this service from the Aspire dashboard to manage data in Redis directly through the browser. I'll cover this topic later.

### 7.4.2 Installing the Redis client for distributed caching

In this section, we install the Redis client in the API application, which will allow us to use distributed caching. The NuGet package we have to install in the `OnlineShop.ApiService` project to enable distributed caching in Redis is `Aspire.StackExchange.Redis.DistributedCaching`.

Then we use the following invocation inside the `Program.cs` file to instantiate the Redis cache client and connect it to the Redis container hosted by Aspire:

```
builder.AddRedisDistributedCache(connectionName: "cache");
```

The `connectionName` parameter matches the name of the Redis resource we registered in the Aspire host. In our example, it's `cache`.

We have a basic application setup. Next, we'll add the distributed cache.

### 7.4.3 Using a distributed cache

It's not every day that new product items are added to our catalog, so we don't have to make a round trip to the database every time we have to retrieve product information. We can cache that information instead. To do so, we'll modify our `/products` endpoint mapping as follows.

**Listing 7.3 Retrieving product items from the cache**

```
app.MapGet("/products",
    async ([FromServices] SqlConnection connection,
        [FromServices] IDistributedCache cache) =>
    {
        const string cacheKey = "Products";

        var cached = await cache.GetStringAsync(cacheKey);
        if (cached is not null)
        {
            var cachedProducts =
                JsonSerializer.Deserialize<ProductDto[]>(cached);

            return Results.Ok(cachedProducts);
        }

        await connection.OpenAsync();

        await using var command = new SqlCommand(@"
            USE Shop;
            SELECT Id, Title, Summary, Price
            FROM Products;", connection);

        var products = new List<ProductDto>();

        await using var reader = await command.ExecuteReaderAsync();
        while (await reader.ReadAsync())
        {
            products.Add(new ProductDto(
                Id: reader.GetInt32(0),
                Title: reader.GetString(1),
                Summary: reader.GetString(2),
                Price: reader.GetDecimal(3)
            ));
        }
```

**Read product data from the Redis cache based on a specific key.**

**If data is returned, return it to the caller right away.**

```
        var serializedProducts = JsonSerializer.Serialize(products.ToArray());

        await cache.SetStringAsync(            <-- If data is retrieved from
            cacheKey,                              the database, cache it
            serializedProducts,                    for quicker retrieval.
            new DistributedCacheEntryOptions
            {
                AbsoluteExpirationRelativeToNow = TimeSpan.FromMinutes(5)
            });

        return Results.Ok(products.ToArray());
    });
```

Here, we're injecting an object of the type `IDistributedCache`, which we registered when we invoked the `AddRedisDistributedCache()` method on the application builder. We use two methods from this object:

- `GetStringAsync()`, which attempts to pull a value from the cache using the specified key that contains the product ID. If no item in the cache matches this key, it returns null.
- `SetStringAsync()`, which adds an item to the cache and assigns a key to it.

Here's what's happening in this method:

1. A request comes in to retrieve the list of products.
2. We check the cache, but it contains no information for a particular key.
3. We pull the product information from the database, which can be slow.
4. The product data is serialized as a JSON string and placed in the cache.
5. When the next request comes, we retrieve the product information from the cache right away.

Our cache is distributed. We can scale out the API application (that is, run multiple instances of it to manage a large volume of requests) and still take full advantage of the caching mechanism regardless of which specific service instance the request hits.

Sometimes, we have to invalidate our cache. If our product list changes, for example, we don't want to return the old product list from the cache. So if we remove or add an item or modify any item data, we can call the `RemoveAsync()` method on the `cache` object. The entry will be removed from the cache and repopulated automatically on the first retrieval.

### 7.4.4 Using a distributed lock

Our example uses distributed locking to make sure that nothing interferes with order placement while it's in progress. If one thread is doing an update, no other threads (or services) will attempt to do it until the update is complete.

This makes our flow thread-safe. If multiple users try to buy the same product at the same time, we have to make sure that the stock is adjusted consistently. The easiest way to achieve this is to ensure that only one thread at a time can adjust the stock. The first thread enters and applies the lock. The next thread waits until the lock is removed. It enters and applies its own lock until it's done.

To see how this works, we'll modify our order-placement endpoint method in the API application's `Program.cs` file as shown in the next listing. This is a simplified version in which only one thread can place an order.

**Listing 7.4 Using the distributed lock during product modification**

```
app.MapPost("/api/orders", async (
    Dictionary<int, int> basket,
    [FromServices] SqlConnection dbConnection,
    [FromServices] QueueServiceClient queueServiceClient,
    [FromServices] IDistributedCache cache,
    [FromServices] IConnectionMultiplexer redis) =>
{
    if (basket is null || basket.Count == 0)
        return Results.BadRequest("Basket is empty.");

    var items = basket
        .Where(kvp => kvp.Value > 0)
        .ToDictionary(kvp => kvp.Key, kvp => kvp.Value);

    if (items.Count == 0)
        return Results.BadRequest("Basket contains no items with quantity > 0.");

    IDatabase db = redis.GetDatabase();

    List<string> lockKeys = [];

    foreach (var productId in items.Keys)
    {
        string lockKey = $"product_lock_{productId}";

        bool lockAcquired = await db.LockTakeAsync(        ◁ Try to set a lock based on a product key.
            lockKey,
            Environment.MachineName,
            TimeSpan.FromSeconds(10));

        if (!lockAcquired)
        {
            return Results.StatusCode(423);        ◁ If the lock exists, exit with 423 to indicate the resource is locked by another process.
        }

        lockKeys.Add($"product_lock_{productId}");
    }

    if (dbConnection.State != ConnectionState.Open)
        await dbConnection.OpenAsync();

    int orderId;
    decimal totalAmount;
```

```
await using var tx =
    (SqlTransaction)await
 dbConnection.BeginTransactionAsync(IsolationLevel.ReadCommitted);

try
{
    var productIds = items.Keys.ToList();
    var inParams = string.Join(", ", productIds.Select((_, i) => $"@p{i}"));

    var priceLookup = new Dictionary<int, decimal>();

    await using (var cmd = new SqlCommand($@"
        SELECT Id, Price
        FROM Products
        WHERE Id IN ({inParams});",
        dbConnection, tx))
    {
        for (int i = 0; i < productIds.Count; i++)
            cmd.Parameters.AddWithValue($"@p{i}", productIds[i]);

        await using var reader = await cmd.ExecuteReaderAsync();
        while (await reader.ReadAsync())
            priceLookup[reader.GetInt32(0)] = reader.GetDecimal(1);
    }

    totalAmount = items.Sum(i => priceLookup[i.Key] * i.Value);

    await using (var cmd = new SqlCommand(@"
        INSERT INTO Orders (TotalAmount)
        VALUES (@totalAmount);
        SELECT CAST(SCOPE_IDENTITY() AS INT);",
        dbConnection, tx))
    {
        var p = cmd.Parameters.Add("@totalAmount", SqlDbType.Decimal);
        p.Precision = 18;
        p.Scale = 2;
        p.Value = totalAmount;

        orderId = (int)(await cmd.ExecuteScalarAsync() ?? 0);
    }

    if (orderId <= 0)
        return Results.Problem("Failed to create order.");

    await using (var cmd = new SqlCommand(@"
        INSERT INTO OrderItems (OrderId, ProductId, Quantity)
        VALUES (@orderId, @productId, @quantity);",
        dbConnection, tx))
    {
        cmd.Parameters.Add("@orderId", SqlDbType.Int).Value = orderId;
        var pProductId = cmd.Parameters.Add("@productId", SqlDbType.Int);
        var pQuantity = cmd.Parameters.Add("@quantity", SqlDbType.Int);
```

```
            foreach (var (productId, qty) in items)
            {
                pProductId.Value = productId;
                pQuantity.Value = qty;
                await cmd.ExecuteNonQueryAsync();
            }
        }

        await tx.CommitAsync();
    }
    catch (Exception ex)
    {
        await tx.RollbackAsync();
        return Results.Problem($"Order creation failed: {ex.Message}");
    }
    finally
    {
        foreach (var lockKey in lockKeys)
        {
            await db.LockReleaseAsync(
                lockKey,
                Environment.MachineName);
        }
    }

    var queueClient = queueServiceClient
        .GetQueueClient("orders-created");
    queueClient.CreateIfNotExists();

    var message = JsonSerializer.Serialize(new { orderId });

    queueClient.SendMessage(
        message);

    return Results.Created($"/api/orders/{orderId}", new
    {
        OrderId = orderId,
        TotalAmount = totalAmount
    });
});
```

Release all the locks once the functionality is completed or errored.

Here, in addition to injecting an instance of the `IDistributedCache` type, we're injecting an instance of the `IConnectionMultiplexer` type, which is registered the same way and related to the same Redis connection. To use the lock, we invoke the `GetDatabase()` method on this new object to create an abstraction of the Redis database. We use the following code on this database object to attempt to acquire the lock:

```
bool lockAcquired =
    await db.LockTakeAsync(
        lockKey,
        Environment.MachineName,
        TimeSpan.FromSeconds(10));
```

The `LockTakeAsync()` method creates a lock in a Redis database. It uses the following three parameters:

- *Lock key*—The lock key can be any string; we have to make sure that it's tied to the entity we want to lock. In our example, it contains the specific product ID.
- *Lock value*—This value can be anything.
- *Lock expiry time*—This parameter is necessary in case the application that can remove the lock fails. Expiry time prevents the resource from being locked indefinitely.

This method returns a Boolean value. It returns `true` if the lock was placed successfully, which happens only if another lock with the same key isn't already in place. If the lock already exists, the method returns `false`. In our example, if the lock is in place when we attempt to apply it, we exit early and return the `423` HTTP status code to the client, indicating that the requested resource is locked.

In real-life commercial applications, the locking mechanism is more complex. Still, this example is sufficient to demonstrate the fundamental principles.

To remove the lock, we use the `LockReleaseAsync()` method on the Redis database object. We use it inside the `finally` block to make sure that we release the lock whether the update operation succeeds or fails.

You've looked at caches and locks. But did you know that you can view and manage this data directly in the Redis database? That's what you'll do next.

## 7.5 Managing the Redis cache

Remember how we installed Redis Commander while configuring the Aspire host application? We can find it as a separate service in the Aspire dashboard, as shown in figure 7.5.

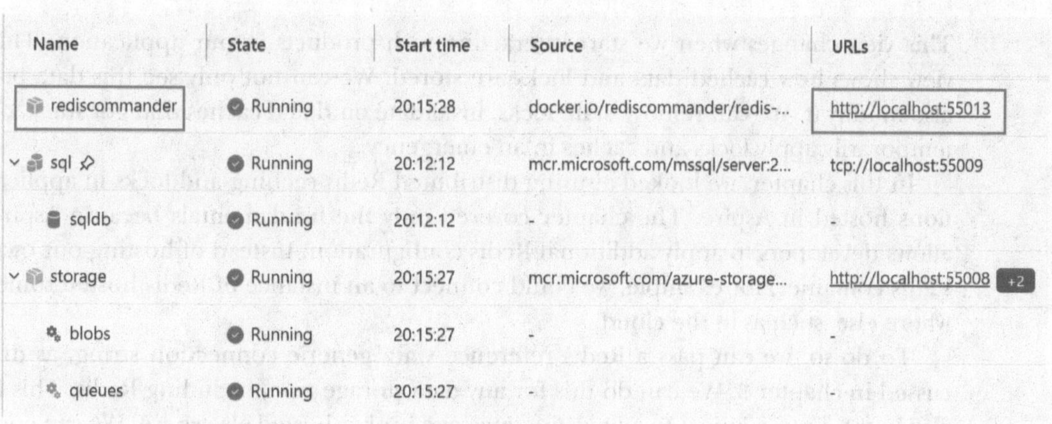


**Figure 7.5 Redis Commander endpoint in the Aspire dashboard**

If we navigate to this resource, we see the Redis Commander window, which we can use to view and interact with data stored in Redis. It includes both a visual interface and a command-line interface, as figure 7.6 shows.

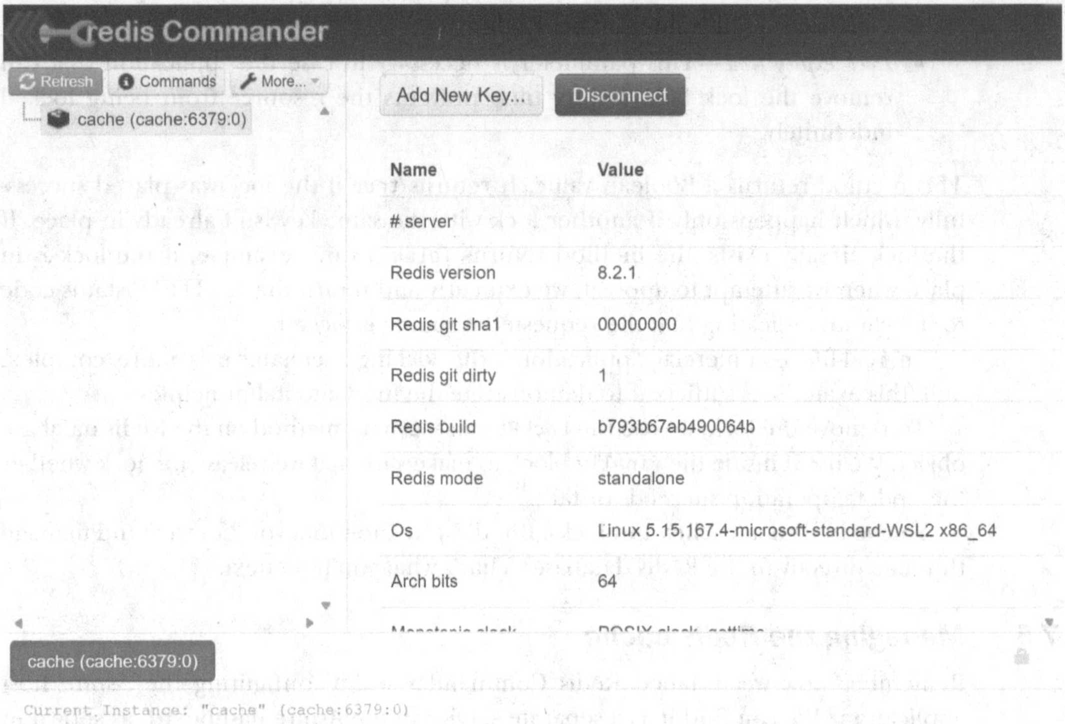


**Figure 7.6 Redis Commander interface**

This view changes when we start interacting with products in our application. This view shows how cached data and locks are stored. We can not only see this data but also modify it. We can remove stale locks, invalidate outdated caches that got stuck, or temporarily apply locks and caches in an emergency.

In this chapter, we looked at using distributed Redis caching and locks in applications hosted in Aspire. The chapter covered only the fundamentals because Aspire allows developers to apply additional Redis configuration. Instead of hosting our own Redis container, for example, we could connect to an instance of Redis hosted somewhere else, such as in the cloud.

To do so, we can pass a Redis reference via a generic connection string, as discussed in chapter 3. We can do this for any data storage type, including Redis. This is also how we can connect to an existing message broker hosted elsewhere. We can connect to any external resource via the `builder.AddConnectionString()` method in the `AppHost` as long as it uses a connection string.

## Summary

- Message brokers transfer data between applications and services via message queues. Although message-broker technologies are built differently, their underlying operational principles are similar.
- Aspire supports a wide variety of message-broker integrations:
  - RabbitMQ is a popular technology-agnostic message broker that is highly configurable.
  - Azure Queue Storage, as the name suggests, is specific to Azure and is part of an Azure Storage account.
- Azure Queue Storage may be preferable to RabbitMQ in some situations because it's significantly easier to set up and work with, though it loses some of RabbitMQ's flexibility.
- A cache is an in-memory data store from which data can be retrieved more quickly than from a database. Caching is useful for storing data temporarily so that it can be retrieved faster, which results in better user experience.
- A distributed cache is an in-memory data store that multiple services on the network can access.
- A distributed lock can be implemented with a caching mechanism and shared among services to ensure that only one thread at a time can access a resource. Locking functionality is useful while particular data is being updated because it ensures that no other processes try to update it.
- Aspire can host a Redis component, which can be used for both distributed caching and locking. It's the same component that can be used for output caching, but the locking and distributed caching functionality use a different client library from the one used for output caching.
- Redis Commander is a tool that allows users to manage Redis directly. It can integrate with Aspire natively.

# 8 Application security in Aspire

***This chapter covers***

- Understanding the fundamentals of application security
- Getting an overview of single sign-on
- Implementing OpenID Connect authentication in Aspire
- Using OAuth authorization in Aspire
- Securing the Aspire dashboard

We briefly viewed application security in chapter 2 by adding a Keycloak container to an Aspire instance. In this chapter, we'll delve deeper into application security concepts. We'll enforce authentication and authorization end to end so that they apply when the user interacts with the UI and when the frontend interacts with the backend API.

If you publish a web application and make it publicly accessible, you'll want to make sure that only authorized users can access it—unless, of course, your application is a trivial website. Applications orchestrated by Aspire are no exceptions. Because Aspire is a platform for building complex distributed applications, chances are that you aren't using it to build trivial websites. Therefore, knowing how to secure your orchestrated application is a must.

Whether you use an external authentication provider like Google or Okta or your own locally hosted Keycloak container, such as the one you configured in chapter 2, you'll rely on the same authentication and authorization protocols. You'll have to connect to a fixed endpoint outside your system and apply the appropriate configuration in the appropriate place. This is why this chapter's approach to securing applications is universally applicable, regardless of which authentication provider you choose and whether it's external or self-hosted.

Also, while using Aspire, you'll want to know how to secure your dashboard. After all, you don't want just anyone to manage your applications and view their internal logs. Aspire has a separate mechanism for securing the dashboard, and this chapter covers it as well.

## 8.1 A brief introduction to single sign-on

Before we talk about securing Aspire applications, let's briefly discuss one of the most popular technologies used to secure applications: single sign-on (SSO). Because it's one of the most popular ways to secure applications, I'll use it as a specific example when discussing how to secure Aspire applications.

SSO allows users to authenticate into an entire ecosystem of applications after they've authenticated into one application. If you logged in to your Chrome browser via your Google account, for example, you can reuse your credentials to log in to any website that has the Sign in with Google option.

This mechanism is typically enabled by storing users' credentials in a dedicated service known as an *identity provider* (IdP). Services that require authentication for access can communicate with this service and verify that the user is authenticated.

The process normally works as follows. Although this description is simplified, it provides a good high-level overview:

1. A user tries to access a secure resource without being logged in.
2. The application doesn't detect any login information and redirects the user to the login page managed by the IdP.
3. The user authenticates by entering their username and password and maybe providing a single-use code from an authenticator app.
4. Upon successful login, the user is redirected to the original page, which is now accessible.
5. While the redirect happens, a special token is sent in the redirection request, containing the user's details and confirming that the user is authenticated.
6. The token is stored in temporary storage (such as a browser cookie). While the token is present, the user is authenticated and can access the page without logging in.
7. The token can be used to authenticate with any app protected by the same IdP, which is why it's called *single sign-on.*
8. The token eventually expires, and the user has to log in again. But if the user keeps accessing the page before it expires, the token keeps refreshing.

Figure 8.1 shows how the process works.

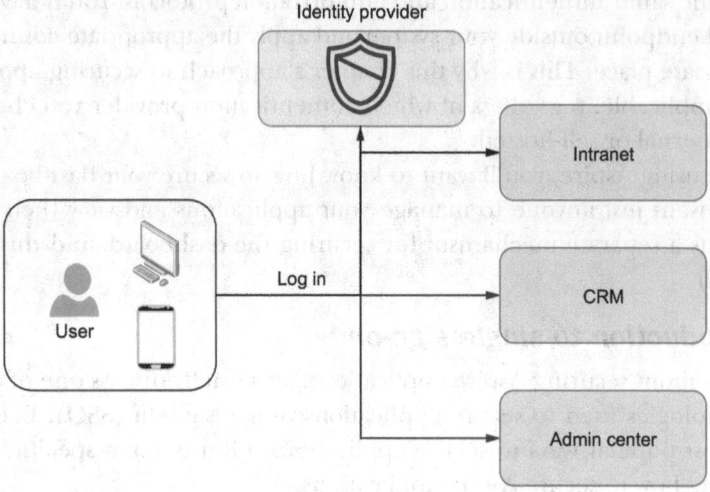


**Figure 8.1 SSO flow**

Several popular protocols enable this type of authentication. Among the most popular are OpenID Connect (OIDC) and OAuth, which often work together.

The OIDC part is responsible for *authentication*, which is when users prove that they are who they say they are by providing secret information known only to them, such as a password and a single-use code. The OAuth part is responsible for *authorization*, which is the mechanism that determines whether the user is allowed to access the requested resource. Certain pages may be accessible only by people with the admin role, for example.

These protocols instantiate SSO by obtaining an access token through valid credentials. The session is maintained by refreshing this token. Figure 8.2 demonstrates how this works at a high level.

We don't have to know in detail how either protocol works. A high-level understanding is sufficient to follow this tutorial.

We'll continue building the online-shop application. Authentication matters to our users. Otherwise, it would be impossible for us to know who placed the order and where to send the items. Also, users don't want someone else to impersonate them and use their payment cards. Therefore, they have to be logged in and registered, and their accounts must be protected. The solution that we're building is available at https://mng.bz/oZgd.

We already have a Keycloak container set up that will be acting as the IdP. Our next job is to use the IdP to enforce access security in our application.

When we've applied our changes, we'll still be able to browse the product catalog. But we won't be able to place orders until we register a user and log in as that user,

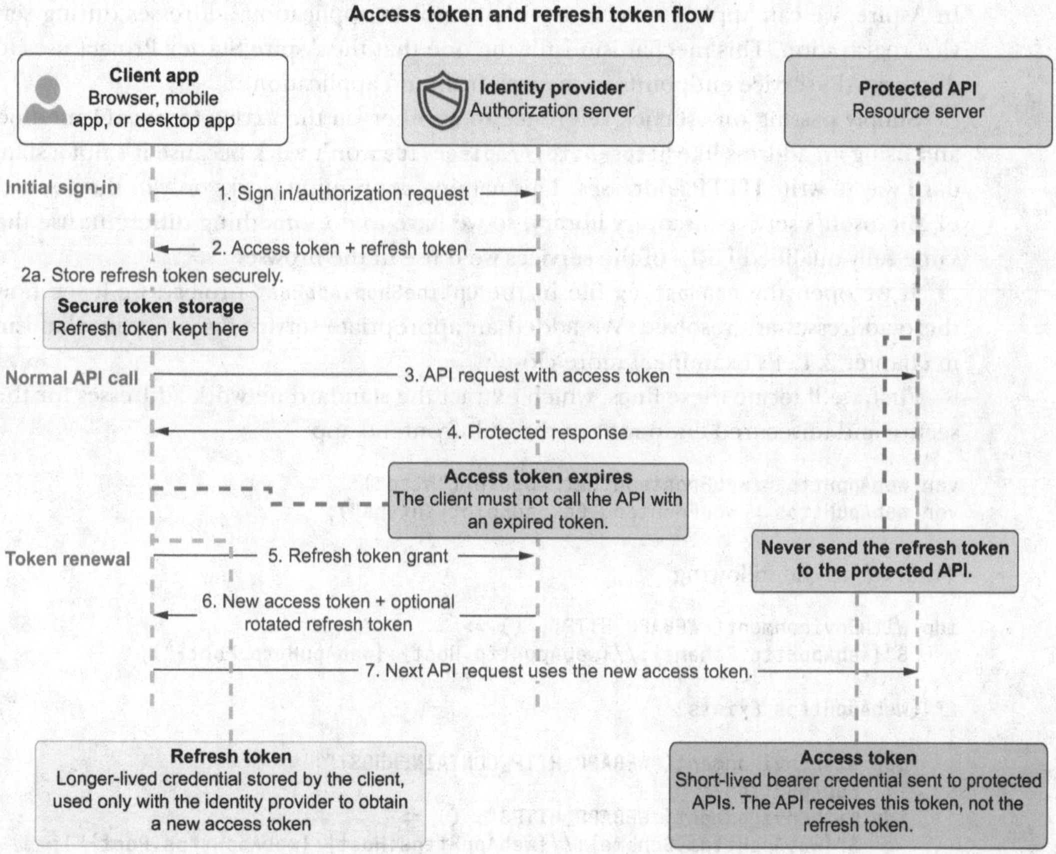


**Figure 8.2 Access-token and refresh-token flow**

which happens automatically when we register a new user. After we do this, we're redirected to the web frontend app and will be able to use all of its functionality.

The REST API endpoints are also secured, but we don't have to do anything special to access them. After we log into the web frontend, our credentials are reused when the web frontend makes an HTTP request to the REST API. In section 8.2, we'll see how it's set up.

## 8.2 Using service discovery in SSO

To make SSO work via OIDC, we have to set up the following:

- The application that uses the IdP for authentication has to know the IdP's publicly accessible address.
- Each application that can redirect to the IdP login page has to be registered with the IdP.
- For each such application, the IdP has to know the application's publicly accessible redirect address.

In Aspire, we can apply a mechanism that resolves application addresses during service registration. This mechanism isn't the one that the Aspire Starter Project uses to discover API service endpoints in the web frontend application.

Simply passing one service reference to another via the `WithReference()` method and using an address like `https+http://apiservice` won't work because it's not a standard way to write HTTP addresses. This naming convention works only in the context of Microsoft's service-discovery library, so we have to do something different: use the same fully qualified URLs of the services we'd use in the browser.

If we open the `AppHost.cs` file in the `OnlineShop.AppHost` project, we'll see how these addresses are resolved. We added an appropriate service-discovery mechanism in chapter 2. Let's examine it more closely.

First, we'll locate these lines, which extract the standard network addresses for the secure and unsecured endpoints of the web frontend app:

```
var webAppHttp = webFrontend.GetEndpoint("http");
var webAppHttps = webFrontend.GetEndpoint("https");
```

Then we do the following:

```
idp.WithEnvironment("WEBAPP_HTTP", () =>
    $"{webAppHttp.Scheme}://{webAppHttp.Host}:{webAppHttp.Port}");

if (webAppHttps.Exists)
{
    idp.WithEnvironment("WEBAPP_HTTP_CONTAINERHOST",
        webAppHttps);
    idp.WithEnvironment("WEBAPP_HTTPS", () =>
        $"{webAppHttps.Scheme}://{webAppHttps.Host}:{webAppHttps.Port}");
}
else
{
    idp.WithEnvironment("WEBAPP_HTTP_CONTAINERHOST",
        webAppHttp);
}
```

Here, we check whether the HTTPS endpoint exists. If so, we assign the URL extracted from this endpoint to the `WEBAPP_HTTP_CONTAINERHOST` environment variable. If this endpoint doesn't exist, we pass the URL of the unsecured HTTP endpoint instead. These environment variables will be used during Keycloak container realm import when the container is launched, so the Keycloak instance will come preconfigured with the exact postlogin redirection address for the UI app.

In a real production environment, we won't be able to use an unsecured HTTP endpoint for authentication, but it's acceptable in a development environment. Also, this code works only in the local development environment, which is why it's hidden behind this condition:

```
if (builder.Environment.IsDevelopment())
```

This is because on a real host, the addresses of the hosted services won't be available by the time it gets here, so the whole orchestrator will crash when it attempts to execute it. But this isn't a problem. In a real hosted environment, user-facing applications have custom HTTP domains assigned to them. You can configure those addresses manually inside your IdP.

The environment-variable name is arbitrary. We need a mechanism to pass the value to the service. Using an environment variable is a convenient way to do so because this value will be accessible to any code in this service. The variable name has to be something that makes sense to us.

Next, we have to make sure that both our UI and the API can talk to the IdP. For this task, we can use the standard service-discovery mechanism if our IdP application is hosted by the same Aspire orchestrator. But there are some caveats. To begin, we'd pass the IdP service reference into both hosted apps, like this:

```
builder.AddProject<Projects.OnlineShop_ApiService>("apiservice")
    .WithHttpHealthCheck("/health")
    .WithReference(idp)
    .WaitFor(idp)...
```

But then we won't be able to use the service-discovery URL as the authority URL in the authentication settings. The URI used in Aspire service discovery isn't a standard URI, so it won't work as one. First, we have to register an HTTP client by using service discovery. Then we use this client for the backchannel in the authentication settings. Chapter 2 covered this process, which we already have configured in our app.

Now the URL of the web frontend can be accessed from the IdP service. The URL of the IdP service can be accessed by both the web frontend and the API. Now we have to configure these services to enable the authentication mechanism and enforce authentication.

## 8.3 Enforcing UI authentication

In the `OnlineShop.Web` project, authentication is configured via the `Microsoft.AspNetCore.Authentication.OpenIdConnect` NuGet package, Microsoft's standard NuGet package for enabling OIDC authentication in ASP.NET Core applications. If we open the `AuthExtensions.cs` file, we should see the following code, which shows how authentication is configured.

**Listing 8.1 Configuring authentication in the UI app startup**

```
public static void ConfigureWebAppOpenIdConnect(this AuthenticationBuilder
    authentication)
{
    // Named options
    authentication.Services
        .AddOptions<OpenIdConnectOptions>(
            OpenIdConnectDefaults.AuthenticationScheme)
        .Configure<
```

```
            IConfiguration,
            IHttpClientFactory,
            IHostEnvironment>(Configure);

    // Unnamed options
    authentication.Services.AddOptions<OpenIdConnectOptions>()
        .Configure<
            IConfiguration,
            IHttpClientFactory,
            IHostEnvironment>(Configure);

    static void Configure(
        OpenIdConnectOptions options,
        IConfiguration configuration,
        IHttpClientFactory httpClientFactory,
        IHostEnvironment hostEnvironment)
    {
        var backchannelHttpClient =
            httpClientFactory.CreateClient(
                "OidcBackchannel");

        options.Backchannel = backchannelHttpClient;
        options.Authority =
            backchannelHttpClient
                .GetIdpAuthorityUri().ToString();
        options.ClientId = "webapp";
        options.ClientSecret =
            Environment
                .GetEnvironmentVariable(
                    "Identity__ClientSecret");
        options.ResponseType =
            OpenIdConnectResponseType.Code;
        options.SaveTokens = true;
        options.RequireHttpsMetadata =
            !hostEnvironment.IsDevelopment();
        options.MapInboundClaims = false;
    }
}
```

This extension method is invoked from this point in the `Program.cs` file:

```
builder.Services.AddAuthentication(options =>
{
    options.DefaultScheme =
        CookieAuthenticationDefaults.AuthenticationScheme;
    options.DefaultChallengeScheme =
        OpenIdConnectDefaults.AuthenticationScheme;
})
.AddCookie(
    CookieAuthenticationDefaults.AuthenticationScheme)
.AddOpenIdConnect()
.ConfigureWebAppOpenIdConnect();
```

Here's a brief explanation of what this code does and how the startup registration and extension method fit together:

- `builder.Services.AddAuthentication()`—This method adds authentication services to the dependency injection container. It configures the authentication options that the application will use.
- `options.DefaultScheme` *and* `options.DefaultChallengeScheme`—`DefaultScheme` is set to the cookie authentication scheme, which means that cookies will be used to store authentication information. `DefaultChallengeScheme` is set to the OIDC scheme. This setting tells the application to use OIDC to challenge (redirect) unauthenticated users when they attempt to access a protected resource.
- `AddCookie()`—This method adds the cookie authentication scheme to the authentication services. The scheme name is defined by `CookieAuthenticationDefaults.AuthenticationScheme`, a constant with the value `Cookies`. This scheme is responsible for managing and validating authentication cookies.

  The authentication scheme is distinct from the challenge scheme. The challenge scheme determines what the system does if the user isn't authenticated, whereas the authentication scheme reads the current identity to determine whether the user is authenticated.
- `AddOpenIdConnect()`—This method adds the OIDC challenge scheme. It configures various options for how the application will interact with an OIDC IdP. Then we will go into individual options in the extension method.
- `options.Backchannel`—This specifies the HTTP client instance that will be used to communicate directly with the IdP.
- `options.Authority`—This sets the authority (issuer) URL of the IdP. The value is retrieved from the backchannel HTTP client and is dynamically constructed in the following method by combining the base address with the special path used in the authentication flow. Add this method to the `Extensions.cs` file in the `OnlineShop.ServiceDefaults` project:

```
public static Uri GetIdpAuthorityUri(this HttpClient httpClient)
{
    var idpBaseUri = httpClient.BaseAddress
        ?? throw new InvalidOperationException(
            $"HttpClient instance does not have a BaseAddress configured.");
    return new Uri(idpBaseUri, "realms/OnlineShop/");
}
```

- `options.ClientId` *and* `options.ClientSecret`—`ClientId` and `ClientSecret` identify the application when communicating with the OIDC provider. The client ID is a unique identifier of the application, and the client secret is a secret password-like value that the client uses to authenticate. These values should be registered with the IdP and used to authenticate the application, as we'll see later. Typically, these values are extracted from application settings. To make things simpler for demonstration purposes, the client ID is hard coded, and the client secret is read from an environment variable in this example.

- `options.ResponseType`—This specifies the response type as `code`, meaning that the application will use the authorization code flow, a secure way to obtain an access token via a server-side exchange of a code for tokens.
- `options.SaveTokens`—This instructs the application to save the tokens received from the IdP, such as the access token, refresh token, and ID token. These tokens can be used for subsequent requests or to access user information.
- `options.MapInboundClaims`—This controls whether ASP.NET Core rewrites claim names from an IdP into .NET-style claim types. Normally, it has to be set to `true` only in older legacy applications.
- `options.RequireHttpsMetadata`—Setting this to `false` allows the application to accept non-HTTPS metadata endpoints, which might be useful for development but isn't recommended in production.

Next, let's look at options we don't have but could have added:

- `options.UsePkce`—Enables Proof Key for Code Exchange (PKCE), an additional layer of security for the authorization code flow, especially for public clients.
- `options.CallbackPath`—Specifies the callback path to which the IdP redirects after the user has authenticated. This endpoint in the application handles the OIDC response. If not set explicitly, it defaults to `/signin-oidc`, the standard redirect path for OIDC.
- `options.SignedOutCallbackPath`—Specifies the path for handling sign-out callbacks from the IdP. After signing out, the IdP can redirect to this path to confirm that the sign-out process is complete. It defaults to the standard `/signout-callback-oidc` path if not explicitly specified.
- `options.GetClaimsFromUserInfoEndpoint`—Instructs the application to retrieve additional claims (user information) from the `UserInfo` endpoint after authentication. It can provide more detailed user information than is available in the ID token alone.

After we configure our authentication mechanism, we have to add authorization dependencies. To do so, we go back to the `Program.cs` file and add the following line before the app variable is instantiated:

```
builder.Services.AddAuthorization();
```

Then we add authentication and authorization to the middleware by placing the following code before any endpoint registration:

```
app.UseAuthentication();
app.UseAuthorization();
```

Finally, we add the following Razor attribute to our order-tracking Razor page, the `OrderTracking.razor` file in the `Pages` folder inside the `Components` folder:

```
@attribute [Microsoft.AspNetCore.Authorization.Authorize]
```

This attribute ensures that only authenticated users can access this page. If a user tries to access a page marked with this attribute without being logged in, the user is automatically redirected to the login page provided by the IdP. The address of the IdP is found via the `Authority` setting configured earlier, and the authentication middleware handles the whole process automatically. Therefore, we don't have to write any code to redirect the user to the login page.

Next, we will do something interesting. If we run an online shop, we still want to make sure that anyone can at least browse the product catalog. Users still have to be registered and authenticated to place orders, but they should be able to see the products even if they haven't registered yet. Otherwise, they'll leave our shop and go somewhere else.

### 8.3.1 Partially enforcing security

Now we'll ensure that only authenticated users can process orders. To do so, open the `Home.razor` page, and add the following namespace reference:

```
@using Microsoft.AspNetCore.Components.Authorization
```

Then inject the navigator so that the user can be redirected to the login endpoint:

```
@inject NavigationManager Nav
```

Locate the `td` element that displays the buttons that allow the user to add items to the basket. The buttons should initially look like this:

```
<div style="display:flex; gap:8px; align-items:center; flex-wrap:wrap;">
    <button class="btn btn-sm btn-primary"
            @onclick="() => AddToBasket(product.Id)">
        Add to Basket
    </button>

    <button class="btn btn-sm btn-outline-danger"
            @onclick="() => RemoveFromBasket(product.Id)"
            disabled="@(qty == 0)">
        Remove From Basket
    </button>

    <span class="btn btn-sm btn-secondary disabled"
          aria-disabled="true"
          style="pointer-events:none;">
        Quantity ordered: @qty
    </span>
</div>
```

These buttons will be displayed only to authenticated users if we wrap them in `AuthorizeView` like this:

```
<AuthorizeView>
    <Authorized>
```

```
            <div style="display:flex; gap:8px; align-items:center; flex-wrap:wrap;">
                <button class="btn btn-sm btn-primary"
                    @onclick="() => AddToBasket(product.Id)">
                    Add to Basket
                </button>

                <button class="btn btn-sm btn-outline-danger"
                    @onclick="() => RemoveFromBasket(product.Id)"
                    disabled="@(qty == 0)">
                    Remove From Basket
                </button>

                <span class="btn btn-sm btn-secondary disabled"
                    aria-disabled="true"
                    style="pointer-events:none;">
                    Quantity ordered: @qty
                </span>
            </div>
        </Authorized>

        <NotAuthorized>
            <span class="text-muted">
                Sign in to order
            </span>
        </NotAuthorized>
    </AuthorizeView>
```

Here's what we've done:

- The `AuthorizeView` element determines which elements are shown only to an authenticated user and which are shown if the user isn't authenticated.
- The `Authorized` element determines what's shown if the user is authenticated.
- The content inside the `NotAuthorized` element is displayed only if the user is not authenticated. In our case, that content is the text *Sign in to order.*

We'll apply the same principle to the Order button, which initially looks like this:

```
<div class="mt-3 p-3 border rounded" style="display:flex; justify-content:space-
    between; align-items:center; gap:12px; flex-wrap:wrap;">
    <div>
        <strong>Total price:</strong> @TotalPrice.ToString("0.00") USD
        <span class="text-muted">(@TotalQuantity item@(TotalQuantity == 1 ? "" :
    "s"))</span>
    </div>

    <button class="btn btn-success"
            @onclick="PlaceOrderAsync"
            disabled="@isPlacingOrder">
        @(isPlacingOrder ? "Placing..." : "Place order")
    </button>
</div>
```

When our changes are applied, the button looks like this:

```
<AuthorizeView>
    <Authorized>
        @if (TotalQuantity > 0)
        {
            <div class="mt-3 p-3 border rounded" style="display:flex; justify-
     content:space-between; align-items:center; gap:12px; flex-wrap:wrap;">
                <div>
                    <strong>Total price:</strong> @TotalPrice.ToString("0.00") USD
                    <span class="text-muted">(@TotalQuantity item@(TotalQuantity ==
     1 ? "" : "s"))</span>
                </div>

                <button class="btn btn-success"
                        @onclick="PlaceOrderAsync"
                        disabled="@isPlacingOrder">
                    @(isPlacingOrder ? "Placing..." : "Place order")
                </button>
            </div>

            @if (!string.IsNullOrWhiteSpace(orderStatus))
            {
                <p class="mt-2">@orderStatus</p>
            }
        }
    </Authorized>
</AuthorizeView>
```

We'll also display Sign In and Sign Out buttons at the bottom. Here's what they'll look like:

```
<div class="d-flex justify-content-between align-items-center mb-3">
    <h1 class="m-0">Products</h1>

    <AuthorizeView>
        <Authorized>
            <form method="post"
                action="@($"/logout?returnUrl={Uri.EscapeDataString(Nav.Uri)}")">
                <button type="submit" class="btn btn-outline-secondary btn-sm">
                    Sign out
                </button>
            </form>
        </Authorized>
        <NotAuthorized>
            <a class="btn btn-outline-primary btn-sm"
               href="@($"/login?returnUrl={Uri.EscapeDataString(Nav.Uri)}")">
                Sign in
            </a>
        </NotAuthorized>
    </AuthorizeView>
</div>
```

Finally, we add the sign-in and sign-out endpoints that will handle authentication by using the SSO middleware. To do so, open the `Program.cs` file in the web frontend application and add the following endpoint mappings immediately before the `app.Run()` invocation:

```
app.MapGet("/login", async (HttpContext ctx, string? returnUrl) =>
{
    returnUrl ??= "/";

    await ctx.ChallengeAsync(OpenIdConnectDefaults.AuthenticationScheme,
        new AuthenticationProperties { RedirectUri = returnUrl });
});

app.MapPost("/logout", async (HttpContext ctx, string? returnUrl) =>
{
    returnUrl ??= "/";

    // sign out of the local cookie and the OIDC provider
    await
     ctx.SignOutAsync(CookieAuthenticationDefaults.AuthenticationScheme);
    await ctx.SignOutAsync(OpenIdConnectDefaults.AuthenticationScheme,
        new AuthenticationProperties { RedirectUri = returnUrl });
});
```

We have one more thing to do. In a Blazor application, `AuthorizeView` won't work unless we pass the authentication state. To do so, we open the `Routes.razor` file and wrap its entire content in the `CascadingAuthenticationState` element, which comes from the `Microsoft.AspNetCore.Components.Authorization` namespace. After that, the file content should look like this:

```
@using Microsoft.AspNetCore.Components.Authorization
<CascadingAuthenticationState>
    <Router AppAssembly="typeof(Program).Assembly">
        <Found Context="routeData">
            <RouteView RouteData="routeData"
     DefaultLayout="typeof(Layout.MainLayout)" />
            <FocusOnNavigate RouteData="routeData" Selector="h1" />
        </Found>
    </Router>
</CascadingAuthenticationState>
```

Now if we launch the application and access its home page, it no longer allows us to place orders, but it displays the sign-in button at the bottom, as figure 8.3 shows.

If the user clicks that button, they're automatically redirected to the IdP-provided login page, where they can register or log in if they're already registered (figure 8.4).

After a successful login, the user is redirected to the product page. This time, they'll be fully authenticated and able to place an order.

What we did is enough to enforce security in the frontend. But to make the app even more secure, we'll apply similar mechanisms to the API to prevent an API endpoint from being triggered by bypassing the UI.

| | | | |
|---|---|---|---|
| 1TB | | 2 support, delivering fast read/write speeds in a compact design. | |
| Noise-Cancelling Headphones | 249.00 | Over-ear wireless headphones with active noise cancellation, high-fidelity sound, and 30-hour battery life. | Sign in to order |
| Webcam Full HD 1080p | 69.99 | Full HD 1080p webcam with built-in microphone, autofocus, and low-light correction for video conferencing. | Sign in to order |
| Gaming Laptop Backpack | 59.95 | Water-resistant backpack designed for gaming laptops up to 17 inches, featuring padded compartments and USB charging port. | Sign in to order |
| Wi-Fi 6 Router | 199.00 | Dual-band Wi-Fi 6 router offering high-speed wireless connectivity, improved range, and support for multiple devices. | Sign in to order |
| Portable Laser Printer | 289.99 | Compact monochrome laser printer suitable for small offices, offering fast printing speeds and wireless connectivity. | Sign in to order |

Products

Sign in

**Figure 8.3 Sign-in button on the products page**

**Figure 8.4 Keycloak-provided login page**

## 8.4 Enforcing API authentication

In this section, we'll enforce authentication in the `OnlineShop.ApiService` app. Because the app is an API app without a user interface, we'll authenticate requests differently. The client that calls the API must already be authenticated, and it must pass a valid JSON Web Token (JWT) in the header of the HTTP request. This mechanism is an incredibly common way to handle API authentication, and the vast majority of organizations use it.

To handle this task, we use the NuGet package `Microsoft.AspNetCore.Authentication.JwtBearer`. Our `AuthExtensions.cs` file contains the configuration shown in the following listing.

**Listing 8.2 Configuring authentication in the API app startup**

```
static void Configure(
    JwtBearerOptions options,
    IConfiguration configuration,
    IHttpClientFactory httpClientFactory,
    IHostEnvironment hostEnvironment)
{
    var backchannelHttpClient =
        httpClientFactory.CreateClient(
            "OidcBackchannel");

    options.Backchannel = backchannelHttpClient;
    options.Authority =
        backchannelHttpClient
            .GetIdpAuthorityUri().ToString();
    options.RequireHttpsMetadata =
        !hostEnvironment.IsDevelopment();
    options.MapInboundClaims = false;
    options.TokenValidationParameters =
        new TokenValidationParameters
        {
            ValidateAudience = false
        };
}
```

This code is similar to what we've seen before but simpler. We use a different authentication scheme because there's no redirect to the IdP login page. We use the same IdP address as the `Authority` setting. This setting is still required because upon receiving the authentication token, the API sends a request to the IdP to check whether the token is valid.

Another setting here is the `ValidateAudience` option in `TokenValidationParameters`. Because the original token would have been issued to the calling client rather than the API application, the token has the `Audience` (`aud`) field set to the address of the calling client, which is different from the address of the API. This is why we don't validate the audience. Still, this example shows how `aud` field validation can be done.

Consider this scenario: an API gateway manages access to multiple microservices, each with its own security requirements. In this setup, a frontend application, such as a single-page application (SPA) or a mobile app, communicates through the gateway.

The microservice or an API gateway sitting in front of it must validate that the token is indeed meant for that specific API. This involves checking the `aud` claim to ensure that it matches the expected value. If the `aud` claim doesn't match, the request should be rejected because it could indicate that the token was issued for a different service and might be used inappropriately.

Because we're talking about authorization now, add the following invocation to register the authorization components:

```
builder.Services.AddAuthorization();
```

Then add authentication and authorization steps to the middleware before any endpoint mappings:

```
app.UseAuthentication();
app.UseAuthorization();
```

Finally, we append the `RequireAuthorization()` invocation to our order placement endpoint, as shown here:

```
app.MapPost("/api/orders", async (
    Dictionary<int, int> basket,
    [FromServices] SqlConnection dbConnection,
    [FromServices] QueueServiceClient queueServiceClient,
    [FromServices] IDistributedCache cache,
    [FromServices] IConnectionMultiplexer redis) =>
{
    // Code inside the endpoint mapping hidden for brevity
    ...
}).RequireAuthorization();
```

This prevents clients from invoking this endpoint unless the request supplies a valid JWT.

### 8.4.1 Passing a JWT to the API

Now let's see how a JWT is passed to the API. If we go back to the `OnlineShop.Web` project, we find a class called `ProductsApiClient`. This class makes an HTTP request to the API. First, we'll modify the constructor so that it accepts authentication state, which is automatically registered by the Blazor Server hosting model:

```
public class ProductsApiClient(
    HttpClient httpClient, AuthenticationStateProvider authStateProvider)
```

Then we modify the `MakeOrder()` method.

**Listing 8.3 Passing the Bearer token to the API**

```
public async Task<HttpResponseMessage> MakeOrder(Dictionary<int, int> basket)
{
    var authState = await authStateProvider.GetAuthenticationStateAsync();
    var user = authState.User;

    if (user.Identity?.IsAuthenticated == true)
    {
        var token = user.FindFirst("access_token")?.Value;

        if (!string.IsNullOrWhiteSpace(token))
        {
            httpClient.DefaultRequestHeaders.Authorization =
                new AuthenticationHeaderValue("Bearer", token);
        }
    }

    return await httpClient.PostAsJsonAsync("/api/orders", basket);
}
```

Get the authentication state.

Check if a user is authenticated.

Extract the token for the authenticated user.

Pass the token into the Authorization header of the HTTP requests made by the client.

First, we extract the access token from the authentication state. The token is present only if the user successfully logged in. Because we've already enforced authentication on all pages, this code won't be invoked if the user isn't logged in.

Then we pass this token into the authorization header of the request. This is the so-called bearer token, which is why we specify the authorization type as `Bearer`.

This concludes full end-to-end authentication among the user, the UI, and the backend API. In section 8.5, we'll see how the Aspire dashboard itself is secured.

## 8.5 Securing the Aspire dashboard

So far, you've learned to secure distributed applications hosted by Aspire. But as you can imagine, securing the Aspire dashboard is just as important. Fortunately, it's not difficult. It's also done automatically when an Aspire application is deployed in Azure, as discussed in chapter 9. Still, you may want to learn how to secure the dashboard in other environments and apply a nondefault security mechanism to it.

There are many ways to secure Aspire dashboards. You can do it inside the following section in the `appsettings.json` file inside the Aspire host project:

```
{
  "Dashboard": {
    "Frontend": {
      "AuthMode": "<Define authentication mode>"
    }
  }
}
```

The `AuthMode` setting in the `Frontend` section of the `Dashboard` block allows us to define the authentication mechanism. Additional settings may be available in the `Frontend` section, depending on the authentication mode we specify. If we specify OpenId-Connect as our `AuthMode`, for example, we can define OIDC settings similar to those we specified earlier for the web frontend client.

> **NOTE** If you choose to secure the Aspire dashboard via OIDC, use an IdP that's hosted outside Aspire. Otherwise, you won't be able to log in to your dashboard if the IdP is down.

If you want to disable security, you can set `AuthMode` to `Unsecured`. You should never do this outside a development environment, however.

By default, the `BrowserToken` option is used as the `AuthMode`. This means that unless you launch your host app from Visual Studio or a similar environment, you have to provide a special token in the request to access it. If you launch the application by executing the `dotnet run` command-line interface (CLI) command and then navigate to its base URL, you see the dialog box shown in figure 8.5.

**Figure 8.5 Aspire dashboard authentication dialog box**

You can obtain the token from the console that's running the app, as shown in figure 8.6.

```
info: Aspire.Hosting.DistributedApplication[0]
      Aspire version: 8.0.0+d215c528c07c7919c3ac30b35d92f4e51a60523b
info: Aspire.Hosting.DistributedApplication[0]
      Distributed application starting.
info: Aspire.Hosting.DistributedApplication[0]
      Application host directory is: C:\Repos\dotnet-aspire-examples\AspireWithSso\AspireApp\AspireApp.AppHost
info: Aspire.Hosting.DistributedApplication[0]
      Now listening on: https://localhost:17099
info: Aspire.Hosting.DistributedApplication[0]
      Login to the dashboard at https://localhost:17099/login?t=0b686a6d6161b525ed49e5496cb8037c
info: Aspire.Hosting.DistributedApplication[0]
      Distributed application started. Press Ctrl+C to shut down.
```

**Figure 8.6 Access token shown in the Aspire host console**

For all the options available for securing the Aspire dashboard, see the official documentation at https://mng.bz/nZaa.

We've covered all the fundamentals of working with Aspire applications in a local development environment. But every commercial application eventually has to be deployed to production. Chapter 9 discusses multiple ways to deploy Aspire applications to production, which should cover any cloud environment. It also discusses other important considerations when the application is running in production, such as scaling it and applying gradual updates to the resources it relies on, including database schema migration.

## Summary

- Authentication is the mechanism that requires users and other clients to prove that they are who they claim to be.
- Authorization is the mechanism that ensures that authenticated clients have the required permission to access the requested resource.
- SSO security is managed by a shared IdP.
- OIDC is a commonly used authentication mechanism. OAuth is an authorization mechanism that can be used alongside OIDC.
- An authenticated UI application can pass credentials and the user's permission information to a backend API via a JWT.
- We can use Aspire's service-discovery feature to secure our hosted applications by using an internally hosted IdP.
- The Aspire dashboard has its own security configuration and several options for securing it. The default security option for the Aspire dashboard is a URL token.

# Part 4

# *Deployment, upgrades, and legacy adoption*

A platform earns its place only when it supports the full life cycle: shipping to production, upgrading safely, and integrating with the systems you already have. This final part focuses on turning Aspire from a local development superpower into a long-term foundation.

You'll deploy Aspire applications in production-ready ways, learn what to standardize and what to keep flexible, and build a repeatable release pipeline mindset. Then you'll tackle a hard (and common) scenario: bringing legacy applications into Aspire incrementally. You'll also explore how AI agents can assist with modernization and operations, especially when they can "see" your system through tools and telemetry, so adopting Aspire becomes not only easier but also faster and more maintainable over time.

# 9 Deploying Aspire apps to production

***This chapter covers***
- Scaling out individual services in Aspire
- Generating Aspire manifests for distributed application deployment
- Deploying Aspire applications to Azure Container Apps
- Using Aspir8 to deploy Aspire apps to a Kubernetes cluster in any cloud environment

So far, we've looked at how Aspire apps can be orchestrated while being built and debugged on a development machine. But eventually, we have to deploy the app to production.

Aspire has some built-in mechanisms for doing this, and we'll look at them in this chapter. The code samples we'll use are available at https://mng.bz/MwaW.

Before we jump into deploying Aspire apps, let's delve into some modifications of our Aspire setup that will make it easier to manage the application after deployment.

## 9.1 Predeployment modifications of Aspire-hosted systems

Why would we modify our system further before deploying it? We might have multiple reasons to do so. We may anticipate that for certain types of services, we'll always run multiple replicas. Perhaps we're expected to deal with high user throughput, and a single replica won't cut it. In Aspire, we can add more replicas to handle the additional load.

Another reason is that we may want to run local substitutes for cloud-hosted services that can't be emulated locally. We may use Service Bus as our message broker in Azure but replace it with RabbitMQ or emulate Azure Queue Storage while the app is running locally. The Aspire host can run different code paths for local and deployed versions of the application.

Something else we may want to consider is database migrations. If we host a database, we may occasionally have to update its schema, which is the structure of its tables. This is especially relevant to SQL databases. Aspire can be configured so that every deployment applies such changes automatically, without any downtime, when a new version is deployed.

The next modification we might make is adding new functionality to the dashboard. When we use message brokers, our message queues may end up with far more messages than the application can handle. We can solve this problem by adding a custom command to the Aspire dashboard that clears the queues in the message broker. The following sections discuss these topics in more detail.

### 9.1.1 Running multiple instances of a service

In a distributed application, services are often expected to scale out by running multiple replicas. A particular service might receive a high number of requests from users, for example. To make sure that the service doesn't grind to a halt, these requests can be distributed among several replicas of the service. Then a special front-facing service called a *load balancer* decides which replica each request should go to.

In an Aspire app, we can run multiple replicas of a service by invoking the `WithReplicas()` method while registering the service in the host application. The number of replicas we need is passed into the method as a parameter in the `AppHost.cs` file. The following example configures the host to run three replicas of the `webfrontend` service:

```
builder.AddProject<Projects.OnlineShop_Web>("webfrontend")
    .WithExternalHttpEndpoints()
    .WithReference(cache)
    .WithReference(apiService)
    .WithReplicas(3)...
```

If we launch the application, we see three separate instances of the service listed, as figure 9.1 shows.

But you may have noticed a strange thing about these instances: all of them have the same endpoint URLs. How can they be different instances if they have the same address and the same port?

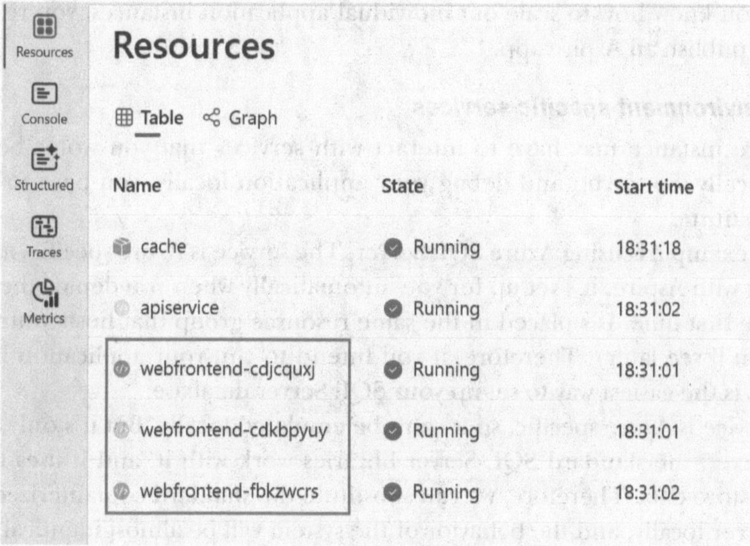


**Figure 9.1 Hosting multiple instances of a service in Aspire**

What you're seeing is load balancing in action. The addresses in the dashboard are the front-facing addresses. The address is the same because it's the address of the load balancer, which routes the request to a specific application instance. If we open the logs for any of these service instances, we see the actual HTTP port the application instance is listening on, as figure 9.2 shows.

If we look at the logs for the other instances of the `webfrontend` service, we see that each has its own unique address.

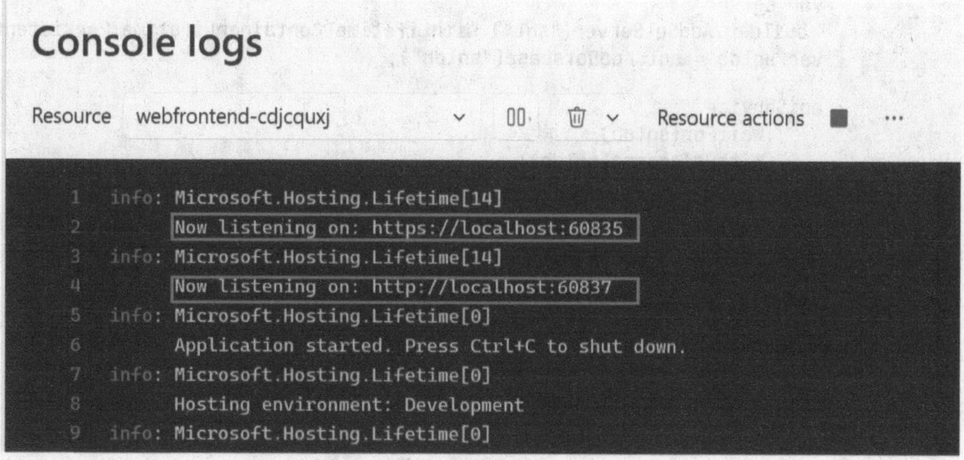


**Figure 9.2 Looking at the internal HTTP ports of individual instances**

Now that you know how to scale out individual application instances, you're ready to see how to publish an Aspire app.

### 9.1.2 Running environment-specific services

Your Aspire instance may have to interact with services that you won't be able to emulate locally. So to run and debug your application locally, you have to find the closest substitute.

A good example is using Azure SQL Server. The service is Azure-specific, and if you integrate it with Aspire, it's set up for you automatically when you deploy the application for the first time. It's placed in the same resource group that hosts your application (as you'll see later). Therefore, if you intend to run your application in Azure, Azure SQL is the easiest way to set up your SQL Server database.

The service is Azure-specific, so it can't be emulated locally. But it's only a variant of SQL Server: the standard SQL Server libraries work with it, and it uses the same schema to store data. Therefore, we can substitute the standard containerized version of SQL Server locally, and the behavior of the system will be almost identical whether it's deployed in Azure or launched locally.

Here's how to do it. In the Aspire host, reference the following NuGet packages:

- `Aspire.Hosting.SqlServer` for the standard SQL Server integration
- `Aspire.Hosting.Azure.Sql` for Azure SQL integration

Then remove the existing SQL Server references from the `AppHost.cs` file, including the following lines and the `WithReference()` and `WaitFor()` invocations:

```
var sql = builder.AddSqlServer("sql").WithLifetime(ContainerLifetime.Persistent);
var sqldb = sql.AddDatabase("sqldb");
After instantiating apiService, add the following condition:
if (builder.ExecutionContext.IsRunMode)
{
    var sql =
     builder.AddSqlServer("sql").WithLifetime(ContainerLifetime.Persistent);
    var sqldb = sql.AddDatabase("sqldb");

    apiService
        .WaitFor(sqldb)
        .WithReference(sqldb);
}
else
{
    var sql = builder.AddAzureSqlServer("sql");
    var sqldb = sql.AddDatabase("sqldb");

    apiService
        .WaitFor(sqldb)
        .WithReference(sqldb);
}
```

We're checking whether the value of the `IsRunMode` property on the builder's `ExecutionContext` property is set to `true`. If so, we're running our application locally, so we set up a standard containerized version of SQL Server. Otherwise, we set up Azure SQL by invoking the `AddAzureSqlServer()` method on the builder.

We can also invert the logic by looking at the `IsPublishMode` property instead of `IsRunMode`. These two Boolean properties have opposite values.

Otherwise, all client libraries remain the same. We don't have to modify the hosted services that connect to the SQL Server instance. Aspire's service discovery and automatic connection string construction mechanism will still work.

To make sure that no other local-only code makes it into the infrastructure deployment scripts, we want to do the same thing for the parts of the code in `AppHost` that are hidden behind `builder.Environment.IsDevelopment()`. This would apply to our original Keycloak-specific URL mappings, for example. We simply replace this condition with `builder.ExecutionContext.IsRunMode`:

```
if (builder.ExecutionContext.IsRunMode)
{
    var webAppHttp = webFrontend.GetEndpoint("http");
    var webAppHttps = webFrontend.GetEndpoint("https");

    idp.WithEnvironment("WEBAPP_HTTP", () =>
        $"{webAppHttp.Scheme}://{webAppHttp.Host}:{webAppHttp.Port}");

    if (webAppHttps.Exists)
    {
        idp.WithEnvironment("WEBAPP_HTTP_CONTAINERHOST",
            webAppHttps);
        idp.WithEnvironment("WEBAPP_HTTPS", () =>
            $"{webAppHttps.Scheme}://{webAppHttps.Host}:{webAppHttps.Port}");
    }
    else
    {
        idp.WithEnvironment("WEBAPP_HTTP_CONTAINERHOST",
            webAppHttp);
    }
}
```

### 9.1.3 Managing database migrations

If you use any databases with a rigid schema in your application, such as SQL-based relational databases, you have to put in place a reliable mechanism for updating that schema safely. .NET has several such mechanisms, and all can be made compatible with Aspire. One popular schema update mechanism is database migrations, which are built into Entity Framework. This is how they work:

1. When the database is created, a snapshot of its schema, known as a *migration*, is taken and given a unique name and timestamp.
2. When the application is deployed for the first time, the schema is applied according to this migration, and the database tracks the name of the migration that was applied.

3 Any necessary modifications are made to the schema (e.g., adding a new field to an entity model representing a table record).
4 The migration includes the new modifications.
5 The redeployment process applies only the new migration because the previous one has already been applied and recorded.
6 After the new changes are applied, the name of the new migration is recorded.

In a nutshell, we're keeping track of the database schema changes that have already been applied, so any new changes are applied in the order in which they were made.

In Aspire, we can set up our system to apply migrations automatically every time a new version of the application is deployed.

First, we install the NuGet package `Microsoft.EntityFrameworkCore.Design` in `OnlineShop.ApiService`, the .NET project that represents the application and relies on the SQL database.

Next, we generate our first migration. To do so, we have to meet the following criteria:

- Entity Framework command-line interface (CLI) tools are installed in our environment.
- Entity Framework's database context class exists.
- At least one entity type is present.

Also, it's important to know that migrations are incompatible with databases that were created by executing the `EnsureCreated()` method on the database context. Such databases lack a special table for storing migration versions. Therefore, we have to make special manual modifications to such a database before we can update it with migrations.

To install the tool globally on your development machine, execute the following CLI command in a terminal:

```
dotnet tool install --global dotnet-ef
```

Then add the database context and at least one table. If we're building an online shop, we can use the following entities to represent database tables:

```
public class Product
{
    [Key]
    public int Id { get; set; }

    [MaxLength(100)]
    public string Title { get; set; } = string.Empty;

    [MaxLength(2100)]
    public string Summary { get; set; } = string.Empty;

    public decimal Price { get; set; }
```

```
    public DateTime DateAdded { get; set; }

    public ICollection<OrderItem> OrderItems { get; set; } = [];
}

public class Order
{
    [Key]
    public int Id { get; set; }

    public double TotalAmount { get; set; }

    public ICollection<OrderItem> Items { get; set; } = [];
}

public class OrderItem
{
    public int OrderId { get; set; }
    public int ProductId { get; set; }
    public int Quantity { get; set; }

    public Order Order { get; set; } = default!;
    public Product Product { get; set; } = default!;
}
```

The database context will look like this:

```
public class ProductsDbContext : DbContext
{
    public ProductsDbContext(
        DbContextOptions<ProductsDbContext> options) : base(options)
    {
    }

    public DbSet<Product> Products { get; set; }
    public DbSet<Order> Orders { get; set; }
    public DbSet<OrderItem> OrderItems { get; set; }

    protected override void OnModelCreating(ModelBuilder modelBuilder)
    {
        base.OnModelCreating(modelBuilder);

        modelBuilder.Entity<OrderItem>(entity =>
        {
            entity.HasKey(x => new { x.OrderId, x.ProductId });

            entity.HasOne(x => x.Order)
                .WithMany(o => o.Items)
                .HasForeignKey(x => x.OrderId)
                .OnDelete(DeleteBehavior.Cascade);

            entity.HasOne(x => x.Product)
                .WithMany(p => p.OrderItems)
                .HasForeignKey(x => x.ProductId)
```

```
                .OnDelete(DeleteBehavior.Restrict);
        });
    }
}
```

Now we can open the folder that contains our .NET project with the startup code in a CLI terminal and execute the following command:

```
dotnet ef migrations add InitialCreate
```

**NOTE** In this example, `InitialCreate` is an arbitrary name we've given our migration. Although the name is arbitrary, it should sufficiently describe what the migration does. In this case, the name makes clear that this migration is the first one added.

This command should create the `Migrations` folder inside the project. This folder contains three files:

- `ProductsDbContextModelSnapshot.cs`—Represents a snapshot of the latest version of the database schema
- `{timestamp}_InitialCreate.cs`—Represents the set of changes specific to the individual migration and has the same suffix as the migration name specified in the command
- `{timestamp}_InitialCreate.Designer.cs`—Provides a more detailed definition of the schema changes applied with the migration

To update the migration, add the following property to the `Order` class:

```
public string? Address{ get; set; }
```

Execute the following CLI command to add this change as a migration:

```
dotnet ef migrations add AddOrderAddress
```

We've updated the snapshot and added a new migration with the following code:

```
protected override void Up(MigrationBuilder migrationBuilder)
{
    migrationBuilder.AddColumn<string>(
        name: "Address",
        table: "Orders",
        type: "nvarchar(max)",
        nullable: true);
}
```

Our migrations are in place. The next step is configuring Aspire to apply them automatically with every deployment. The easiest way is via a background service attached to the application that uses the database. This solution isn't specific to Aspire but works brilliantly with it.

Let's create a class called `DataSeederService`, which inherits from the `BackgroundService` base class. Initially, we'll inject the dependency injection (DI) service provider, so we can resolve scoped and transient dependencies inside this singleton service:

```
public class DataSeederService(IServiceProvider serviceProvider) :
    BackgroundService
{
    private readonly IServiceProvider _serviceProvider = serviceProvider;

    protected override Task ExecuteAsync(CancellationToken stoppingToken)
    {
        throw new NotImplementedException();
    }
}
```

We register this service in the startup code of our API application like this:

```
builder.Services.AddSingleton<DataSeederService>();
builder.Services.AddHostedService(sp =>
    sp.GetRequiredService<DataSeederService>());
```

This code launches the service in the background automatically when the application starts, including when the application is redeployed. The method inside this service that runs on startup is `ExecuteAsync()`. To enable this method to execute database migrations, we have to make sure that we have the following method:

```
private static async Task RunMigrationAsync(
    ProductsDbContext context,
    CancellationToken cancellationToken)
{
    var strategy = context.Database.CreateExecutionStrategy();
    await strategy.ExecuteAsync(async () =>
    {
        await context.Database.MigrateAsync(cancellationToken);
    });
}
```

This code relies on the `Microsoft.EntityFrameworkCore` namespace, which we can add as a `using` statement. Then we can insert another method that seeds the initial data after the migrations have been applied:

```
private static void SeedData(ProductsDbContext context)
{
    if (!context.Products.Any())
    {
        var products = new List<Product>
        {
            new Product
            {
                Title = "Wireless Optical Mouse",
```

```
                Summary = "Ergonomic wireless optical mouse with adjustable
    DPI and long battery life, suitable for everyday office and home use.",
                Price = 24.99m,
                DateAdded = new DateTime(2025, 1, 5)
            },
            new Product
            {
                Title = "Mechanical Gaming Keyboard",
                Summary = "RGB backlit mechanical keyboard with blue
    switches, anti-ghosting keys, and durable aluminum frame.",
                Price = 129.99m,
                DateAdded = new DateTime(2025, 1, 6)
            },
            new Product
            {
                Title = "27-inch 4K Monitor",
                Summary = "27-inch UHD 4K monitor with IPS panel, 3840x2160
    resolution, HDR support, and ultra-thin bezels.",
                Price = 399.00m,
                DateAdded = new DateTime(2025, 1, 7)
            },
            new Product
            {
                Title = "USB-C Docking Station",
                Summary = "Multi-port USB-C docking station with HDMI,
    DisplayPort, Ethernet, USB 3.0 ports, and 100W power delivery.",
                Price = 179.50m,
                DateAdded = new DateTime(2025, 1, 8)
            },
        };

        context.Products.AddRange(products);
        context.SaveChanges();
    }
}
```

**WARNING** We have to make sure that we're no longer attempting to create the database or seed it with data in the Program.cs file because that would conflict with the migration executed in the background service.

Finally, to bring everything together, we modify our ExecuteAsync method to call both the migration execution and the data seeding:

```
protected override async Task ExecuteAsync(CancellationToken stoppingToken)
{
    using var scope = _serviceProvider.CreateScope();
    using var context =
     scope.ServiceProvider.GetRequiredService<ProductsDbContext>();

    await RunMigrationAsync(context, stoppingToken);
    SeedData(context);
}
```

That's it. This is all we have to do to set up automated schema updates with Aspire.

### 9.1.4 Modifying the dashboard

Sometimes, we have to add functionality to the Aspire dashboard. There are many use cases for custom functionality, one of which is resetting the Redis cache. Distributed locks might be blocking some critical part of the application, or the cache must be invalidated because the data in the application has changed.

Let's see how to add functionality. Although the methods we'll use are specific to this task, the principles for adding any custom functionality are the same.

First, we add a static class to our Aspire host project. Let's call it `RedisResourceBuilderExtensions`. Next, we add the following private method to the class:

```
private static async Task<ExecuteCommandResult> RunAsync(
    IResourceBuilder<RedisResource> builder)
{
    var connectionString = await builder.Resource.GetConnectionStringAsync()
        ?? throw new InvalidOperationException(
            "Could not resolve Redis connection string.");

    await using var multiplexer = await
     ConnectionMultiplexer.ConnectAsync(connectionString);
    var db = multiplexer.GetDatabase();

    // Clear everything across all DBs. Prefer FLUSHDB if you only want the
     current DB.
    await db.ExecuteAsync("FLUSHALL");

    return CommandResults.Success();
}
```

This method verifies the current Redis connection and, if an active connection is found, clears all data across all Redis databases by executing the `FLUSHALL` command.

Next, we add the following extension method, which allows us to bind the command to the dashboard and configure how it's displayed in the menu:

```
public static IResourceBuilder<RedisResource> WithClearCacheCommand(
    this IResourceBuilder<RedisResource> builder)
{
    var options = new CommandOptions
    {
        IconName = "Broom",
        IconVariant = IconVariant.Filled,
        UpdateState = commandStateContext =>
            commandStateContext.ResourceSnapshot.HealthStatus ==
     HealthStatus.Healthy
                ? ResourceCommandState.Enabled
                : ResourceCommandState.Disabled
    };

    builder.WithCommand(
        name: "clear-cache",
        displayName: "Clear cache",
```

```
        executeCommand: _ => RunAsync(builder),
        commandOptions: options);

    return builder;
}
```

The `CommandOptions` instance configures which icon is displayed next to the command in the menu and whether the command is enabled. In this example, we use the `Broom` icon. The `WithCommand()` invocation adds the title to the command and binds it to the command options and the actual command code we added earlier.

To enable this command, we call the extension method while configuring the Redis cache resource in the Aspire startup code:

```
var cache = builder.AddRedis("cache").WithClearCacheCommand();
```

Now if we launch the application and wait for the dashboard to load, we can expand the menu next to the cache resource and see our command there, as figure 9.3 shows.

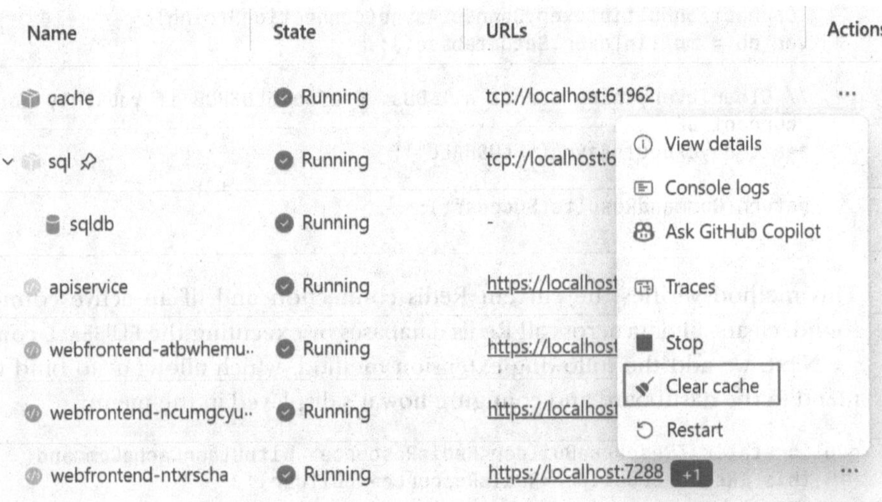


**Figure 9.3 Accessing a custom command from the Aspire dashboard**

This concludes a brief overview of the predeployment modifications we can make in an Aspire setup. Next, we'll see how it's deployed.

## 9.2 Preparing Aspire for deployment

Aspire applications use manifest files as the first step in publishing applications. These files describe the application and all its services in JSON format. To generate such a file, run the following command in the terminal from the Aspire host project folder:

```
dotnet run --publisher manifest --output-path manifest.json
```

This command should generate a file called `manifest.json` in the same folder or a file with a different name if we specify a different value for the `--output-path` option. It begins with the outer `schema` element, which looks like this:

```
"$schema": "https://json.schemastore.org/aspire-8.0.json",
```

Because our JSON must follow a specific structure, this element ensures that structure.

Next is the `resources` element, which contains all the individual services that make up the application. This is how it describes the resource called `cache`, which in our example application is represented by a Redis component:

```
...
"cache": {
    "type": "container.v0",
    "connectionString":
   "{cache.bindings.tcp.host}:{cache.bindings.tcp.port},password={cache-
   password.value}",
    "image": "docker.io/library/redis:8.2",
    "entrypoint": "/bin/sh",
    "args": [
      "-c",
      "redis-server --requirepass $REDIS_PASSWORD"
    ],
    "env": {
      "REDIS_PASSWORD": "{cache-password.value}"
    },
    "bindings": {
      "tcp": {
        "scheme": "tcp",
        "protocol": "tcp",
        "transport": "tcp",
        "targetPort": 6379
      }
    }
  },
...
```

This definition points to a Docker image as the source of the service. Also, the type of the service is `container.v0`, which the Aspire manifest uses to represent a service running as a Docker container.

Then, among the other container references, is the service called `apiservice`. This definition points to the `OnlineShop.ApiService` project in our application, and the `type` is now `project.v0`:

```
"apiservice": {
    "type": "project.v0",
    "path": "../OnlineShop.ApiService/OnlineShop.ApiService.csproj",
    "env": {
      "OTEL_DOTNET_EXPERIMENTAL_OTLP_EMIT_EXCEPTION_LOG_ATTRIBUTES":
   "true",
      "OTEL_DOTNET_EXPERIMENTAL_OTLP_EMIT_EVENT_LOG_ATTRIBUTES": "true",
```

```
        "OTEL_DOTNET_EXPERIMENTAL_OTLP_RETRY": "in_memory",
        "ASPNETCORE_FORWARDEDHEADERS_ENABLED": "true",
        "HTTP_PORTS": "{apiservice.bindings.http.targetPort}",
        "ConnectionStrings__cache": "{cache.connectionString}",
        "CACHE_HOST": "{cache.bindings.tcp.host}",
        "CACHE_PORT": "{cache.bindings.tcp.port}",
        "CACHE_PASSWORD": "{cache-password.value}",
        "CACHE_URI": "redis://:{cache-password-uri-
encoded.value}@{cache.bindings.tcp.host}:{cache.bindings.tcp.port}",
        "ConnectionStrings__queues": "{queues.connectionString}",
        "QUEUES_URI": "{storage.outputs.queueEndpoint}",
        "ConnectionStrings__blobs": "{blobs.connectionString}",
        "BLOBS_URI": "{storage.outputs.blobEndpoint}",
        "ConnectionStrings__tables": "{tables.connectionString}",
        "TABLES_URI": "{storage.outputs.tableEndpoint}",
        "ConnectionStrings__mongodb": "{mongodb.connectionString}",
        "MONGODB_HOST": "{mongo.bindings.tcp.host}",
        "MONGODB_PORT": "{mongo.bindings.tcp.port}",
        "MONGODB_USERNAME": "admin",
        "MONGODB_PASSWORD": "{mongo-password.value}",
        "MONGODB_AUTHENTICATIONDATABASE": "admin",
        "MONGODB_AUTHENTICATIONMECHANISM": "SCRAM-SHA-256",
        "MONGODB_URI": "mongodb://admin:{mongo-password-uri-
encoded.value}@{mongo.bindings.tcp.host}:{mongo.bindings.tcp.port}/
mongodb?authSource=admin\u0026authMechanism=SCRAM-SHA-256",
        "MONGODB_DATABASENAME": "mongodb",
        "IDP_HTTP": "{idp.bindings.http.url}",
        "services__idp__http__0": "{idp.bindings.http.url}",
        "ConnectionStrings__sqldb": "{sqldb.connectionString}",
        "SQLDB_HOST": "{sql.outputs.sqlServerFqdn}",
        "SQLDB_PORT": "1433",
        "SQLDB_URI": "mssql://{sql.outputs.sqlServerFqdn}:1433/sqldb",
        "SQLDB_JDBCCONNECTIONSTRING": "jdbc:sqlserver://
{sql.outputs.sqlServerFqdn}:1433;database=sqldb;encrypt=true;trustServer
Certificate=false",
        "SQLDB_DATABASENAME": "sqldb"
      },
```

The description of the webfrontend service follows the same principles:

```
"webfrontend": {
      "type": "project.v0",
      "path": "../OnlineShop.Web/OnlineShop.Web.csproj",
      "env": {
        "OTEL_DOTNET_EXPERIMENTAL_OTLP_EMIT_EXCEPTION_LOG_ATTRIBUTES": "true",
        "OTEL_DOTNET_EXPERIMENTAL_OTLP_EMIT_EVENT_LOG_ATTRIBUTES": "true",
        "OTEL_DOTNET_EXPERIMENTAL_OTLP_RETRY": "in_memory",
        "ASPNETCORE_FORWARDEDHEADERS_ENABLED": "true",
        "HTTP_PORTS": "{webfrontend.bindings.http.targetPort}",
        "ConnectionStrings__phi35": "{phi35.connectionString}",
        "PHI35_HOST": "{ollama.bindings.http.host}",
        "PHI35_PORT": "{ollama.bindings.http.port}",
        "PHI35_URI": "{ollama.bindings.http.scheme}://
{ollama.bindings.http.host}:{ollama.bindings.http.port}",
```

```
        "PHI35_MODEL": "phi3.5",
        "APISERVICE_HTTP": "{apiservice.bindings.http.url}",
        "services__apiservice__http__0": "{apiservice.bindings.http.url}",
        "APISERVICE_HTTPS": "{apiservice.bindings.https.url}",
        "services__apiservice__https__0": "{apiservice.bindings.https.url}",
        "IDP_HTTP": "{idp.bindings.http.url}",
        "services__idp__http__0": "{idp.bindings.http.url}",
        "Identity__ClientSecret": "some_secret",
        "ConnectionStrings__cache": "{cache.connectionString}",
        "CACHE_HOST": "{cache.bindings.tcp.host}",
        "CACHE_PORT": "{cache.bindings.tcp.port}",
        "CACHE_PASSWORD": "{cache-password.value}",
        "CACHE_URI": "redis://:{cache-password-uri-
    encoded.value}@{cache.bindings.tcp.host}:{cache.bindings.tcp.port}"
      },
```

Section 9.3 shows how to use this manifest to deploy the app.

## 9.3 Deploying to Azure Container Apps

Although Aspire is designed to be a cloud-agnostic system, at this writing, the Aspire manifest on its own can be used only to deploy services to Azure Container Apps. There are ways to deploy it to other types of environments and on different cloud providers, but I'll cover those topics later.

For now, let's talk about Azure Container Apps deployments. For this kind of deployment, you have to install a tool called the Azure Developer CLI. You can download and install this tool from the following web page: https://mng.bz/a9r7.

If you're a Windows user, execute the following command:

```
winget install microsoft.azd
```

If you use Linux for development, install it by running the following command:

```
curl -fsSL https://aka.ms/install-azd.sh | bash
```

To install it on a macOS machine, run the following command:

```
brew tap azure/azd && brew install azd
```

After we've downloaded and installed the tool according to the instructions, we can use it to deploy our app.

### 9.3.1 Using the Azure Developer CLI

Before we can deploy our application, we have to run the following terminal command inside the Aspire host project folder and follow the prompts:

```
azd init
```

This command creates some additional files we'll need for deployment to Azure Container Apps. Those files are

- `azure.yaml`—Configuration for the Aspire host project that's used to deploy it to Azure Container Apps
- `next-steps.md`—Detailed documentation of the commands we can execute next and what they do

We can follow the onscreen instructions, but setting the default options should be sufficient. Next, we log in to our Azure environment by executing the following command:

```
azd login
```

After configuring our Azure Container Apps instance and logging in, we execute the following command:

```
azd up
```

Once again, we can follow the prompt and get the application deployed to the correct Azure Container Apps instance.

### 9.3.2 Deploying from Visual Studio

If you prefer not to use the command line, you can deploy the Aspire app to an Azure Container Apps resource through Visual Studio. You still need the Azure Developer CLI, but you can do the deployment through a graphical user interface.

To deploy the app from Visual Studio, you right-click the App Host project in Visual Studio and choose the Publish option (figure 9.4).

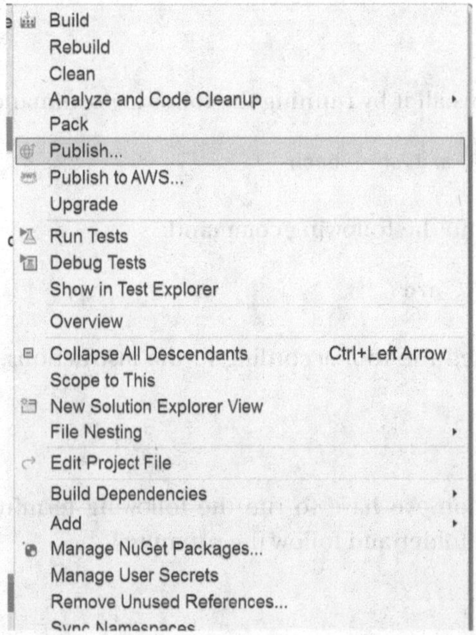


**Figure 9.4 Publishing Aspire apps from Visual Studio**

The Azure Container Apps option should appear, as figure 9.5 shows.

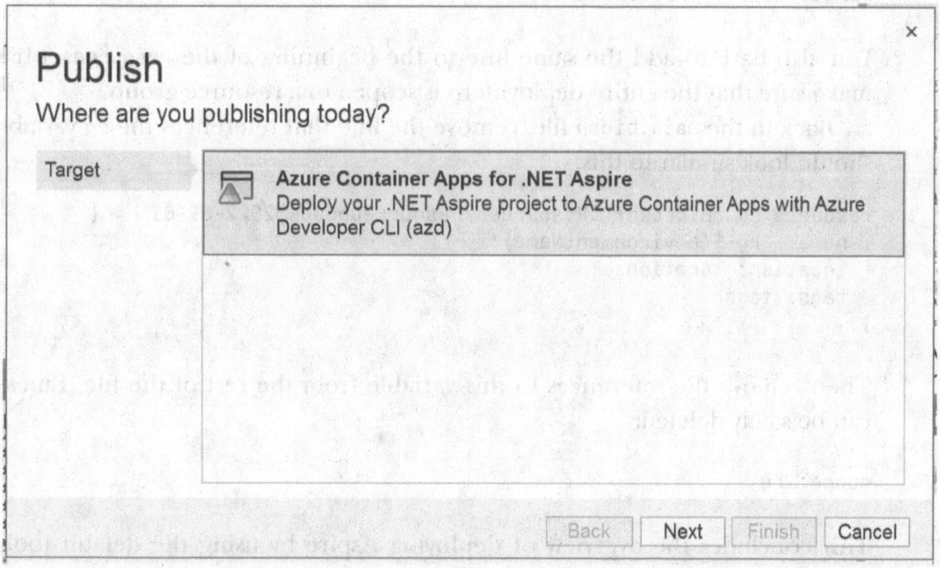


**Figure 9.5 Selecting Azure Container Apps as a deployment target**

Follow the onscreen instructions by selecting the right Azure subscription, the right Azure Container Apps instance, and so on. The instructions should be straightforward to navigate.

### 9.3.3 *Obtaining the deployment files*

By default, Aspire applies all deployment files in memory, but this gives you limited control. By default, the in-memory files assume that either you or the agent you're using for the deployment has contributor and role manager access at the subscription level in Azure. This will not always be the case. Quite often, you have such access only at the resource group level. If you want to generate infrastructure deployment files that you can modify, run the following command:

```
azd infra generate
```

You can also use `azd infra gen` as an alias. This command generates a folder called `infra`, in which all deployment scripts are placed.

You have multiple ways to deploy services to Azure. The AZD CLI utility uses Bicep files, for example, which you can examine in the `infra` folder. You can modify the generated files to scope them to a resource group. If you open the `main.bicep` file in the `infra` folder, you see the following line:

```
targetScope = 'subscription'
```

To scope the deployment to a resource group, replace it with this:

```
targetScope = 'resourceGroup'
```

You also have to add the same line to the beginning of the `resources.bicep` file to make sure that the entire deployment is scoped to a resource group.

Back in the `main.bicep` file, remove the line that references the `rg` variable, which should look similar to this:

```
resource rg 'Microsoft.Resources/resourceGroups@2022-09-01' = {
  name: 'rg-${environmentName}'
  location: location
  tags: tags
}
```

Then remove the references to this variable from the rest of the file. Lines like this can be safely deleted:

```
scope: rg
```

This concludes the overview of deploying Aspire by using the default tools. But as mentioned earlier, Azure Container Apps isn't our only option for deploying Aspire apps. We can convert our Aspire manifest into alternative Infrastructure as Code (IaC) formats. Section 9.4 shows how to deploy Aspire apps with Terraform.

## 9.4 Converting Aspire manifest to Terraform

Terraform is an alternative to Bicep. Unlike Bicep, it's not Azure-specific and can be used to deploy services in any cloud, including Google Cloud Platform (GCP) and Amazon Web Services (AWS).

Converting Bicep to Terraform is fairly straightforward. Several tools can do the job. Microsoft Copilot, for example, has been trained to handle this task reasonably well. But it's also possible to convert a raw Aspire manifest file directly to Terraform without producing the Bicep files first by using a tool called `Aspire.Terraform`.

> **WARNING** Before you use this tool, there's a caveat: it's not officially supported by Microsoft. It may lack some functionality or produce unpredictable results. If you ever have to use this tool, make sure to verify the outputs.

To install this tool, run the following CLI command:

```
dotnet tool install --global Aspire.Terraform
```

Then go to your Aspire host project folder and run the following command to scaffold the necessary folders and initial files:

```
aspire-tf init
```

Finally, to generate the Terraform files based on the current Aspire manifest, execute this command:

```
aspire-tf generate
```

Your Terraform scripts should be ready for deployment.

## 9.5 Converting Aspire manifest to Kubernetes

Terraform isn't the only IaC technology we can use to deploy Aspire apps; we can deploy them to a Kubernetes cluster too. If you're new to Kubernetes, it's an open source platform for automating the deployment, scaling, and management of containerized applications. It groups containers into logical units called *pods* and provides tools for managing their life cycle across a cluster of machines. It's widely used for building and managing modern, cloud-native applications. Key features include

- *Scaling*—Automatically adjusts the number of running containers based on demand
- *Load balancing*—Distributes traffic across containers to ensure high availability
- *Self-healing*—Restarts failed containers and replaces unresponsive ones
- *Service discovery*—Provides Domain Name System (DNS) and IP management for locating services within the cluster
- *Declarative configuration*—Uses YAML/JSON files to define desired states, which Kubernetes continuously works to maintain

To deploy our Aspire application to a Kubernetes cluster, we have to convert our Aspire manifests to a format that Kubernetes can understand. We can do this with a tool called Aspir8.

### 9.5.1 Using Aspir8

Aspir8 is designed to streamline the deployment of Aspire applications to Kubernetes clusters. It automates the generation of Kubernetes deployment YAML files based on an Aspire App Host manifest. To install the tool, run the following CLI command:

```
dotnet tool install --global aspirate
```

When Aspir8 is installed, we can use it by running the following command inside the Aspire App Host project folder, leaving all default options selected:

```
aspirate init
```

This command should create the `aspirate.json` file. If we selected the default options, its content should look like this:

```
{
 "TemplatePath": null,
 "ContainerSettings": {
```

```
    "Registry": null,
    "RepositoryPrefix": null,
    "Tags": [
      "latest"
    ],
    "Builder": "docker"
  }
}
```

To convert the Aspire manifest to Kubernetes deployment files, execute the following command:

```
aspirate generate
```

This command should create the `aspirate-output` folder, which will contain a hierarchy of folders filled with YAML and JSON files. The top-level folder should contain the following files:

- `dashboard.yaml`—Contains the configuration for the Aspire dashboard
- `kustomization.yaml`—Describes the hierarchy of the entire setup by pointing to `dashboard.yaml` and all the subfolders inside the folder

The folder also contains subfolders, each named after an individual service hosted by our Aspire app. In our case, the subfolders are `apiservice`, `cache`, and `webfrontend`. Each subfolder contains additional YAML files that describe the service in a way that Kubernetes can understand. Next, we'll use those files to deploy the services to a Kubernetes cluster.

### 9.5.2 Deploying to a Kubernetes cluster

To deploy resources to a Kubernetes cluster, we use a CLI tool called kubectl that interacts with Kubernetes clusters. It allows users to manage Kubernetes resources, deploy applications, inspect and troubleshoot problems, and perform cluster maintenance tasks.

For detailed instructions on installing kubectl in any supported operating system, see https://mng.bz/gm2V.

When the tool is installed, we can configure it to connect to a specific Kubernetes cluster. The exact command and its parameters depend on the kind of Kubernetes cluster to which we want to connect. To connect to a Kubernetes cluster hosted in Azure, we can use the following command (assuming that we have the Azure CLI tool installed):

```
az aks get-credentials --resource-group <resource-group> --name <cluster-name>
```

If our Kubernetes cluster is hosted by AWS, we have to install the AWS CLI tool, and the command follows this format:

```
aws eks update-kubeconfig --region <region> --name <cluster-name>
```

For GCP, we use the gcloud CLI tool, and the command looks like this:

```
gcloud container clusters get-credentials <cluster-name> --region <region>
```

To verify that the connection was successful, run the following command to get the connection information:

```
kubectl config get-contexts
```

This command gives us more information about the specific Kubernetes nodes, which are typically virtual machines (although they can be physical machines):

```
kubectl get nodes
```

After we've configured our kubectl instance to connect to a Kubernetes cluster and the verification commands run without errors, we can deploy the Aspire resources. All we have to do is point our kubectl tool to the appropriate YAML files and execute the `apply` command.

If we're in the root of the `aspirate-output` folder, we can execute the following command to deploy the entire setup to a Kubernetes cluster:

```
kubectl apply -k .
```

The `kustomization.yaml` file in the folder should help the kubectl tool determine the hierarchy of our distributed app, so we don't need to execute any other commands. This single command should be sufficient to deploy the entire distributed app.

Although we've created deployment scripts for a wide range of platforms, we don't want to run those scripts manually; we want to automate our deployments. That's why we have to integrate these scripts into continuous integration/continuous delivery (CI/CD) pipelines, which we'll look at in section 9.6.

## 9.6 Building CI/CD pipelines for Aspire

CI/CD pipelines provide automation for the whole end-to-end build and deployment process for our solutions. The process can be configured to be fully automated, such as when it gets triggered by a commit or an opened pull request (PR). The process can involve many steps, including the following:

- Performing various prebuild checks, such as verification of library versions
- Building the software
- Running automated tests
- Checking code for various problems, such as code smells and excessive complexity
- Deploying the software to a specified environment

Several environments allow us to configure and run such pipelines. Fortunately, Aspire supports some of the most popular ones out of the box. Here, we'll look at two examples: GitHub Actions and Azure DevOps. We'll follow the process of building a standard Azure Container Apps pipeline that's built into the AZD CLI tool.

Before we do, though, we have to take some common steps:

1. Execute the `azd init` command inside the Aspire host project directory to make sure that the AZD config files have been set up.
2. Execute the `azd login` command to log in to Azure.

We can also run the `azd up` command as a sanity check to make sure that we can deploy to Azure, but that step isn't strictly necessary.

### 9.6.1 Creating a GitHub Actions pipeline

GitHub Actions is the CI/CD mechanism available by default in GitHub. To build a pipeline for GitHub Actions, execute the following command:

```
azd pipeline config --provider github
```

You're asked to select the Azure subscription, select the region, and log in to your GitHub account. After you follow all the prompts to the end, the script creates a pipeline YAML file inside the `workflows` folder in the `.github` folder at the root of your repository. By default, the file is called `azure-dev.yml`, which is initially specific to the development environment. But you can reconfigure this file to build a production instance of your software, or you can have separate YAML files for different environments, such as test and staging.

The default pipeline configuration should be generic enough to be compatible with any environment. Most if not all configurations are identical, and environment-specific settings are controlled by environment variables. The following listing shows what this file might look like.

**Listing 9.1 GitHub Actions pipeline**

```
# Run when commits are pushed to main
on:                                    <- The block that controls what triggers the execution of the pipeline
  workflow_dispatch:                   <- The block that controls the specific trigger behavior
  push:                                <- Indicates that the pipeline is triggered automatically when new changes are pushed
    # Run when commits are pushed to mainline branch (main or master)
    # Set this to the mainline branch you are using
    branches:
      - main                           <- Indicates that the branch that is monitored for changes is main

# Set up permissions for deploying with secretless Azure federated credentials
# https://learn.microsoft.com/en-us/azure/developer/github/connect-from-
  azure?tabs=azure-portal%2Clinux#set-up-azure-login-with-openid-connect-
  authentication
```

```
permissions:
  id-token: write
  contents: read

jobs:
  build:
    runs-on: ubuntu-latest
    env:
      AZURE_CLIENT_ID: ${{ vars.AZURE_CLIENT_ID }}
      AZURE_TENANT_ID: ${{ vars.AZURE_TENANT_ID }}
      AZURE_SUBSCRIPTION_ID: ${{ vars.AZURE_SUBSCRIPTION_ID }}
      AZURE_ENV_NAME: ${{ vars.AZURE_ENV_NAME }}
      AZURE_LOCATION: ${{ vars.AZURE_LOCATION }}
    steps:
      - name: Checkout
        uses: actions/checkout@v4
      - name: Install azd
        uses: Azure/setup-azd@v1.0.0
      - name: Install .NET Aspire workload
        run: dotnet workload install aspire

      - name: Log in with Azure (Federated Credentials)
        run: |
          azd auth login `
            --client-id "$Env:AZURE_CLIENT_ID" `
            --federated-credential-provider "github" `
            --tenant-id "$Env:AZURE_TENANT_ID"
        shell: pwsh

      - name: Provision Infrastructure
        run: azd provision --no-prompt
        env:
          AZD_INITIAL_ENVIRONMENT_CONFIG: ${{
    secrets.AZD_INITIAL_ENVIRONMENT_CONFIG }}

      - name: Deploy Application
        run: azd deploy --no-prompt
```

- Sets the operating system for the build agent (runs-on)
- Sets the environment variables from the variables that were passed into the pipeline (env)
- Sets the pipeline execution steps (steps)
- Provisions the system by using the AZD CLI (azd provision)
- Deploys the system to the specified Azure location by using AZD CLI (azd deploy)

After this pipeline is checked in, you can configure it to run from the GitHub UI. The official document at https://mng.bz/eBZQ explains how.

Although this pipeline is good, a crucial component is missing. The default pipeline that was created only builds and deploys the solution. At minimum, we want our pipeline to run the automated tests to ensure that our new set of changes hasn't broken anything. If any test fails, the build stops. We have to address the problem and push the fix before the build can rerun. The next listing shows how our pipeline might look after we add the steps that run the tests.

**Listing 9.2 GitHub Actions pipeline with tests**

```
on:
  workflow_dispatch:
  push:
    # Run when commits are pushed to mainline branch (main or master)
    # Set this to the mainline branch you are using
    branches:
      - main

permissions:
  id-token: write
  contents: read

jobs:
  build:
    runs-on: ubuntu-latest
    env:
      AZURE_CLIENT_ID: ${{ vars.AZURE_CLIENT_ID }}
      AZURE_TENANT_ID: ${{ vars.AZURE_TENANT_ID }}
      AZURE_SUBSCRIPTION_ID: ${{ vars.AZURE_SUBSCRIPTION_ID }}
      AZURE_ENV_NAME: ${{ vars.AZURE_ENV_NAME }}
      AZURE_LOCATION: ${{ vars.AZURE_LOCATION }}
    steps:
      - name: Checkout
        uses: actions/checkout@v4

      # Make sure the right .NET SDK is available
      - name: Setup .NET
        uses: actions/setup-dotnet@v4
        with:
          dotnet-version: '10.0.x'

      - name: Install azd
        uses: Azure/setup-azd@v1.0.0

      - name: Install .NET Aspire workload
        run: dotnet workload install aspire

      # ---------- CI: build & test ----------
      - name: Restore
        run: dotnet restore ./AspireApp.sln

      - name: Build
        run: dotnet build ./AspireApp.sln --configuration Release --no-restore

      - name: Test
        run: dotnet test ./AspireApp.sln --configuration Release --no-build
      # If tests fail here, the job stops and nothing below runs
      # --------------------------------------

      - name: Log in with Azure (Federated Credentials)
        run: |
          azd auth login `
```

Install the .NET SDK into the pipeline environment, as the tests rely on the dotnet CLI.

Execute dotnet restore, pointing to the location of your .NET solution.

Build your solution.

Execute tests and short-circuit the pipeline if any of them fail.

```
      --client-id "$Env:AZURE_CLIENT_ID" `
      --federated-credential-provider "github" `
      --tenant-id "$Env:AZURE_TENANT_ID"
  shell: pwsh

- name: Provision Infrastructure
  run: azd provision --no-prompt
  env:
    AZD_INITIAL_ENVIRONMENT_CONFIG: ${{
 secrets.AZD_INITIAL_ENVIRONMENT_CONFIG }}

- name: Deploy Application
  run: azd deploy --no-prompt
```

We can make other useful modifications in our pipelines. We've already seen that we can modify the Bicep files to scope the deployment to an Azure resource group rather than a subscription. To do so, add the following line to the step with the `azd provision` command:

```
azd config set alpha.resourceGroupDeployments on
```

If our infrastructure provisioning doesn't work as intended, we have to find out why. To do so, we add the `--debug` flag to the `azd provision` command.

Finally, if environment variables are available in the pipeline, remember that they won't be passed in to the Bicep templates and the deployed application automatically. To pass these variables, we have to set them in the `azd` environment by executing the following command:

```
azd env set <in-application environment variable name> <pipeline environment
  variable>
```

Suppose that we want to make the value of the `STORAGE_BLOBENDPOINT` pipeline variable accessible inside the deployed application. Here's what we do:

```
azd env set STORAGE_BLOBENDPOINT "$STORAGE_BLOBENDPOINT"
```

You can apply many more improvements to the pipeline. To find out what else you can do, see the official GitHub Actions documentation at https://docs.github.com/en/actions.

### 9.6.2 Creating an Azure DevOps pipeline

In this section, we look at how to use another popular CI/CD provider: Azure DevOps, a Microsoft product that's tightly integrated with Azure and used by many enterprises. It offers many features in addition to deployment pipelines, such as a task management system and wiki pages.

This step is most relevant if you host your Git repo in Azure DevOps. Still, you can use Azure DevOps for a CI/CD pipeline even if you host your repository elsewhere, such as GitHub, GitLab, or Bitbucket. The only limitation is that if you don't host your repo in Azure DevOps, you won't be able to complete all of the following steps via the CLI. You'll still be able to generate the YAML file that represents your pipeline steps, but you'll have to apply some additional manual configurations to connect it to the repo.

Assuming that you've already used AZD to initialize the environment and log in to Azure, you can run the following command in the Aspire host project directory to create an Azure DevOps pipeline:

```
azd pipeline config --provider azdo
```

This step creates the `.azdo` folder inside the root of your repository, creates the `pipelines` folder inside it, and generates the `azure-dev.yml` file inside this folder. The next listing shows what the content of this file might look like.

**Listing 9.3 Azure DevOps pipeline**

```
# Run when commits are pushed to main
trigger:
  - main

pool:
  vmImage: ubuntu-latest

steps:
  # setup-azd@0 needs to be manually installed in your organization
  # if you can't install it, you can use the below bash script to install azd
  # and remove this step
  - task: setup-azd@0
    displayName: Install azd

  # If you can't install above task in your organization, you can comment it
     and uncomment below task to install azd
  # - task: Bash@3
  #   displayName: Install azd
  #   inputs:
  #     targetType: 'inline'
  #     script: |
  #       curl -fsSL https://aka.ms/install-azd.sh | bash

  # azd delegate auth to az to use service connection with AzureCLI@2
  - pwsh: |
      azd config set auth.useAzCliAuth "true"
    displayName: Configure AZD to Use AZ CLI Authentication.
  - task: Bash@3
    displayName: Install .NET Aspire workload
    inputs:
      targetType: 'inline'
      script: |
        dotnet workload install aspire

  - task: AzureCLI@2
    displayName: Provision Infrastructure
```

- Trigger the pipeline when anything is pushed into main branch.
- Set the operating system of the build agent.
- Install AZD CLI.
- Install Aspire workload.

```
    inputs:
      azureSubscription: azconnection
      scriptType: bash
      scriptLocation: inlineScript
      keepAzSessionActive: true
      inlineScript: |
        azd provision --no-prompt          <-- Provision the Aspire application.
    env:
      AZURE_SUBSCRIPTION_ID: $(AZURE_SUBSCRIPTION_ID)
      AZURE_ENV_NAME: $(AZURE_ENV_NAME)
      AZURE_LOCATION: $(AZURE_LOCATION)
      AZD_INITIAL_ENVIRONMENT_CONFIG: $(AZD_INITIAL_ENVIRONMENT_CONFIG)

  - task: AzureCLI@2
    displayName: Deploy Application
    inputs:
      azureSubscription: azconnection
      scriptType: bash
      scriptLocation: inlineScript
      keepAzSessionActive: true
      inlineScript: |
        azd deploy --no-prompt             <-- Deploy the Aspire application.
    env:                                   <-- Set the required environment variables.
      AZURE_SUBSCRIPTION_ID: $(AZURE_SUBSCRIPTION_ID)
      AZURE_ENV_NAME: $(AZURE_ENV_NAME)
      AZURE_LOCATION: $(AZURE_LOCATION)
```

As you can see, the pipeline is conceptually similar to a GitHub Actions workflow. It uses YAML and largely follows the same steps, though the steps are defined differently. The following listing shows what this pipeline might look like if you added tests to it.

**Listing 9.4 Azure DevOps pipeline with tests**

```
trigger:
  - main

pool:
  vmImage: ubuntu-latest

steps:
  # setup-azd@0 needs to be manually installed in your organization
  # if you can't install it, you can use the below bash script to install azd
  # and remove this step
  - task: setup-azd@0
    displayName: Install azd

below task to install azd
  # - task: Bash@3
  #   displayName: Install azd
  #   inputs:
  #     targetType: 'inline'
  #     script: |
  #       curl -fsSL https://aka.ms/install-azd.sh | bash
```

```
# Make sure the right .NET SDK is available
- task: UseDotNet@2
  displayName: 'Setup .NET SDK'
  inputs:
    packageType: 'sdk'
    version: '10.0.x'                      <-- Installs the .NET SDK

- pwsh: |
    azd config set auth.useAzCliAuth "true"
  displayName: Configure AZD to Use AZ CLI Authentication.

- task: Bash@3
  displayName: Install .NET Aspire workload
  inputs:
    targetType: 'inline'
    script: |
      dotnet workload install aspire

# ---------- CI: build & test BEFORE provision/deploy ----------
- task: Bash@3
  displayName: Restore
  inputs:
    targetType: 'inline'
    script: |
      dotnet restore ./AspireApp.sln       <-- Restores the .NET solution

- task: Bash@3
  displayName: Build
  inputs:
    targetType: 'inline'
    script: |
      dotnet build ./AspireApp.sln --configuration Release --no-restore    <-- Builds the .NET solution

- task: Bash@3
  displayName: Test
  inputs:
    targetType: 'inline'
    script: |
      dotnet test ./AspireApp.sln --configuration Release --no-build --
  logger "trx;LogFileName=test_results.trx"     <-- Runs the tests and stops the pipeline if any tests fail

- task: PublishTestResults@2
  displayName: 'Publish test results'
  condition: succeededOrFailed()   # still publish even if tests fail
  inputs:
    testResultsFormat: 'VSTest'
    testResultsFiles: '**/test_results.trx'
    searchFolder: '$(System.DefaultWorkingDirectory)'
    testRunTitle: 'Unit Tests'
# If tests fail, later steps won't run because the job fails by default
# --------------------------------------------------------------

- task: AzureCLI@2
  displayName: Provision Infrastructure
```

```
    condition: succeeded()    # only if build+tests passed
    inputs:
      azureSubscription: azconnection
      scriptType: bash
      scriptLocation: inlineScript
      keepAzSessionActive: true
      inlineScript: |
        azd provision --no-prompt
    env:
      AZURE_SUBSCRIPTION_ID: $(AZURE_SUBSCRIPTION_ID)
      AZURE_ENV_NAME: $(AZURE_ENV_NAME)
      AZURE_LOCATION: $(AZURE_LOCATION)
      AZD_INITIAL_ENVIRONMENT_CONFIG: $(AZD_INITIAL_ENVIRONMENT_CONFIG)

  - task: AzureCLI@2
    displayName: Deploy Application
    condition: succeeded()    # only if previous steps passed
    inputs:
      azureSubscription: azconnection
      scriptType: bash
      scriptLocation: inlineScript
      keepAzSessionActive: true
      inlineScript: |
        azd deploy --no-prompt
    env:
      AZURE_SUBSCRIPTION_ID: $(AZURE_SUBSCRIPTION_ID)
      AZURE_ENV_NAME: $(AZURE_ENV_NAME)
      AZURE_LOCATION: $(AZURE_LOCATION)
```

For more information on how to run and further modify such a pipeline, see the official documentation at https://learn.microsoft.com/en-us/azure/devops/pipelines.

This is how you scaffold the CI/CD pipelines for the standard Azure Container Apps deployment of Aspire. But what if you want to deploy to other clouds or other systems, such as Kubernetes? In that case, you can modify the pipelines manually. After all, the pipelines are flexible and can run almost any arbitrary CLI commands, including ones that let you deploy to other environments.

### 9.6.3 Building pipelines for Kubernetes deployment

Now that we know how to use Aspir8 to deploy to Kubernetes, let's see how to set up pipelines for it. If we use Kubernetes, it still makes sense to scaffold the initial pipeline structure, saving us the manual effort of writing the boilerplate YAML. After the YAML file is created, we can modify it manually. The next listing shows how to modify a GitHub Actions pipeline to build a Kubernetes deployment.

**Listing 9.5 GitHub Actions pipeline for Kubernetes**

```
on:
  workflow_dispatch:
  push:
```

```
    branches:
      - main

permissions:
  contents: read

jobs:
  build:
    runs-on: ubuntu-latest
    env:
      CONTAINER_REGISTRY: myregistry.azurecr.io
      ASPIRATE_ENVIRONMENT: production
    steps:
      - name: Checkout
        uses: actions/checkout@v4

      - name: Setup .NET SDK
        uses: actions/setup-dotnet@v4
        with:
          dotnet-version: '10.0.x'

      - name: Install .NET Aspire workload
        run: dotnet workload install aspire

      - name: Install Aspirate CLI
        run: dotnet tool install --global aspirate --prerelease

      - name: Add .NET tools to PATH
        run: echo "$HOME/.dotnet/tools" >> $GITHUB_PATH

      - name: Restore
        run: dotnet restore ./AspireApp.sln

      - name: Build
        run: dotnet build ./AspireApp.sln --configuration Release --no-restore

      - name: Test
        run: dotnet test ./AspireApp.sln --configuration Release --no-build

      - name: Docker login
        run: |
          echo "${{ secrets.REGISTRY_PASSWORD }}" | docker login ${{
     env.CONTAINER_REGISTRY }} \
            --username "${{ secrets.REGISTRY_USERNAME }}" --password-stdin

      - name: Aspirate generate (build images & manifests)
        working-directory: ./AspireApp.AppHost
        run: |
          aspirate generate \
            --container-registry "${{ env.CONTAINER_REGISTRY }}" \
            --environment "${{ env.ASPIRATE_ENVIRONMENT }}" \
            --output ./k8s \
            --non-interactive
```

- Set your container registry. (CONTAINER_REGISTRY)
- Install Aspir8 CLI. (dotnet tool install --global aspirate)
- Log in to Docker by using credentials from environment variables. (--password-stdin)
- Generate build manifests by providing the location of the Aspire Host folder. (working-directory)

```
- name: Setup kubectl
  uses: azure/setup-kubectl@v4
  with:
    version: 'latest'

- name: Configure kubeconfig
  run: |
    mkdir -p $HOME/.kube
    echo "${{ secrets.KUBECONFIG_CONTENT }}" > $HOME/.kube/config

- name: Deploy to Kubernetes with Aspirate
  working-directory: ./AspireApp.AppHost
  run: |
    aspirate apply --non-interactive
```

Set up kubectl for Kubernetes deployment.

Configure kubectl.

Deploy the application to the Kubernetes cluster.

Now let's look at the equivalent changes for an Azure DevOps pipeline. The next listing shows how they're done.

**Listing 9.6 Azure DevOps pipeline for Kubernetes**

```
trigger:
  - main

pool:
  vmImage: ubuntu-latest

steps:
  - task: UseDotNet@2
    displayName: 'Setup .NET SDK'
    inputs:
      packageType: 'sdk'
      version: '10.0.x'         # or 8.0.x / whatever you target

  - task: Bash@3
    displayName: Install .NET Aspire workload
    inputs:
      targetType: 'inline'
      script: |
        dotnet workload install aspire

  - task: Bash@3
    displayName: Install Aspirate CLI
    inputs:
      targetType: 'inline'
      script: |
        dotnet tool install --global aspirate --prerelease
        echo "##vso[task.prependpath]$HOME/.dotnet/tools"

  - task: Bash@3
    displayName: Restore
    inputs:
      targetType: 'inline'
```

Install Aspir8 CLI.

```
      script: |
        dotnet restore ./AspireApp.sln

  - task: Bash@3
    displayName: Build
    inputs:
      targetType: 'inline'
      script: |
        dotnet build ./AspireApp.sln --configuration Release --no-restore

    displayName: Test
    inputs:
      targetType: 'inline'
      script: |
        dotnet test ./AspireApp.sln --configuration Release --no-build --
     logger "trx;LogFileName=test_results.trx"

  - task: PublishTestResults@2
    displayName: 'Publish test results'
    condition: succeededOrFailed()
    inputs:
      testResultsFormat: 'VSTest'
      testResultsFiles: '**/test_results.trx'
      searchFolder: '$(System.DefaultWorkingDirectory)'
      testRunTitle: 'Unit Tests'

  - task: Bash@3
    displayName: Docker login (container registry)     <-- Log into Docker by using credentials from environment variables.
    condition: succeeded()
    inputs:
      targetType: 'inline'
      script: |
        echo "$(REGISTRY_PASSWORD)" | docker login "$(CONTAINER_REGISTRY)" \
          --username "$(REGISTRY_USERNAME)" --password-stdin
    env:
      REGISTRY_USERNAME: $(REGISTRY_USERNAME)
      REGISTRY_PASSWORD: $(REGISTRY_PASSWORD)
      CONTAINER_REGISTRY: $(CONTAINER_REGISTRY)

  - task: Bash@3
    displayName: Aspirate generate (build images & manifests)     <-- Use Aspir8 to generate the manifest and build containers.
    condition: succeeded()
    inputs:
      targetType: 'inline'
      workingDirectory: ./AspireApp.AppHost
      script: |
        aspirate generate \
          --container-registry "$(CONTAINER_REGISTRY)" \
          --environment "$(ASPIRATE_ENVIRONMENT)" \
          --output ./k8s \
          --non-interactive
    env:
      CONTAINER_REGISTRY: $(CONTAINER_REGISTRY)
      ASPIRATE_ENVIRONMENT: $(ASPIRATE_ENVIRONMENT)
```

```
- task: Bash@3
  displayName: Configure kubeconfig        <-- Configure kubeconfig.
  condition: succeeded()
  inputs:
    targetType: 'inline'
    script: |
      mkdir -p $HOME/.kube
      printf '%s\n' "$(KUBECONFIG_CONTENT)" > $HOME/.kube/config
  env:
    KUBECONFIG_CONTENT: $(KUBECONFIG_CONTENT)

- task: Bash@3
  displayName: Deploy to Kubernetes with Aspirate     <-- Deploy the app to a Kubernetes cluster.
  condition: succeeded()
  inputs:
    targetType: 'inline'
    workingDirectory: ./AspireApp.AppHost
    script: |
      aspirate apply --non-interactive
```

This concludes the overview of how to scale, modify, and build Aspire apps. Chapter 10 covers migrating existing apps to Aspire and old Aspire 8/9 apps to the most recent evergreen Aspire 13. The chapter also covers moving existing apps to an Aspire host.

## Summary

- Aspire can scale out individual services by running multiple instances of them. You can have separate logic for the local Aspire instance and the deployed application.
- The Aspire dashboard can be extended with additional custom commands.
- When multiple instances of a service are hosted in Aspire, load balancing is handled automatically.
- Aspire can be integrated with a variety of other tools for deployment to various cloud environments, such as the Azure Developer CLI.
- JSON files known as Aspire manifests describe all individual services hosted by Aspire.
- Aspire can be deployed in Azure Container Apps via the Azure Developer CLI. If we want to deploy it to a Kubernetes cluster in a cloud-agnostic way, we can convert Aspire manifests to YAML files that Kubernetes can understand by using a tool called Aspir8.

# 10 Adding legacy apps to Aspire and working with AI agents

**This chapter covers**

- Upgrading from Aspire 8 and 9 to Aspire 13
- Adding existing .NET projects to Aspire
- Moving existing infrastructure components to Aspire
- Integrating Aspire with AI coding agents

So far, we've seen how to build distributed applications with Aspire. We've also looked at how to create deployment scripts for such applications and extend Aspire functionality. But all these examples involved the evergreen Aspire 13.

But Aspire has been production-ready since version 8 was released in 2023. Version 9 was released in 2024, and many systems in the wild still use one of these versions. How do you modernize these systems and make them run on Aspire 13? We'll learn how in this chapter.

But that's not all. What if your application wasn't on Aspire to begin with, even though it would have benefited from being hosted on Aspire? Tooling is available that makes adding existing applications to Aspire easy. This includes adding the infrastructure components you may have distributed throughout your system, such as databases and message brokers. You'll see how easy it is to convert these components to Aspire integrations while keeping the existing production versions intact.

Finally, the chapter covers integrating Aspire solutions with AI coding assistants. Agentic coding assistants are transforming the way software is developed by automating tasks that used to be tedious and time-consuming, leaving developers to focus on the most exciting parts, such as problem-solving. Aspire has tools that make it work nicely with popular coding assistants, such as Claude Code. We'll examine how these tools work.

## 10.1 Migrating old .NET Aspire projects

When Aspire first appeared, it was a game changer for cloud-application development, but it lacked many useful features that are in the current version. Things have changed significantly between versions.

But because even the initial version simplified cloud-first development so much, many development teams started to adopt it. That's why you may still encounter an organization that runs its system on an old version of Aspire.

Fortunately, migrating to the new version is easy enough. The process differs slightly depending on whether your system runs version 8 or 9, but the steps are simple enough in either case.

**NOTE** Aspire has no version 10, 11, or 12; version 13 came after version 9. The team chose 13 instead of 10 to break out of sequential version updates and signal that Aspire is now evergreen, like Windows 11. The .NET part was removed because Aspire is no longer .NET-exclusive. It supports JavaScript and Python, and other languages may be supported in the future.

### 10.1.1 Migrating from .NET Aspire 8

Let's see how the migration process is done with both major versions of Aspire. You can upgrade a .NET Aspire 9 application to Aspire 13, for example, by executing a single command-line interface (CLI) command. But this command doesn't work in .NET Aspire 8, so if you have a legacy application on this Aspire version, you have to upgrade it manually. Here's how.

A .NET Aspire 8 application is available at https://mng.bz/Nwg1. It's a simple Aspire app with a standard web frontend service, an API service, and an additional SQL Server integration. The integration is included to demonstrate how integration libraries are updated during the process to match the Aspire version.

The following listing shows the `.csproj` file for the Aspire host project.

**Listing 10.1 .NET Aspire 8 project definition**

```
<Project Sdk="Microsoft.NET.Sdk">

  <PropertyGroup>
    <OutputType>Exe</OutputType>
    <TargetFramework>net8.0</TargetFramework>
    <ImplicitUsings>enable</ImplicitUsings>
    <Nullable>enable</Nullable>
```

```
    <IsAspireHost>true</IsAspireHost>
    <UserSecretsId>b6070f86-3ef8-4a16-bc70-cdeed5b2851f</UserSecretsId>
  </PropertyGroup>

  <ItemGroup>
    <ProjectReference
     Include="..\AspireApp.ApiService\AspireApp.ApiService.csproj" />
    <ProjectReference Include="..\AspireApp.Web\AspireApp.Web.csproj" />
  </ItemGroup>

  <ItemGroup>
    <PackageReference Include="Aspire.Hosting.AppHost" Version="8.0.0" />
    <PackageReference Include="Aspire.Hosting.SqlServer" Version="8.1.0" />
  </ItemGroup>

</Project>
```

The property defines that the project is Aspire Host.

.NET Aspire 8 host package

.NET Aspire 8 SQL Server integration package

It's also important to know that the startup and orchestration code for Aspire 8 applications is located in the `Program.cs` file instead of `AppHost.cs`. It follows the same pattern and format (albeit with fewer features), but the filename is different.

**NOTE** If we want to upgrade this project to Aspire 13, it would be better to upgrade it to Aspire 9 first. This approach is recommended for Aspire's built-in upgrade tools.

To begin, we add the following element to the `.csproj` file immediately after the opening `Project` tag:

```
<Sdk Name="Aspire.AppHost.Sdk" Version="9.0.0" />
```

Then we upgrade all Aspire-specific packages to the latest version that starts with 9. This applies to the core `Aspire.Hosting.AppHost` package, any hosted integration packages, and any Aspire-specific client packages used to connect to the Aspire-hosted integration components.

If our original solution was on .NET version 8, it may also be a good idea to update it to at least version 9 because Aspire version 9 came out at the same time as .NET version 9. To see what the solution looks like after being updated to Aspire 9, go to https://mng.bz/EwoO.

The next listing shows the `.csproj` file of the Aspire host project after the update.

**Listing 10.2 .NET Aspire 9 project definition**

```
<Project Sdk="Microsoft.NET.Sdk">

  <Sdk Name="Aspire.AppHost.Sdk" Version="9.0.0" />

  <PropertyGroup>
    <OutputType>Exe</OutputType>
    <TargetFramework>net9.0</TargetFramework>
```

Aspire 9 SDK reference

```
    <ImplicitUsings>enable</ImplicitUsings>
    <Nullable>enable</Nullable>
    <IsAspireHost>true</IsAspireHost>
    <UserSecretsId>b6070f86-3ef8-4a16-bc70-cdeed5b2851f</UserSecretsId>
  </PropertyGroup>

  <ItemGroup>
    <ProjectReference
     Include="..\AspireApp.ApiService\AspireApp.ApiService.csproj" />
    <ProjectReference Include="..\AspireApp.Web\AspireApp.Web.csproj" />
  </ItemGroup>

  <ItemGroup>
    <PackageReference Include="Aspire.Hosting.AppHost" Version="9.2.1" />     Updated Aspire Host package
    <PackageReference Include="Aspire.Hosting.SqlServer" Version="9.2.1" />   Updated Aspire SQL Server integration package
  </ItemGroup>

</Project>
```

In the Aspire 9 host project, the file that contains the startup and orchestration code can be called `Program.cs` or `AppHost.cs`. Either name will work.

Now, we are ready to do a clean upgrade to Aspire 13.

### 10.1.2 Migrating from .NET Aspire 9 to Aspire 13

You can do the Aspire 13 update manually, the same way you updated version 8 to version 9. The same packages and SDK elements can be upgraded to a version that starts with 13.

If your legacy Aspire system runs on version 9, however, the upgrade process is easy: install the `aspire` CLI tool, which will do the job for you. You can get it at https://aspire.dev/get-started/install-cli/. After the tool is installed, navigate to your .NET solution containing the Aspire setup and execute the following command:

```
aspire update
```

This process automatically updates everything in your entire solution related to Aspire, including the SDK, the host package, and the client packages. If you have to update the CLI tool itself, run the following command:

```
aspire update --self
```

You can find the upgraded solution at https://mng.bz/Dw6w. The next listing shows what the file looks like after the upgrade.

**Listing 10.3 Aspire 13 project definition after update**

```
<Project Sdk="Microsoft.NET.Sdk">

  <Sdk Name="Aspire.AppHost.Sdk" Version="13.3.5" />     Updated Aspire SDK version
```

```
  <PropertyGroup>
    <OutputType>Exe</OutputType>
    <TargetFramework>net10.0</TargetFramework>
    <ImplicitUsings>enable</ImplicitUsings>
    <Nullable>enable</Nullable>
    <IsAspireHost>true</IsAspireHost>
    <UserSecretsId>b6070f86-3ef8-4a16-bc70-cdeed5b2851f</UserSecretsId>
  </PropertyGroup>

  <ItemGroup>
    <ProjectReference
    Include="..\AspireApp.ApiService\AspireApp.ApiService.csproj" />
    <ProjectReference Include="..\AspireApp.Web\AspireApp.Web.csproj" />
  </ItemGroup>
                                        Updated core Aspire Host package
  <ItemGroup>
    <PackageReference Include="Aspire.Hosting.AppHost" Version="13.3.5" />
    <PackageReference Include="Aspire.Hosting.SqlServer" Version="13.3.5" />
  </ItemGroup>
                                        Updated SQL Server
</Project>                              integration package
```

**NOTE** The exact version of Aspire packages may be different because packages are updated regularly.

Still, you may find this structure substantially different from Aspire 13 projects you've built from scratch. This is nothing to worry about. Aspire supports both approaches; they're just syntactic sugar for the same thing. You can modernize the Aspire project further by doing the following:

1. Remove the `IsAspireHost` element.
2. Remove the `Sdk` element that references `Aspire.AppHost.Sdk`.
3. Remove the reference to the `Aspire.Hosting.AppHost` package.
4. Replace the value of the `Sdk` attribute of the top-level `Project` element from `Microsoft.NET.Sdk` to `Aspire.AppHost.Sdk/`, followed by the latest Aspire SDK version number.

These changes will make the project file less verbose without changing any of its behavior. The next listing shows how the file will look after the changes.

**Listing 10.4 Modernized Aspire 13 project format**

```
<Project Sdk="Aspire.AppHost.Sdk/13.1.0">       Aspire 13 SDK defined at
                                                the project type level
  <PropertyGroup>
    <OutputType>Exe</OutputType>                No explicit IsAspireHost
    <TargetFramework>net10.0</TargetFramework>  property set
    <ImplicitUsings>enable</ImplicitUsings>
    <Nullable>enable</Nullable>
    <UserSecretsId>2f2ef062-99af-422f-b6a5-1094759553e7</UserSecretsId>
  </PropertyGroup>
```

```
<ItemGroup>
  <ProjectReference
   Include="..\AspireApp.ApiService\AspireApp.ApiService.csproj" />
  <ProjectReference Include="..\AspireApp.Web\AspireApp.Web.csproj" />
</ItemGroup>

<ItemGroup>
  <PackageReference Include="Aspire.Hosting.SqlServer" Version="13.3.5" />
</ItemGroup>

</Project>
```

Only Aspire integration components are referenced, no Aspire Host package

**TIP** You can use the same `aspire update` command to keep updating the Aspire version when a new version comes out.

Finally, Aspire 13, like Aspire 9 before it, supports both `Program.cs` and `AppHost.cs` files as its startup code file but not both at the same time.

Upgrading Aspire from an older version is easy. Next, we'll see how to add existing projects to Aspire orchestration.

## 10.2 Enrolling existing projects in Aspire orchestration

Most .NET applications in the wild aren't hosted on Aspire. Typically, they're executed individually and configured to connect to overly specific localhost addresses when run locally. The deployment scripts are usually tedious to construct, but Aspire simplifies the process.

When I worked at Microsoft, we were building a large distributed system that processed huge quantities of weather data. When I joined the project, it was difficult to run locally. We could launch only a handful of applications at a time and emulate everything else. Some services couldn't be launched locally at all, which made problems harder to fix if we discovered them after the services were deployed in a real cloud environment.

Aspire changed this situation. Despite the complexity of the system, the enrollment process didn't take long, and when it was complete, it eliminated many problems. The whole system could be launched easily on a single development machine, including the services that previously couldn't be launched in a meaningful way. Manual address configuration was no longer required because service discovery handled it. The number of problems decreased because everything could be thoroughly tested before it was committed to the main branch.

This chapter won't look at a system as complex as this one, but it will cover the same fundamental principles. Our starting point is the distributed system at https://mng.bz/lZ78. It's a standard application that consists of the following components:

- Hosted Blazor application acting as a frontend
- Backend API application from which the frontend application retrieves the data

The backend API application gets its data from a SQL Server database via a standard connection string. The database itself isn't part of the setup; it can be hosted anywhere. Figure 10.1 shows the initial setup.

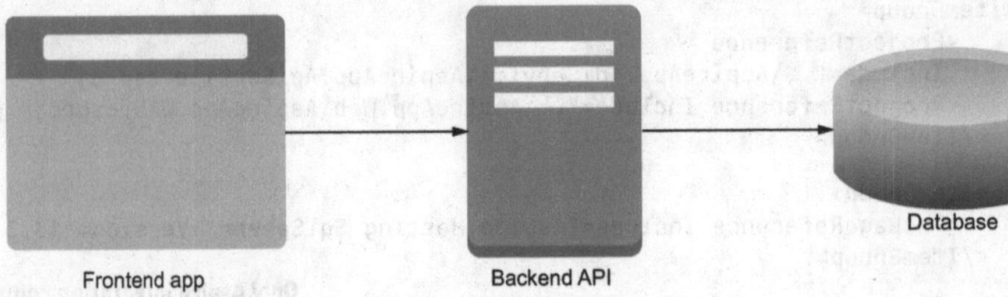


**Figure 10.1 A system without Aspire orchestration**

There's an official name for the process of enrolling existing apps in Aspire orchestration: *aspirification*. The systems that have been moved to Aspire are known as *aspirified*.

You can go about it in different ways:

- Open an IDE such as Visual Studio or Rider, add the Aspire Host and Aspire Service Defaults projects to the solution, and then integrate all existing projects with them manually.
- Execute the following command in the solution folder, assuming that we've installed the `aspire` CLI tool:

  ```
  aspire init
  ```

The tool guides you through choosing the kind of Aspire setup you want. You may not want to include the standard Service Defaults package, for example; perhaps you have your own metrics and health-check mechanisms. But in most cases, you want to include it.

After creating the Aspire host project, you can add references to the projects you want to orchestrate and then reference these projects in the orchestrator inside the `AppHost.cs` file. The next listing shows the code.

**Listing 10.5 Adding project references to the Aspire host**

```
var builder = DistributedApplication.CreateBuilder(args);

var apiService =
    builder.AddProject<Projects.OnlineShop_ApiService>("apiservice")
    .WaitFor
    .WithReference;

builder
    .AddProject<Projects.OnlineShop_Web>("webfrontend")
    .WithExternalHttpEndpoints()
    .WithReference(apiService)
    .WaitFor(apiService);

builder.Build().Run();
```

If you chose not to add the service defaults, you can do so later by executing the following command, replacing `<Your Solution Name>` and `<Your Project Name>` parts with the name of your solution and the name of the project to which you want to add the service discovery, telemetry, and health-check capabilities:

```
dotnet new aspire-servicedefaults -n <Your Solution Name>.ServiceDefaults
dotnet sln add <Your Solution Name>.ServiceDefaults
dotnet add <Your Project Name> reference <Your Solution Name>.ServiceDefaults
```

After adding your projects to the Aspire orchestrator and referencing service defaults, you can modify the startup code inside the `Program.cs` file in each of these services to use the shared Aspire dependencies. First, add the following line anywhere in the builder phase:

```
builder.AddServiceDefaults();
```

Then add this code to the request-processing pipeline to expose the health-check endpoints and any other shared endpoints:

```
app.MapDefaultEndpoints();
```

Finally, now that the health-check endpoint is exposed, add this line to the `AppHost.cs` file of the Aspire host project below the service reference:

```
.WithHttpHealthCheck("/health")
```

Figure 10.2 demonstrates a high-level architecture of the systems that you will end up with after completing these setup steps.

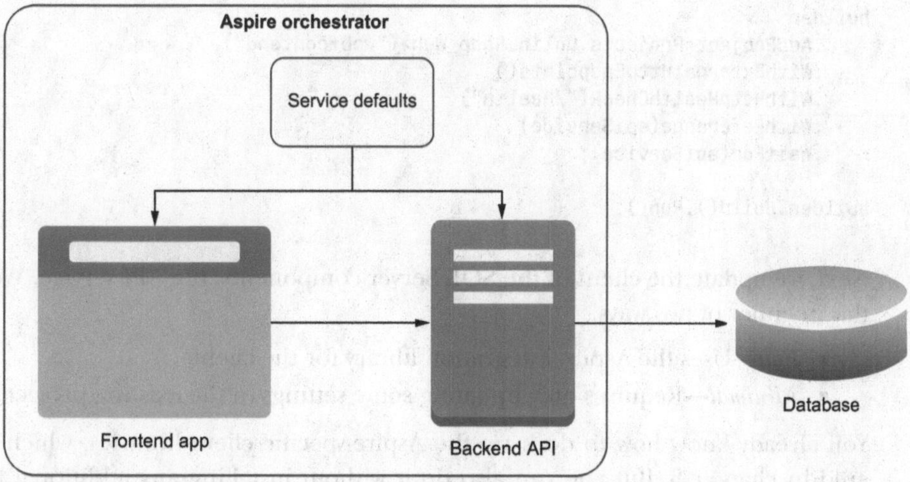


**Figure 10.2 The topology of our system after the Aspire orchestrator is added**

You may have noticed that SQL Server is still being hosted externally. Although this is OK, your life would be easier if you hosted the database inside Aspire itself. You can still do this in a way that won't affect the application's interoperability with the existing production database hosted elsewhere.

## 10.3 Reconfiguring the infrastructure components

The setup at https://mng.bz/BzJ8 shows our original application after the SQL Server database was migrated to Aspire integration.

You're probably already familiar with the process because it was covered in chapter 3. But let's look at it from the perspective of aspirifying the existing apps.

First, we install the appropriate integration components in the Aspire host project. Because our example relies on a SQL Server database, we'll install the `Aspire.Hosting.SqlServer` package.

Then we instantiate the SQL Server object in the `AppHost.cs` file, create a database, and pass the database reference to the API service. The next listing shows what our `AppHost.cs` will look like when these changes are applied.

**Listing 10.6 Full Aspire host with a SQL Server integration**

```
var builder = DistributedApplication.CreateBuilder(args);

var sql = builder.AddSqlServer("sql").WithLifetime(ContainerLifetime.Persistent);
var sqldb = sql.AddDatabase("sqldb");

var apiService = builder.AddProject<Projects.OnlineShop_ApiService>("apiservice")
    .WithHttpHealthCheck("/health")
    .WaitFor(sqldb)
    .WithReference(sqldb);

builder
    .AddProject<Projects.OnlineShop_Web>("webfrontend")
    .WithExternalHttpEndpoints()
    .WithHttpHealthCheck("/health")
    .WithReference(apiService)
    .WaitFor(apiService);

builder.Build().Run();
```

Next, we update the client of the SQL Server components, the API service. We can do this in either of two ways:

- *Full*—Uses the Aspire integration library for the client
- *Minimal*—Requires only updating some settings in the existing project

You already know how to do it via the Aspire-specific client libraries, which was covered in chapter 3. But you can also do it without installing any additional libraries. The code is slightly more verbose, but it works. Also, the code is only slightly different from what you have in your existing application.

Navigate to the application that connects to the database, which in this example is the API service application. Then locate where the database connection string is configured. In our example, that location is the following lines in the `Program.cs` file:

```
builder.Services.AddDbContext<ProductsDbContext>(options =>
    options.UseSqlServer(builder.Configuration.GetConnectionString(
     "DefaultConnection")));
```

In this case, the connection string is obtained from the settings, which are defined in the environment-specific `appsettings.json` files, such as `appsettings.Development.json`, `appsettings.Production.json`, and so on. The `builder.Configuration.GetConnectionString()` method looks for a setting with a particular name inside the `ConnectionStrings` section of the settings file. So in the preceding example, which looks at the `DefaultConnection` setting, this is how the settings will look:

```
{
    ...
    "ConnectionStrings": {
        "DefaultConnection": "<some connection string>",
        ...
    }
}
```

The good news is that we don't necessarily have to change this approach for an Aspire-hosted SQL Server instance. When we did this

```
var sqldb = sql.AddDatabase("sqldb")
```

and followed it with this,

```
builder.AddProject<Projects.OnlineShop_ApiService>("apiservice")
    .WaitFor(sqldb)
    .WithReference(sqldb);
```

Aspire created an entry inside the `ConnectionStrings` section of the API service named sqldb—the same name we gave the SQL Server database reference. The entry was already populated with the correct connection string. So all we have to do on the API service side is change the name of the connection string in the code. Instead of `DefaultConnection`, the name will be `sqldb`. Our code looks like this:

```
builder.Services.AddDbContext<ProductsDbContext>(options =>
    options.UseSqlServer(builder.Configuration.GetConnectionString("sqldb")));
```

That code is slightly more verbose than this, which you get with the Aspire-specific client package, but it still works:

```
builder.AddSqlServerDbContext<ProductsDbContext>("sqldb");
```

What if we already have an active production database? In that case, we'd want to connect to a SQL Server container only when we run our system locally. For the production deployment, we'd still want to connect to production. We can do this easily by adding a condition based on the `IsRunMode` property (chapter 9) and the `AddConnectionString()` method (chapter 3):

```
if (builder.ExecutionContext.IsRunMode)
{
    var sql =
     builder.AddSqlServer("sql").WithLifetime(ContainerLifetime.Persistent);
    var sqldb = sql.AddDatabase("sqldb");
    apiService
        .WaitFor(sqldb)
        .WithReference(sqldb);
}
else
{
    var sqldb = builder.AddConnectionString("sqldb");

    apiService
        .WaitFor(sqldb)
        .WithReference(sqldb);
}
```

In our pipeline, we have the existing connection string labeled `sqldb`, which will be used only in production because only in production will our system connect to an external SQL Server instance. The API service doesn't have to be updated because it will resolve its connection string normally. Its label is still the same. Figure 10.3 shows the topology of our system after we do all this.

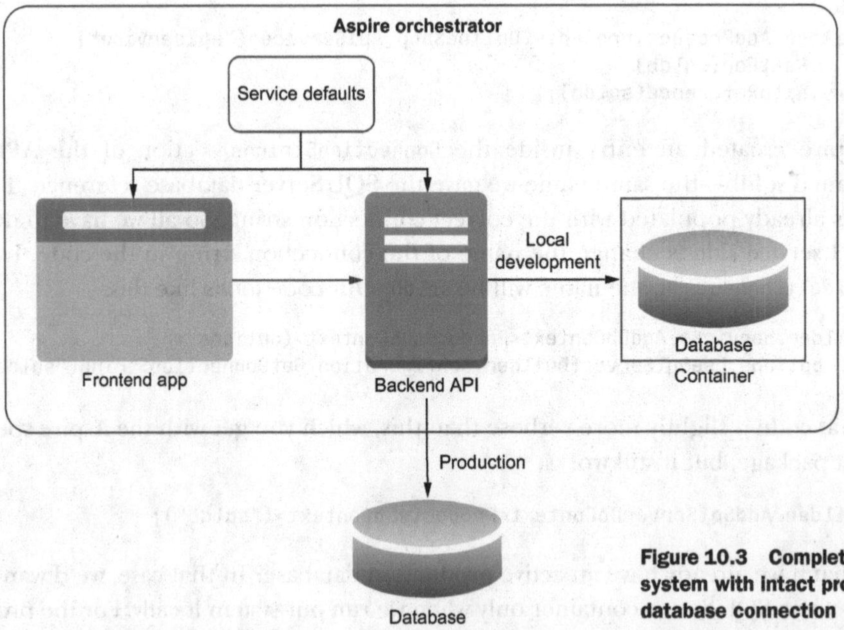


**Figure 10.3 Complete aspirified system with intact production database connection**

This concludes the overview of how existing legacy systems can be aspirified. We looked at a simple example, and although the process was manual, it was relatively easy. But most legacy applications aren't as simple as this example. They come with many moving parts and many domain-specific gotchas that make the manual migration process much harder.

This is where AI coding assistants come to the rescue. They can automate the tedious manual steps so that you can focus on the more interesting parts and step in only when you have to. Aspire has tools that help it integrate with AI agents, as you'll see in section 10.4.

## 10.4 Integrating Aspire with AI coding agents

As AI code assistants, such as Claude Code, Cursor, and Codex, become more powerful, more software developers choose to use these tools instead of writing all their code the old-fashioned way.

But AI agents are only as good as their understanding of the tech stack the application is built on. How do they deal with fairly recent libraries and frameworks that are updated regularly, such as Aspire?

The answer is tool calling. Agents can use various tools to retrieve the most up-to-date information about the system so they can make the best decisions while writing code for it. They don't try to invoke obsolete methods or hallucinate phantom invocations into existence just because they aren't familiar with the technology.

For Aspire in particular, coding agents get the most up-to-date information through a technology called Model Context Protocol (MCP).

To see how coding agents can work with Aspire, aspirify the existing application that you aspirified manually earlier. This application is available at https://mng.bz/lZ78.

Next, install an appropriate AI assistant. If you're familiar with agentic AI coding tools, you can use any tool you like. If you're new to these tools, Claude Code is a good choice because it's one of the most popular tools among software developers. You can find the installation instructions at https://code.claude.com/docs/en/quickstart.

Run the `claude` command (a single word) in the directory of your .NET solution and log in when prompted. Then instantiate the Aspire host project and launch it. To do so, execute the `aspire init` command inside the solution, followed by `aspire run`. This command launches the Aspire dashboard, which is blank because you haven't added any projects to it. Leave it running while you set up MCP and finish setting up the AI assistant.

### 10.4.1 Configuring MCP in Aspire

In Aspire, the MCP server is configured to work with a particular type of coding agent. To set it up, navigate to the folder containing the Aspire host project and execute the following command:

```
aspire mcp init
```

You'll be guided through setting up the MCP server for a particular type of coding assistant and given options such as Claude Code, Codex, and Copilot CLI. When the server is configured, the following tools will be available to your coding assistant while it's working in the repo folder:

- `list_resources`—Lists all services hosted by the current Aspire instance
- `execute_resource_command`—Executes a specific command supported by a specific resource hosted by the current Aspire instance
- `list_console_logs`—Lists console logs so that the agents can identify any problems with the system
- `list_structured_logs`—Lists structured logs for more detailed diagnostics
- `list_traces`—Lists traces so each operation can be tracked end to end through its steps
- `list_trace_structured_logs`—Combines traces with detailed log information for each event
- `list_integrations`—Discovers all available up-to-date versions of the integration packages so that agents can add infrastructure components to Aspire
- `get_integration_docs`—Gets the documentation for the integration packages so the agents know what to do with them
- `list_apphosts`—If there are multiple Aspire hosts in the folder you're looking at, helps the agents identify the right one in the context of their instructions
- `select_apphost`—Allows agents to select a specific Aspire app host

This list of tools is likely to be expanded in the future, so don't treat it as definitive or exhaustive. Just remember the general principle: these tools show you how to work with Aspire and how your current setup is doing.

When the Aspire MCP server is configured, you can start working with the agentic AI assistant to make the required updates. The flow will be the same regardless of which agentic coding assistant you use.

### 10.4.2 Using agentic AI to work with Aspire

To start, launch the coding assistant in the folder containing the .NET solution, including the Aspire host and any projects we want to aspirify. In the case of Claude Code, this would be the `claude` CLI command. Now we're ready to instruct the agents to make the appropriate changes.

The first step is asking our coding agent to analyze the codebase so we can make sure that it understands it correctly. To do so, we can use a prompt similar to this: *Inspect this solution and propose an Aspire AppHost model (projects+dependencies) and the order to implement it.*

The agent should provide detailed solution information and a proposed plan of action. The next listing shows what the first part of the CLI output might look like, describing what the agent understood about your project structure. The output may differ depending on the AI tool and its version.

**Listing 10.7 Claude output describing the solution structure**

```
Claude: I'll scan the repo structure, solution/projects, and configuration
    files (appsettings, launchSettings, docker-compose) to infer runtime
    dependencies and propose an Aspire AppHost model + an incremental
    implementation plan.

? Searching for .sln files...
- Found: OnlineShop.slnx

? Parsing solution projects...
- OnlineShop.ApiService/OnlineShop.ApiService.csproj
- OnlineShop.Web/OnlineShop.Web.csproj

? Checking configuration and local orchestration files...
- Found: OnlineShop.ApiService/appsettings.json
- Found: OnlineShop.Web/appsettings.json
- Found: OnlineShop.ApiService/appsettings.Development.json
- Found: OnlineShop.Web/appsettings.Development.json
- Found: OnlineShop.ApiService/Properties/launchSettings.json
- Found: OnlineShop.Web/Properties/launchSettings.json

? Inferring dependencies from config...
- Database: SQL Server (ConnectionStrings:DefaultConnection ->
    Server=(localdb)\\mssqllocaldb;Database=OnlineShopDb;...)

? Inferring service-to-service calls...
- OnlineShop.Web calls OnlineShop.ApiService:
  - Found HttpClient named "ProductsApiClient" base URL: https://
    localhost:7465 (appsettings.Development)

? Proposed Aspire AppHost model

Projects:
1) web      -> OnlineShop.Web              (external http endpoint)
2) api      -> OnlineShop.ApiService       (internal http endpoint)
```

Later in the output, the tool may propose the structure of the Aspire AppHost file. The next listing shows what the file might look like.

**Listing 10.8 Claude output proposing AppHost structure**

````
Suggested AppHost.cs (initial sketch)

```csharp
var builder = DistributedApplication.CreateBuilder(args);

var sql = builder.AddSqlServer("sql").WithLifetime(ContainerLifetime.Persistent);
var sqldb = sql.AddDatabase("sqldb");

var apiService = builder.AddProject<Projects.OnlineShop_ApiService>("apiservice")
    .WithReference(sqldb);
````
````

```
builder
    .AddProject<Projects.OnlineShop_Web>("webfrontend")
    .WithExternalHttpEndpoints()
    .WithReference(apiService);

builder.Build().Run();
```
```

This example is probably fairly close to what we did but may not be right. In particular, it doesn't suggest adding the health-check endpoints and invoking `WaitFor()` while creating the services to make sure that they don't start until the services they depend on are running.

That's all right because we can tell the agent to add these parts. Still, never trust your agents blindly. AI makes mistakes, and even if the code has been AI-generated, it's still yours, and you're still responsible for it. Therefore, always verify it before you ship.

The coding agent should come up with a plan that you can review. The next listing shows what the plan might look like.

**Listing 10.9 Example plan produced by Claude Code**

```
? Order to implement (incremental)

Step 1 — Scaffold + run API only
- Run: aspire init
- Add only OnlineShop.ApiService to AppHost and confirm it starts under `aspire
     run`
- Verify dashboard shows "api" healthy, endpoints exposed

Step 2 — Add SQL Server + wire API
- Add SQL Server resource + database
- Replace local connection string usage with Aspire-injected config
- Decide migration approach:
   - Option A: run migrations on startup in dev only
   - Option B: separate migration project/command
- Validate API connects; check logs for EF Core connectivity

Step 3 — Add Web frontend
- Add web project
- Update web's ProductsApiClient base address to use Aspire service discovery
- Validate UI -> API calls through Aspire-provided endpoint

Step 4 — Optional hardening
- Add health checks / readiness probes
- Add secrets strategy (user-secrets locally; Key Vault in cloud)
- Add structured log correlation IDs for web -> api

Potential migration notes
- Current configs assume localhost ports; under Aspire use references instead.
- Replace configured `https://localhost:7465` with `http://apiservice` (or
     injected endpoint config).
```
```

```
If you want, I can apply this plan by editing the AppHost for Step 1 and Step 2
    (API + SQL Server) and show the diffs.
```

You can approve the plan and prompt the agent to follow it autonomously, but this action is recommended only if you're an experienced AI-first developer and have various guardrails in place, such as linting rules and tests. If you're new to these tools, it would be safer to move in small iterations and examine the changes from each individual prompt.

If you choose to work incrementally, a good follow-up prompt would be similar to this: *Add one project to AppHost and make it run.*

Also, because the MCP server provides information about the Aspire stack and lets you debug an application running locally, you can prompt your agents with the following questions:

- *Are all my resources running? Which are unhealthy and why?*
- *Show me recent logs for the API resource and summarize the failure.*
- *Find slow HTTP requests for RESOURCE_NAME and suggest fixes.*

### 10.4.3 What are MCP and agentic tool calling?

Before we finish, it would be useful to understand how MCP works. Agentic coding assistants rely on the same types of large language models (LLMs) covered in chapter 5. On its own, however, an LLM wouldn't be able to automate the process of writing code and placing it in the right files. To do that, it needs tools that extend its capabilities.

Agentic tool calling and MCP are two closely related concepts that shape how modern coding assistants operate. They move AI systems from passive text generators to active participants in a development workflow.

*Agentic tool calling* refers to a pattern in which a language model can decide when and how to use external tools to complete a task. Instead of producing only text, the model can invoke structured actions such as reading a file, running a test suite, executing a shell command, querying a database, and calling an API. The model analyzes the user request, determines whether additional information or computation is required, selects the appropriate tool, and then incorporates the result back into its reasoning. This gives the assistant a form of agency: it can plan, act, observe the result, and refine its next step.

In the context of coding assistants, agentic tool calling enables much more than code completion. Consider an assistant integrated into an editor. When a developer asks it to refactor a class, the assistant might first read the relevant files from the repository. Then it might search for references across the codebase, generate updated implementations, run the test suite, and inspect failures. If tests fail, it can iterate by adjusting the code and rerunning tests until they pass. Each step is a tool invocation. The model orchestrates actions in a loop rather than responding with a single block of text.

Claude Code is an example of a coding assistant that uses this pattern. When asked to implement a feature, it can inspect the project structure, read specific files, and propose changes grounded in the actual codebase. It can run commands such as linters or tests and adapt its output based on the results. This transforms the assistant into a collaborative agent that operates within the developer's environment.

Underneath these systems, the model needs a standardized way to discover and use tools. This is where MCP becomes relevant. MCP is a specification that defines how tools, resources, and contextual information are exposed to a language model. Think of it as an API for AI agents. Instead of hardcoding tool integrations for each assistant, MCP provides a consistent contract. Tools describe their capabilities, input schema, and output schema in a structured way. Then the model can select and call them through a predictable interface.

As with an interaction using a REST API or gRPC, there's the concept of a server and a client. The AI agent acts as the client. The MCP server, as the name suggests, acts as the server. The API is what the agent can access, a facade that delivers data from a variety of sources, such as databases, files, and documents. It's not conceptually different from the REST APIs we've looked at many times throughout this book. Figure 10.4 shows how an agent interacts with the MCP server.

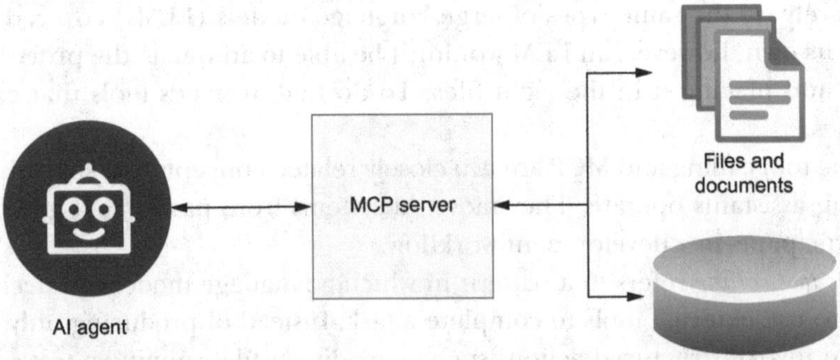


**Figure 10.4 Data flow between the agent and the MCP server**

In a coding environment, MCP can expose tools that read files, write files, search a repository, run tests, and execute a command. Each tool advertises what arguments it expects and what kind of result it returns. The model receives this catalog of capabilities as part of its context. When it determines that it needs more information, it issues a tool call that conforms to the protocol. The host system executes the tool and feeds the result back to the model. This loop continues until the task is complete.

## 10.5 Closing thoughts

When you opened this book, Aspire might have felt like just another tool in the .NET ecosystem—another framework, another abstraction, another dashboard. But now you know it's more.

Aspire isn't about adding complexity; it's about making distributed systems understandable. It brings structure to chaos. It turns a collection of services, databases, queues, and containers into something you can reason about, run locally, observe, and evolve with confidence.

That shift is the real takeaway. Now you think in distributed systems.

Earlier in your career, you may have built single applications: one project, one database, one deployment. With Aspire, you learned to think differently:

- Services are independent.
- Infrastructure is part of the application.
- Observability isn't optional.
- Configuration is explicit.
- Local development should mirror production as closely as possible.

You didn't just learn the framework and APIs; you also learned architecture. You saw how to define resources declaratively. You connected services through clear contracts. You configured databases, storage, messaging, and identity consistently. You used the dashboard to understand what's happening inside your system.

Aspire teaches its biggest lesson beyond tooling. It reinforces three important principles:

1. *Infrastructure is code.* Your application doesn't end at `Program.cs`. Your databases, queues, identity providers, and caches are part of the system. Treat them as such.
2. *Observability is a feature.* If you can't see what your system is doing, you're guessing. Aspire encourages visibility from the beginning.
3. *Local confidence enables production confidence.* If code works reliably on your machine in a realistic setup, deployment becomes an execution detail, not a leap of faith.

These principles will serve you even outside Aspire. This book gave you the foundation. What you build next is up to you. You might refactor an existing system into clearer service boundaries. You might introduce structured observability into a legacy app. Maybe you want to standardize how your team defines infrastructure. The world is your oyster.

The final thought is that technology will evolve, frameworks will change, versions will move forward, and Aspire itself will continue to grow.

If this book helped you move from experimenting with distributed applications to confidently building them, it has done its job. Now it's your turn. Build something meaningful.

## Summary

- You can upgrade Aspire from versions 8 and 9 to the evergreen version 13 manually by updating the SDK and packages or via the `aspire` CLI tool.
- Aspirification is the process of adding non-Aspire applications to Aspire. Aspirification is done by adding the Aspire host and service defaults and then integrating both projects with the existing projects.
- The Service Defaults package doesn't have to be added to the aspirified system, but it helps because it comes with health checks and metrics.
- The existing connection strings can be left intact for aspirified applications so they still work with the existing production resources.
- Aspire can integrate with AI-based coding assistants via MCP and tool calling.

# appendix
# Setting up the development environment

Before using Aspire, you have to set up your development machine. This appendix covers all prerequisites, starting with basic system requirements. We'll go through the components to preinstall, including the .NET SDK and appropriate code editors or IDEs we can use, depending on the machine's operating system.

Then we'll install Aspire itself and make sure that we have all the available project templates. Finally, we'll get familiar with the process of creating a new Aspire project.

## A.1 Minimal system requirements

Before we can work with Aspire, we have to install the following components on our development machine:

- .NET 10 SDK or later
- A suitable IDE or code editor (Visual Studio, Visual Studio Code, or JetBrains Rider)
- A container runtime, such as Docker or Podman

The main dependency is the .NET SDK (preferably the latest version), which you can download at https://dotnet.microsoft.com/.

The easiest way to start with Aspire is through Visual Studio. The latest version of Visual Studio includes all the relevant components. The caveat is that it's available only in Windows. If your development environment is on a Windows machine, you can download the latest version of Visual Studio at https://visualstudio.microsoft.com/. Alternatively, you can download JetBrains Rider, which is available for any operating system that supports .NET.

Unlike Visual Studio, which has a free Community Edition, JetBrains Rider is a premium IDE that requires a paid license. You can download it at https://www.jetbrains.com/rider/.

Finally, there's Visual Studio Code, a lightweight code editor rather than an IDE. Despite its name, it doesn't resemble Visual Studio even though both tools are made by Microsoft.

As a code editor, it lacks some advanced functionality that an IDE has, such as certain debugging and performance analytics capabilities. But its main advantage is that it is much more lightweight than any IDE, runs faster, and doesn't require as much disk space. It's also highly customizable.

Visual Studio Code is available for all major operating systems and can be downloaded for free at https://code.visualstudio.com/.

## A.2 Installing Aspire project templates

After installing all the required development tools, you can set up Aspire. If you're using Visual Studio 2026 or JetBrains Rider, the Aspire SDK should already be installed, and you'll be able to use it right away. If you prefer to use a simple code editor, such as Visual Studio Code, you have to install the appropriate project templates via the `dotnet` command-line interface (CLI). To do so, execute the following command:

```
dotnet new install Aspire.ProjectTemplates
```

To verify that the Aspire project templates have been installed, execute the following command:

```
dotnet new list aspire
```

If the installation worked successfully, some items that contain `aspire` in the name should be listed.

## A.3 Creating an Aspire project

All you have to do in Visual Studio is choose the Create New Project option, find the Aspire Starter Project template, and follow the instructions. Figure A.1 shows what the project template looks like.

The process is similar in JetBrains Rider, but you have to install the Aspire plugin before the appropriate project template is available.

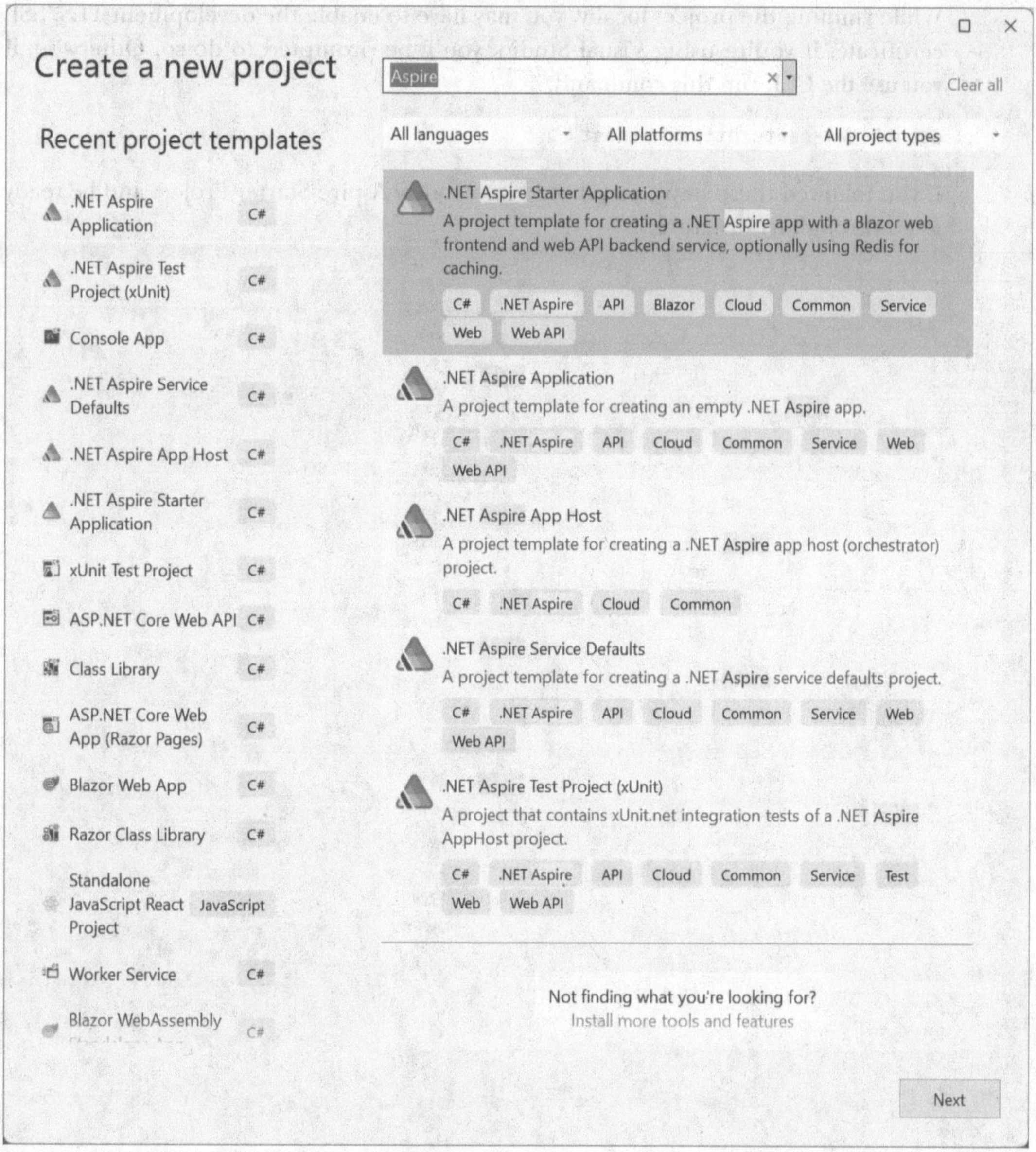


**Figure A.1 Creating a new Aspire project in Visual Studio**

If you're using the CLI for application development and setup, you can create a new Aspire Starter Project by running the following command in the folder of your choice:

```
dotnet new aspire-starter
```

While running the project locally, you may have to enable the development TLS/SSL certificate. If you're using Visual Studio, you'll be prompted to do so. Otherwise, if you use the CLI, run this command:

```
dotnet dev-certs https --trust
```

If you followed these steps, you should have a new Aspire Starter Project and be ready to go through its structure.

# index

## A

## U



## V



## W

*(continued from back cover)*

AI agents. This modern approach to intelligent systems ensures you can safely build smart, responsive applications that are fully prepared for next-generation enterprise workloads.

Because graceful failure is mandatory for distributed systems, you'll explore asynchronous message queues, distributed locking, and end-to-end token security. Reviewer David Sellen of Sweet Systems pointed out that "even for simple applications, visibility into logs, traces, and metrics is essential, and this book is a great introduction to observability!" By learning to construct robust integration tests, configure OpenTelemetry, and secure microservices via OIDC and JWT token propagation, you ensure your applications are resilient, highly observable, and production-ready. As you build your distributed application in Aspire, author Fiodar Sazanavets carefully expands each concept so you can reproduce it in your framework of choice.

For .NET developers, this book is a practical guide to Aspire's dashboard, AppHost, and service defaults. Developers and DevOps practitioners from other ecosystems will also gain transferable insight into orchestrating, observing, testing, and deploying multiservice applications—though the hands-on examples use .NET and Aspire.

**"A comprehensible practical guide to mastering .NET Aspire, from local orchestration to secure, scalable cloud deployments."**
**—Roman Fedytskyi, ORSNN**

**"Clear, to the point, and fun."**
**—Ronald Goodwin, Seven 30 Games**

**"A great resource to learn what Aspire does."**
**—Andy Robinson, Viewsource Ltd.**

www.ingramcontent.com/pod-product-compliance
Lightning Source LLC
LaVergne TN
LVHW040319201026
850649LV00007B/25